A Book Of

MANAGEMENT ACCOUNTING

For
B.B.M., Semester – III (Course Code 306)
As Per New Syllabus of Savitribai Phule Pune University, June 2014

Dr. Suhas Mahajan
B.A., M.Com., Ph.D.
Research Guide, University of Pune and YCMOU Nashik.

Dr. Mahesh Kulkarni
M.Com., M.Phil., L.L.B., D.T.L., Ph.D.
Research Guide, University of Pune and YCMOU, Nashik

N2190

BBM (IB) - III MANAGEMENT ACCOUNTING　　　　ISBN 978-93-5164-040-0

Second Edition : June 2015

© : Authors

The text of this publication, or any part thereof, should not be reproduced or transmitted in any form or stored in any computer storage system or device for distribution including photocopy, recording, taping or information retrieval system or reproduced on any disc, tape, perforated media or other information storage device etc., without the written permission of Authors with whom the rights are reserved. Breach of this condition is liable for legal action.

Every effort has been made to avoid errors or omissions in this publication. In spite of this, errors may have crept in. Any mistake, error or discrepancy so noted and shall be brought to our notice shall be taken care of in the next edition. It is notified that neither the publisher nor the authors or seller shall be responsible for any damage or loss of action to any one, of any kind, in any manner, therefrom.

Published By :
NIRALI PRAKASHAN
Abhyudaya Pragati, 1312, Shivaji Nagar,
Off J.M. Road, PUNE – 411005
Tel - (020) 25512336/37/39, Fax - (020) 25511379
Email : niralipune@pragationline.com

Printed By :
Repro Knowledgecast Limited,
Thane

DISTRIBUTION CENTRES
PUNE

Nirali Prakashan
119, Budhwar Peth, Jogeshwari Mandir Lane
Pune 411002, Maharashtra
Tel : (020) 2445 2044, 66022708, Fax : (020) 2445 1538
Email : niralilocal@pragationline.com

Nirali Prakashan
S. No. 28/25, Dhyari,
Near Pari Company, Pune 411041
Tel : (020) 24690204Fax : (020) 24690316
Email : bookorder@pragationline.com

MUMBAI
Nirali Prakashan
385, S.V.P. Road, Rasdhara Co-op. Hsg. Society Ltd.,
Girgaum, Mumbai 400004, Maharashtra
Tel : (022) 2385 6339 / 2386 9976, Fax : (022) 2386 9976
Email : niralimumbai@pragationline.com

DISTRIBUTION BRANCHES

NAGPUR
Pratibha Book Distributors
Above Maratha Mandir, Shop No. 3, First Floor,
Rani Jhanshi Square, Sitabuldi, Nagpur 440012,
Maharashtra, Tel : (0712) 254 7129

BENGALURU
Pragati Book House
House No. 1, Sanjeevappa Lane, Avenue Road Cross,
Opp. Rice Church, Bengaluru – 560002.
Tel : (080) 64513344, 64513355,
Mob : 9880582331, 9845021552
Email:bharatsavla@yahoo.com

JALGAON
Nirali Prakashan
34, V. V. Golani Market, Navi Peth, Jalgaon 425001,
Maharashtra, Tel : (0257) 222 0395
Mob : 94234 91860

KOLHAPUR
Nirali Prakashan
New Mahadvar Road,
Kedar Plaza, 1st Floor Opp. IDBI Bank
Kolhapur 416 012, Maharashtra. Mob : 9850046155

CHENNAI
Pragati Books
9/1, Montieth Road, Behind Taas Mahal, Egmore,
Chennai 600008 Tamil Nadu, Tel : (044) 6518 3535,
Mob : 94440 01782 / 98450 21552 / 98805 82331, Email : bharatsavla@yahoo.com

RETAIL OUTLETS
PUNE

Pragati Book Centre
157, Budhwar Peth, Opp. Ratan Talkies,
Pune 411002, Maharashtra
Tel : (020) 2445 8887 / 6602 2707, Fax : (020) 2445 8887

Pragati Book Centre
Amber Chamber, 28/A, Budhwar Peth,
Appa Balwant Chowk, Pune : 411002, Maharashtra,
Tel : (020) 20240335 / 66281669
Email : pbcpune@pragationline.com

Pragati Book Centre
676/B, Budhwar Peth, Opp. Jogeshwari Mandir,
Pune 411002, Maharashtra
Tel : (020) 6601 7784 / 6602 0855

PBC Book Sellers & Stationers
152, Budhwar Peth, Pune 411002, Maharashtra
Tel : (020) 2445 2254 / 6609 2463

MUMBAI
Pragati Book Corner
Indira Niwas, 111 - A, Bhavani Shankar Road, Dadar (W), Mumbai 400028, Maharashtra
Tel : (022) 2422 3526 / 6662 5254, Email : pbcmumbai@pragationline.com

www.pragationline.com　　　　info@pragationline.com

Preface ...

A number of books are available on the subject of Management Accounting in the market but they do not meet the basic requirements of B.B.M. (IB) students of Savitribai Phule Pune University. This book is written as per the revised syllabus prescribed for B.B.M. (IB) Semester III, students by Savitribai Phule Pune University from June, 2014. We do hope that this book will definitely help to meet the growing requirements of the students of Management Accounting from the faculty of Business Management (International Business). This book adopts a modern and novel approach towards the study of Management Accounting in view with the specific requirements of the readers and practitioners of this subject.

All the topics included in the syllabus are explained in simple but apt language. Equal stress is also given for necessary accounting theory and wide variety of practical problems. We have taken appropriate care to incorporate basic accounting concepts, accounting standards and tabular representation of classified financial statements. Proper emphasis is also given on charts and graphs to simplify the accounting theories and practices. This book has been designed to serve as a self sufficient text for B.B.M (IB) students. It will definitely add to our satisfaction if this book would be more useful as a guide for practicing accountants, professional managers, dynamic entrepreneurs and enthusiastic teachers of the subject concern.

We sincerely thank the senior faculty members from various Colleges, Management Institutes and Accounting Associations for guiding and constantly encouraging us in our enterprise and the dynamic students community who inspired us to write this book.

We are very much thankful to Shri. Dineshbhai Furia and Shri. Jigneshbhai Furia, Mr. Malik Shaikh, Mr. Prasad Chintakindi and the entire staff of Nirali Prakashan, Pune for their earnest help in bringing out this book with vigour and accuracy. We have taken maximum efforts to make the text error free. Nevertheless, we do not rule out the possibility of certain shortcomings or misprints still remaining, we will be grateful to the reader if such errors are pointed out from time to time.

We must concede that this book would never have been written without the whole hearted support, continuous encouragement and inspiration of our family members many, many thanks to them.

Any criticism or valuable suggestion for further improvement of this book will be gratefully acknowledged and highly appreciated.

1st July, 2015
Pune.

Dr. Suhas Mahajan
Dr. Mahesh Kulkarni

Syllabus ...

Sr. No.	Content	Number of Lecture
Unit 1	**Introduction :** Major Types of Accounting – 1) Financial Accounting 2) Cost Accounting 3) Management Accounting Management Accounting: Need, Essentials of Management Accounting, Importance, Objectives, Scope, Functions, Principal Systems and Techniques, Advantages, Limitations, Distinction between Financial Accounting and Management Accounting, Distinction between Cost Accounting and Management Accounting	10
Unit 2	**Analysis and Interpretation of Financial Statements :** **Methods of Analysis :** Comparative Statements, Common Size Statements, Trend Percentage or Trend Ratios (Horizontal Analysis). **Ratio Analysis:** Meaning of Ratio, Necessity and Advantages of Ratio.	4

Unit 3	**Analysis and Interpretation of Ratios:**
	Types of Ratio :
	i) **According to the nature of items :**
	   a) Balance Sheet Ratios
	   b) Revenue Statements or Profit and Loss Account Ratios
	   c) Inter Statement or Composite Ratios
	ii) **Functional Classification**
	   a) Liquidity Ratios
	   b) Leverage Ratios
	   c) Activity Ratios
	   d) Profitability Ratios
		12

Unit 4	**Fund Flow Statement and Cash Flow Statement :** Meaning of Funds, Fund Flow Statement, Flow of Funds, Working Capital, Causes of Changes in Working Capital, Proforma of Sources and Application of Funds, Proforma of Adjusted Profit and Loss Account, Proforma of Cash Flow Statement	4
Unit 5	**Marginal Costing :** Meaning and Definition of Marginal Cost and Marginal Costing, Contribution, Profit Volume Ratio, Advantages of Marginal Costing, Limitations	12

Unit 6	**Budget and Budgetary Control :**
	Meaning of Budget and Budgetary Control, Definition, Nature of Budget and Budgetary Control, Objective of Budget and Budgetary Control, Limitations of Budget and Budgetary Control, Steps in Budgetary Control.
	Types or Classification or Budgets:
	   According to Time: i) Short-Term, ii) Long-Term.
	   According to Flexibility: i) Fixed, ii) Flexible
		6

	Total	48

Problem Areas : i) Computation of Ratio, ii) Marginal Costing, iii) Flexible Budget.

***

Contents ...

1.	Introduction	1.1 - 1.26
2.	Analysis and Interpretation of Financial Statements	2.1 - 2.20
3.	Analysis and Interpretation of Ratios	3.1 - 3.58
4.	Fund Flow Statement and Cash Flow Statement	4.1 - 4.24
5.	Marginal Costing	5.1 - 5.88
6.	Budget and Budgetary Control	6.1 - 6.28

At a Glance

✱	Glossary	G.1 - G.4
✱	Objective Questions	O.1 - O.8
	i) True or False Statements	
	ii) Fill in the Blanks	
✱	Formulae	F.1 - F.4
✱	Bibliography	B.1 - B.1
•	April 2015 University Question Paper	P.1 - P.2

***

List of Figures, Graphs and Charts ...

1.1	Phases in the Evolution of Accounting	1.3
1.2	Scope of Management Accounting	1.14
2.1	Steps involved in Financial Statement Analysis	2.4
2.2	Methods of Financial Analysis	2.6
3.1	Types of Ratio	3.2
4.1	Meaning of Funds	4.2
4.2	Uses of Funds Flow Statement	4.4
4.3	Utility of Cash Flow Statement	4.15
6.1	Organisational Chart	6.9
6.2	Types of Budget	6.10

***

UNIT 1

INTRODUCTION

SYNOPSIS

1.1 Major Types of Accounting
    1.1.1 Financial Accounting
    1.1.2 Cost Accounting
    1.1.3 Management Accounting

1.2 Management Accounting
    1.2.1 Need
    1.2.2 Essentials
    1.2.3 Importance
    1.2.4 Objectives
    1.2.5 Scope
    1.2.6 Functions
    1.2.7 Principal Systems and Techniques
    1.2.8 Advantages
    1.2.9 Limitations

1.3 Distinction between Financial Accounting and Management Accounting

1.4 Distinction between Cost Accounting and Management Accounting

- Questions for Self-Study

Management Accounting is a segment of accounting that deals specifically with the accounting and reporting of information to management regarding the detailed operations of the company for decisions to be taken in various areas of business. It is oriented primarily towards managerial control and other decision-making groups inside the organisation. Management frequently requires timely financial information that deals with different aspects of the firm, ranging from special purpose reports for a specific department's operating performance to the preparation of annual budgets and forecasts which encompass the entire business.

Managers in all types of organisations need frequent information about business activities to plan accurately for the future, to control business results, to direct an enterprise toward achieving its goals and to make decisions that affect the operations of the business. Information is vital for the management process i.e. for functions carried out by the managers viz. planning, controlling and decision-making. In the goal of providing information, **Management Accounting** identifies, collects, measures, classifies and reports information that is useful to managers in fulfilling the management process.

Management Accounting is that field of accounting which deals with providing information including financial accounting, information to managers for their use in planning, decision-making, performance evaluation, control, management of cost and cost determination for financial reporting. Managerial Accounting thus contains reports prepared to fulfill the needs of the management of any organisation.

Management Accounting was not known to the business world until 1950. The term was first formally described in a report entitled 'Management Accounting' in 1950. The report was published by the **Anglo-American Council of Productivity Management Accounting Team** after its visit to United States during April, May and June 1950.

The team in its report defines **Management Accounting** as,

"the presentation of accounting information in such a way so as to assist management in the creation of policy and in the day-to-day operation of an undertaking".

Thereafter, a number of attempts were and are being made by various professional associations and authorities on the subject to define Management Accounting in its right perspective.

Phases in the Evolution of Accounting

The history of accounting indicates the evolutionary pattern which focuses changing socio-economic conditions and enlarged purposes to which accounting is applied.

In the present situation, nine phases in the Evolution of Accounting can be distinguished viz. Stewardship Accounting, Financial Accounting, Cost Accounting, Management Accounting, Environmental Accounting, Social Responsibility Accounting, Inflation Accounting, Human Resource Accounting, Taxation Accounting etc.

The **Phases in the Evolution of Accounting** are shown in Figure 1.1 as follows.

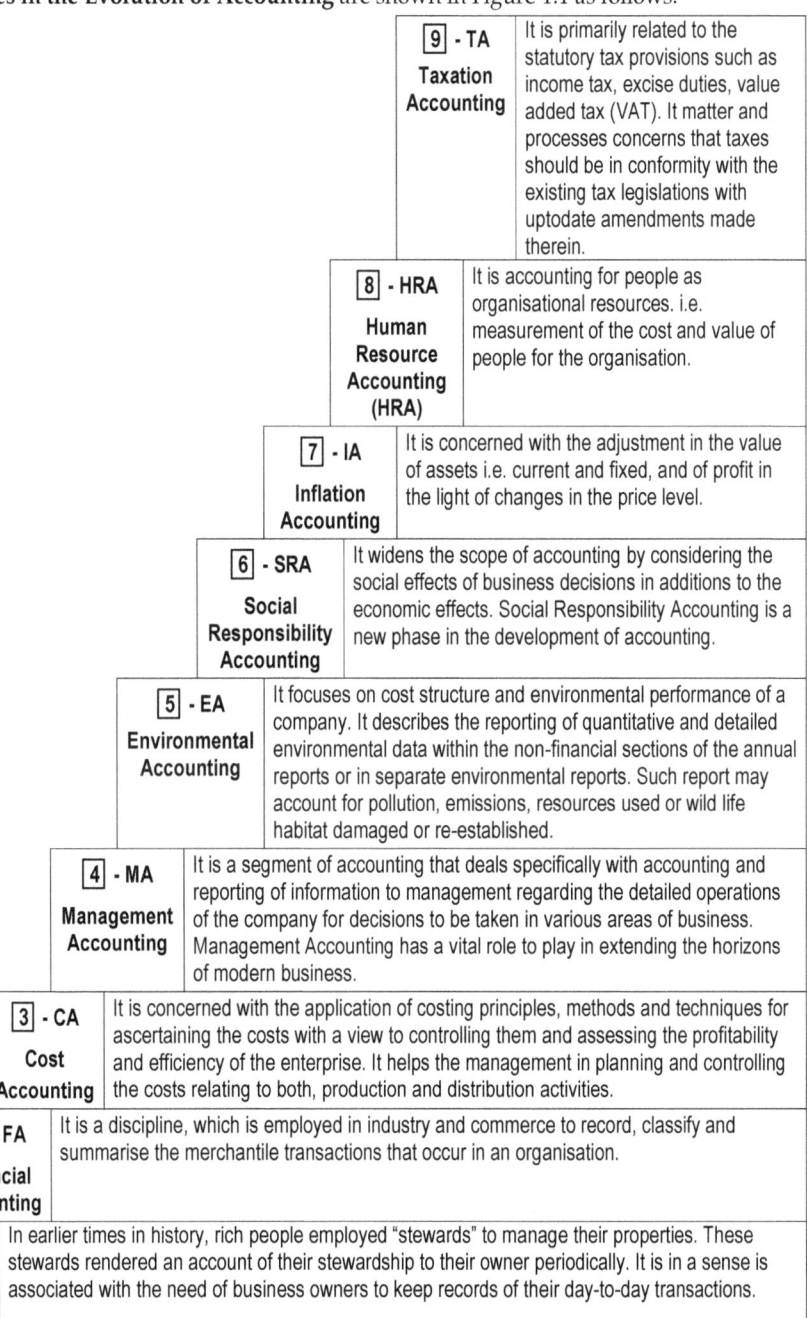

Fig. 1.1 : Phases in the Evolution of Accounting

1.1 MAJOR TYPES OF ACCOUNTING

Accounting plays a critical role in the efficient use of a firm's resources. Decision-makers operate in a complex economic environment that is constantly changing. Their information needs change with the environment, and accounting must adapt to satisfy these changing needs. The importance of sound financial information has always been recognised, but, in the light of today's conditions, such information has become crucial to the survival of business and industry.

Accounting can be broadly classified into three types i.e. 1) Financial Accounting, 2) Cost Accounting and 3) Management Accounting. These three cannot be put in a water-tight compartment classification. Each one supplements the other. In fact, Financial Accounting provides the basics for Cost Accounting as well as Management Accounting and in the ultimate analysis Management Accounting includes part of Cost Accounting.

1.1.1 Financial Accounting

Meaning

Accounting is the language effectively employed to communicate the financial information of a business unit to various parties interested in its progress such as proprietors, creditors, investors, employees, consumers, and the government etc. **Financial Accounting** is concerned with that part of accounting which is meant to serve all parties externally to the operating responsibility of the firm, e.g. creditors, investors, employees, regulatory bodies and the general public. But Management Accounting is designed for use in operational needs of the firm.

Financial Accounting is a discipline which is employed in industry and commerce to record, classify and summarise the mercantile transactions that occur in an organisation. The **American Accounting Association** has defined accounting as the process of identifying, measuring and communicating economic information to permit informed judgements and decisions by users of the information.

Definition

The **American Institute of Certified Public Accountants**, (USA) has defined **Financial Accounting** as, "the art of recording, classifying and summarising in a significant manner and in terms of money transactions and events which are in part at least of a financial character and interpreting the results thereof".

Features

The analysis of the above definitions brings the following **features of Financial Accounting** to the light :
   i)   Art of recording and classifying business transactions and events in a systematic manner;
   ii) Transactions to be recorded in monetary terms;
   iii) Summarising, analysing and interpreting the results of accounting information; and
   iv) Communicating and explaining the information to decision-makers.

Objectives

A modern **Financial Accounting** system has to accomplish the following **objectives** :
   i) To identify financial events and transactions that occur in an organisation.
   ii) To measure the value of these occurrences in terms of money.

iii) To organize the accumulated financial data into meaningful information and
iv) To analyse, interpret and communicate that information to a broad range of persons and groups, both within and outside the organisation.

Functions

The major **functions** of **Financial Accounting** are summarised below :

i) **Recording :**

Since all business transactions cannot be kept in memory, they have got to be systematically recorded and pass through journals, ledgers and work sheets before they could take the forms of final accounts. This aspect of financial accounting has assumed considerable importance with the limitation of human memory.

ii) **Validating :**

With the universal acceptance and enforcement of accounting principles, every recorded entry in the books of accounts maintained by a business unit gives validity or authenticity to all such transactions so recorded.

iii) **Communicating :**

This is an important function of financial accounting. Accounting serves as a language for communicating the financial facts about the enterprise or activity most effectively to all concerned interested in using and interpreting them.

iv) **Interpreting :**

These aspects helps in unfolding the total financial picture of an undertaking and interpreting the same with more meaning.

Limitations

Financial Accounting like any other branch of knowledge, is not without limitations. The fast changing conditions and environmental factors have brought the **Limitations of Financial Accounting** to the fore.

i) It does not provide detailed cost information for different departments, processes, products, jobs in the production divisions. Similarly, separate cost data are not available for different services and functions in the administration division. Management may need information about different products, sales territories and sales activities which are also not available in Financial Accounting.

ii) It does not set up a proper system of controlling materials and supplies. Undoubtedly, if material and supplies are not controlled in a manufacturing concern, they will lead to losses on account of misappropriation, misutilisation, scrap, defectives etc. They may, in turn, influence the estimated net income of a business enterprise.

iii) The recording and accounting for wages and labour is not carried out for different jobs, processes, products, departments. This creates problems in analysing the cost associated with different activities. This also does not provide a basis for rewarding workers and employees, for the above-average performance.

iv) It contains historical cost information which is accumulated at the end of the accounting period. This accounting does not provide day-to-day information about costs and expense. This is the reason why much dissatisfaction has been shown with external financial reporting. The historical cost is not a reliable basis for predicting future earnings, solvency, or overall managerial effectiveness. Historical cost information is relevant but not adequate for all purpose. It is now rightly contended that current cost information should be reported along with historical cost information.

v) It is difficult to know the behaviour of costs in financial accounting as expenses are not assigned to the product at each stage of production. Expenses are not classified into direct and indirect and therefore cannot be classified as controllable and uncontrollable. Control of cost which is the most important objective of all business enterprise, cannot be achieved with the aid of financial accounting alone.

vi) It does not possess an adequate system of standards to evaluate the performance of departments and employees working in departments. Standardisation is now applied to all elements of business. Standards need to be developed for materials, labour and overheads so that a firm can compare the work of labourers, workers, supervisors and executives with what should have been done in an allotted period of time.

vii) It does not provide information to analyse the losses due to various factors, such as idle plant and equipment, seasonal fluctuations in volume of business etc. It does not help management in taking important decisions about expansion of business, dropping of a product line, starting a new product, alternative methods of production, improvement in product etc. The managerial decisions about these business matters have now become vital to the survival and growth of business enterprises.

viii) It does not provide cost data to determine the price of the product being manufactured or the service being rendered to the consumers. It is also not possible to prepare detailed cost reports for the purpose of comparison and analysis between two periods of time within an enterprise and also for making inter-firm comparison.

ix) Change in the economic conditions of the country have direct impact on the business position of an organisation. The conditions of inflation or deflation change the value of the business significantly. Such a change is not depicted in the financial accounts as the accounts of the business have to be maintained on the basis of cost concept. With the result the balance sheet of an organisation fails to give true and fair view of the business.

x) It can only be understood by such persons who have accounting knowledge.

1.1.2 Cost Accounting

Meaning

Cost Accounting is an extension of general accounting systems which have as a goal the gathering, classifying, and analysing cost data that management needs in search for the most efficient methods of operating, achieving control of costs and reducing expenses. Cost accounting is the provision of such analysis and classification of expenditure as will enable the total cost of any particular unit of production to be ascertained with reasonable degree of accuracy and at the same time to disclose exactly how such total cost is constituted'.

Definitions

According to the **Institute of Cost and Works Accountants**, London, **Cost Accounting** is, "the process of accounting for cost from the point at which expenditure is incurred or committed to the establishment of its ultimate relationship with cost centres and cost units. In its widest usage it embraces the preparation of statistical data, the application of cost control methods and the ascertainment of the profitability of activities carried out or planned".

W. J. Morse defines Cost Accounting as, "the processing and evaluation of monetary and non-monetary data to provide information for external reporting, internal planning and control of business operations and special analysis and decisions".

Thus, **Cost Accounting** is the branch of accounting designed to determine the costs of manufactured products and to report cost information to management. It provides the means to gather the data needed to determine unit costs and to prepare reports, schedules, statements and analyses that are relevant to management. Cost Accounting procedures and routines are used as a means of accumulating and allocating all elements of manufacturing cost in a manner that will produce meaningful data for the use of management.

Objectives

The main **Objectives of Cost Accounting** are as follows :

i) To aid in the development of long-range plans by providing cost data that acts as a basis for projecting data for planning.

ii) To ensure efficient cost control by communicating essential costs data at regular intervals.

iii) To determine cost of products or activities.

iv) To identify profitable areas of business.

v) To provide management with information in connection with various operational problems.

1.1.3 Management Accounting

Meaning

The term Management Accounting refers to accounting for the management i.e. accounting which provides necessary information to the management for discharging its functions.

Definitions

Some important definitions given by the professional institutes and renowned authors are given below :

i) **The National Association of Accountants, US :**

"**Management Accounting** is, the process of identification, measurement, accumulation, analysis, preparation and communication of financial information used by management to plan, evaluate, and control within the organisation and to assure appropriate use and accountability for its resources".

ii) **The Chartered Institute of Management Accountants, UK :**

"**Management Accounting** is an integral part of management, concerned with identifying, presenting and interpreting information used for : i) formulating strategy, ii) planning and controlling activities, iii) decision-making, iv) optimising the use of resources, v) disclosure to shareholders and others external to the entity, vi) disclosure to employees, vii) safeguarding assets.

iii) **American Accounting Association :**

"**Management Accounting** is the application of appropriate techniques and concepts in processing historical and projected economic data of an entity to assist management in establishing plans for reasonable economic objectives in the making of rational decisions with a view towards the objectives".

iv) **AACA, USA :**

"Management Accounting is the application of accounting and statistical techniques to the specified purpose of producing and interpreting information designed to assist management in its functions of promoting maximum efficiency and in envisaging, formulating and co-ordinating their execution".

v) **H. M. Treasury :**

"**Management Accounting** is, the application of accounting knowledge to the purpose of producing and of interpreting accounting and statistical informations designed to assist management in its function of promoting maximum efficiency and in formulating and co-ordinating future plans and subsequently in measuring their execution".

vi) **J. Batty :**

"**Management Accounting** is the term used to describe the accounting methods, system and techniques which, coupled with special knowledge and ability, assist management in its task of maximising profits or minimising losses".

vii) **ICMA, London :**

"**Management Accounting** is the application of professional knowledge and skill in the preparation of accounting information in such a way so as to assist management in the formation of policies and in the planning and control of the operations of the undertaking".

viii) **R. L. Smith :**

"**Management Accounting** is a more intimate merger of the two older professions of management and accounting wherein the informational needs of the manager determine the accounting means for their satisfactions".

ix) **Brown and Howard :**

"**Management Accounting** is concerned with the efficient management of a business through the presentation to management of such information as will facilitate efficient and opportune planning and control".

x) **Robert N. Athony :**

"**Management Accounting** is concerned with accounting information which is useful to management".

xi) **Broad and Carmichael :**

"**Management Accounting** covers all those services by which the accounting department can assist top management and other departments in the formation of policy, the control of its execution and appreciation of its effectiveness".

xii) **Shilling Law :**

"Accounting which serves management by providing information as to the cost of profit associated with some portion of firm's total operations, is called **Management Accounting**".

xiii) **T. G. Rose :**

"**Management Accounting** is the adaptation and analysis of accounting information and its diagnosis and explanation in such a way so as to assist management".

xiv) **R. H. Garrison :**

"**Management Accounting** is concerned with providing information to managers; that is to those who are inside of an organisation and who are charged with directing and controlling its operations".

xv) **ICA England and Wales :**

"Any form of accounting which enables a business to be conducted more efficiently can be regarded as **Management Accounting**".

Features

All these definitions of **Management Accounting** reveal the following salient **features** :

i) It is a merger of 'management' and 'accounting'.

ii) It is concerned with accounting information which is useful to management in maximising profits or minimising losses.

iii) It is concerned with the improvement in the efficiency of the various phases of management.

Briefly Management Accounting with all its paraphernalia, does not supplant Financial Accounting as is erroneously misunderstood, but supplements the basic structure of traditional package of accounts to cater to the diversified requirements of modern management.

Thus, Management Accounting emphasises on the information that management requires to make specific intra-firm resource allocations. Such emphasis assumes that accounting must perform the two separate, distinct functions of financial and management reporting and that the data needs for each are often different. 'Few intelligent financial and economic decisions can be made in the absence of the information reservoir. Involvement with both time dimensions, past and future, places the executive near the centre of the control and decision-making processes in any organisation.

Characteristics

The above definitions clearly indicate the following **Characteristics of Management Accounting**.

i) It is the application of professional knowledge and skill in the preparation of accounting information in such a way so as to assist management in the formation of policies and in the planning and control of the operations of the undertaking.

ii) Management Accounting is the application of appropriate techniques and concepts in processing historical and projected economic data of an entity to assist management in establishing plans for reasonable economic objectives in the making of rational decisions with a view towards achieving the objectives.

iii) Management Accounting rearranges for management control to a great extent the accounting information provided by the financial accounting. It, therefore, lies between the following two activities i.e. i) Completing the accounting results on one hand, and ii) Controlling the business by the management, on the other.

iv) Management Accounting actually covers all rearrangement, combination or adjustment of the orthodox accounting figures which may be required to provide the chief executive with the information from which he can control the business.

v) It comprises accounting methods, systems and techniques which coupled with special knowledge and ability, assist management in its task of maximising profits or minimising losses.

vi) Management Accounting is the presentation of accounting information in such a way as to assist management in the creation of policy and in the day-to-day operations of an undertaking.

vii) Management Accounting is concerned with accounting information which is useful to the management. Efficiency of the various phases of management is, as a matter of fact, the common thread which underlies all these definitions. However, it should be clearly understood that it does not supplant financial accounting but rather it supplements it in order to serve the diverse requirements of modern management.

viii) The functions of the management are planning, organising, directing and controlling. Management Accounting helps in the performance of each of these functions in the meaningful way.

ix) Management Accounting serves as a vital source of data for management planning. The accounts and documents are a repository of a vast quantity of data about the past progress of the enterprise which are a must for making forecasts for the future.

1.2 MANAGEMENT ACCOUNTING

Management Accounting deals with the internal reporting. On the basis of the nature of these reports and their contents and the parties who receive these reports, it may be said that the management accounting deals primarily with the furnishing of required and relevant data to the managerial personnel for the purpose of planning, controlling and decision making. The type of accounting information required by the management differs from one type of decision to another. It is not necessarily confined to the financial accounting information but it is much more than this depending upon the type, importance, complexity, etc. of the problem.

The financial accounting and the cost accounting lay emphasis on different objectives. Management cannot base its decision only on the information furnished by the financial and cost accounting. Therefore, there is a need for a system which views, utilises and analyses the abundant data which is generated by financial and cost accounting, with the sole objective of furnishing the relevant data to the management for the purpose of assisting it to take a number of appropriate decisions. **Management Accounting** furnishes only those data which are relevant to the decision under consideration and these relevant data may include the data collected from both financial and cost records and other sources.

1.2.1 NEED

The following points highlight the **Need of Management Accounting** :

i) Management Accounting includes all those accounting services by means of which assistance is rendered to the management in their managerial functions i.e. decision making, profit planning, control etc. It also helps management for execution of their plans and measurement of performance.

ii) Financial Accounting in its traditional form cannot the information supply necessary to the management for functioning efficiently and effectively. Management Accounting is the accounting which provides in non-technical language, cost, profits and other information necessary to the management for discharging their functions.

iii) Management Accounting is the presentation of accounting information in such a way as to assist management in the creation of policy in the day to day operation of undertakings.

iv) Management Accounting goes beyond the figures provided by financial accounting which are mute in nature and makes them self explainatory.

v) Management Accounting is an extension of the managerial aspects of cost accounting. It utilises the principles and practices of both Cost Accounting and Financial Accounting.

vi) The term accounting is used in a more broad scene in Management Accounting so that the scope of management is very wide and the term comprises of every activity of a business.

vii) Since the managerial personnel are accountable to the owners of the company and since their very continuation in the company depends upon the results produced which in turn depends upon the quality of decisions and their implementation, the managerial personnel need a system which furnishes the relevant information to them to take decisions. Therefore, the need for Management Accounting is to serve the management through various reports required by them.

viii) It is very well known that planning, controlling, co-ordinating, organising, motivating and communicating are the six important managerial functions. Management Accounting helps the managerial personnel to perform each one of these functions more effectively and profitably by providing relevant information at the right time. For this purpose, management accountant collects the information from different sources, analyses them systematically to find out their relevance to the decision under consideration and supplies only the relevant information to the management to take proper decisions. The work of the management is made easy by the management accountant. Because, the management accountant will carry out a comprehensive evaluation of all the possible and available alternatives and will suggest the best alternative. This way, management accounting renders a very valuable service to the management in all its fields of activity. It is because of this reason that management accounting has rightly been interpreted as accounting for management, management-oriented accounting, etc.

ix) 'Since the decisions have a number of implications on the determinants of profit, performance, etc., it is necessary to have a comprehensive evaluation of each of the possible and available alternatives so that the management selects the best alternative. In order to evaluate the alternatives, it is necessary to consider all the influencing factors. The influencing factors include both the quantitative and the qualitative factors. Quantitative factors are those factors whose effect can easily be measured in terms of monetary units. They are therefore called monetary factors. e.g. material cost, labour, cost, etc. On the other hand, qualitative factors are those factors whose effect can not easily and directly be measured in terms of monetary units e.g. labour relation. Of course, these qualitative factors, also known as non-monetary factors, influence the quantitative factors indirectly. For instance, labour relation has an impact on wages, production, idle time wages, over time costs, labour productivity etc.

From the above analysis, it is obvious that the management has to take a number of decisions and to take decisions, it i.e. management needs information about the relevant influencing factors. There is therefore a need for a system of accounting which ensures the furnishing of relevant information to the management so that the management undertakes a comprehensive evaluation of the problem and takes the most appropriate decision. Hence, there is a need for an accounting system for management'.

x) Management Accounting, focussing on internal user, measures and reports financial and other information that assist managers in fulfilling the goals of organisation. This furnishes the necessary informations to the management frequently i.e. as and when required and also it points out that what should happen.

1.2.2 ESSENTIALS

With the advancement of science and technology more sophisticated equipments and gadgets have been put into operation in the realm of accounting as well. This has changed the accounting from a mere device of recording to a powerful tool of forecasting, budgeting and budgetary control. Thus, financial accounting has been supplemented with financial and cost control, budgeting and budgetary control and also production planning and control besides reporting on business performance. Precisely, it has led to the emergence of **Management Accounting**.

The term **Management Accounting** is of recent origin even in the U.S.A. This term was first coined and used by the British Team of Accountants that visited United States in 1950 under the auspices of Anglo-American Productivity Council. Since then management accounting has grown into a full fledged subject as is looked upon as a subject distinct from accounting in recent years. It is also otherwise known as "**Management-Oriented Accounting**" or "**Accounting for Management**".

The **Essentials** of an effective and efficient system of **Management Accounting** are as follows :

i) the analytical study of basic needs of business concerns.
ii) a systematic research approach towards 'management' and their 'accounting'.
iii) providing utmost importance to 'human' as an important factor in the professional management.
iv) introducing a sound system of financial accounting.
v) selecting appropriate method for supply of useful accounting information to the management for effective planning, accurate decision-making and absolute control.

vi) existence of method and technique of cost accounting.

vii) a systematic method of reporting to fulfil the needs of modern management.

viii) the use of a scientific method for performance evaluation.

ix) a moderate method of communicating required data to assist the management in the creation of business policies and practices.

x) selection of modern accounting and mathematical techniques for cost control purposes.

1.2.3 IMPORTANCE

Management Accounting, an emerging branch of accounting is **important** because of the following basic reasons:

i) It helps in effective planning for future which is basically required for developing the appropriate strategy to be adopted in achieving the targets set.

ii) It collects relevant and useful accounting data, utilise the same for preparing various periodical reports, which facilitates in time decision-making.

iii) It provides the most innovative tools and scientific techniques for further critical analysis and interpretation of collected data.

iv) It helps in controlling business activities more effectively and efficiently through the traditional techniques like standard costing, budgetary control etc.

v) It provides further scope for the rapid growth and overall development of the organisation by adopting ratio analysis as a suitable technique to evaluate the business performances more critically.

vi) It provides valuable guidance to the management in giving their well thoughout judgements about financial position and profitability of the business.

vii) It helps in reducing costs substantially, providing quality products at reasonably affordable prices, that results in rendering best possible valuable services to prosumers and make them happy.

viii) It helps in systematic planning, appropriate decision-making and effective control which ultimately helps in increasing managerial efficiency.

1.2.4 OBJECTIVES

Management Accounting primarily aims at serving the people who are internal to the business entity. This means, it furnishes the most pertinent facts and figures to the managerial personnel and assists them to take various decisions. For this purpose, it collects the data from different sources and presents the same to the management whenever required and in the suitable form. By doing so, management accounting aims at assisting management to take appropriate decisions and discharging their responsibility satisfactorily. Hence, management accounting is called management-oriented accounting or accounting for management. In order to accomplish this aim, management accounting has to perform a number of functions and process. These, functions may also be called as objectives of management accounting. Because these functions of management accounting may also be interpreted as the factors which high-lights the need for management accounting. However, the following are the major **Objectives** of **Management Accounting.**

i) Providing managers with useful information for decision-making and planning aims at modifying the data to suit the requirements of the decision.

ii) With the help of the tools of financial analysis to analyse and interpret the data and present the results with necessary comments, conclusion etc. to the management.

iii) Assisting managerial personnel in directing and controlling operations with the help of standard costing, budgetary control and responsibility accounting.

iv) Motivating managers and other employees towards the organisations goals.

v) Measuring the performance of sub units, managers and other employees within the organisation.

vi) To submit comprehensive reports which includes both the quantitative and the qualitative information.

1.2.5 SCOPE

Management Accounting covers not only the use of financial data and a part of costing theory but may extend beyond the boundaries of accounting and costing. It requires the aid of techniques of other disciplines such as economic, finance, mathematics, statistics and operations research. Figure 1.2 summarises the **Scope of Management Accounting** as follows :

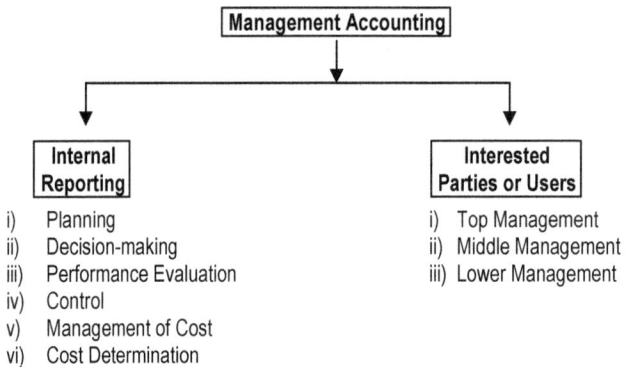

Fig. 1.2 : Scope of Management Accounting

The following are some of the areas of specification included within the ambit of Management Accounting.

i) **Financial Accounting :**

Financial Accounting is an essential pre-requisite of any discussion on management accounting. Financial statements contain enough information that is used by management for decision-making. Management Accounting contains only tool and techniques and it gets the data for interpretation and analysis mainly from financial accounting. Thus, without efficient **Financial Accounting** system, management accounting cannot operate.

ii) **Cost Accounting :**

Business executives depend heavily on accounting information in general and on cost information in particular, because any activity of an organisation can be described by its cost. They make use of various cost data in managing organisations effectively. **Cost Accounting** is considered as backbone of management accounting as it provides the analytical tools such as budgetary control, standard costing, marginal costing, inventory control, operating costing etc. which are used by management to discharge its responsibilities efficiently.

iii) **Financial Statement Analysis :**

Frequently, the various users of financial statements may need access to information that can be obtained only by selecting individual numbers from the statements and by developing certain trends and ratios. Any attempt in this direction is referred to as **Financial Statement Analysis**. A person can gain meaningful insights and conclusions about the firm with the help of analysis and interpretation of the information contained in financial statements. Numerous techniques have been developed which can be used for proper interpretation and analysis of financial statements.

iv) **Forecasting and Budgeting :**

This refers to the formulation of **Budgets and Forecasts**, using standard norms in co-operation with operating and other departments of a business concern. This ultimate success of any budgeting depends on the proper setting of target figures in the budgets and the actual realisation of the same in practice, without even a slight deviation due to external reasons beyond the control of the management.

v) **Cost Control Techniques :**

These serve as effective tool for comparing the actual results with the predetermined figures as laid down in budgets. They greatly help in translating the budgets into operating plans.

vi) **Inflation Accounting :**

Inflation Accounting attempts to identify certain characteristics that tend to distort the reporting of financial results during periods of rapidly changing prices. It devises and implements appropriate methods to analyse and interpret the impact of inflation on the financial information.

vii) **Management Reporting :**

Clear, informative, timely reports are essential management tools in machine decisions that make the best use of a company's resources. Thus, one of the basic responsibility of management accounting is to keep the management well informed about the operations of the business. To discharge this responsibility efficiently, he has to prepare quarterly, half-yearly and other interim reports and submit the same to the management.

viii) **Quantitative Techniques :**

Modern managers believe that the financial and economic data available for managerial decisions can be more useful when analysed with more sophisticated and evaluation techniques. Quantitative analysis methods allow managers to develop information from their financial database that is not otherwise available. The techniques such as time series, regression analysis and sampling techniques are commonly used for this purpose. Further, managers also use techniques such as linear programming, game theory, queuing theory etc. in their decision-making process.

ix) **Taxation :**

Taxation plays an important role in the profitability of a commercial concern. Therefore, it is essential for a management accountant to have a complete knowledge of business taxation. The business profit and the tax thereon is to be ascertained as per the provision of taxation. The filing of tax returns and the payment of tax in due time is exclusively the responsibility of management accountant.

x) **Internal Audit :**

The **Internal Audit** as a discipline of management accounting makes arrangements for performance appraisal of the company's various departments. Thus, a management accountant must possess knowledge about the fixation of responsibilities and measurement of results.

xi) **Office Services :**

To discharge the responsibilities efficiently, a management accountant has to deal with data processing, filing, copying, duplicating. His area of responsibilities also includes the evaluation and reporting about the utility of different office procedures and machines.

1.2.6 FUNCTIONS

Broadly speaking the functions of management accounting embrace all activities concerning with satisfying the needs of different levels of management. The primary objective of a management accounting system is to supply meaningful information the management. To achieve this goal, it has to carry out many activities which are normally referred to as functions of management accounting. The major **Functions of Management Accounting** are summarised below :

i) **Planning and Forecasting :**

Planning is an activity of the management that requires an efficient system of decision-making. In any type of enterprise, plans should be made to guide future operations of the business. Thus, one of the major functions of the management accountant is to help management in the selection of company goals and in the formulation of policies and strategies to allocate resources to achieve these goals. Different accounting techniques are used by the management to discharge the function of planning efficiently. The important among them are financial statement analysis, budgeting, direct costing, capital budgeting and standard costing.

ii) **Furnishes Information as per Requirements :**

Management Accounting furnishes statistical information according to the varying requirements of the different levels of management at periodic intervals. The three-tier management which is in vogue in recent times requires information of various types at different intervals, e.g. the top level management requires information in a capsule form covering all aspects of the business at relatively long intervals whilst, detailed analysis relating to a particular aspect of the business at short intervals will suffice for the persons in the lower rungs of the management ladder.

iii) **Not Confined merely to Financial Data :**

Management Accounting does not confine itself merely to financial data to assist the management in the decision-making process but frequently draws upon various sources other than accounting for qualitative information, which cannot be converted into monetary terms. For this purpose, engineering records, case studies, minutes of meetings, productivity reports, special surveys and other business documents are greatly relied upon.

iv) **Analysis and Interpretation :**

The economic and financial data as collected from various statements do not have much management utility unless it is properly analysed in the light of the nature of the decisions. In fact process of analysis and interpretation puts life in available data to speak about future trends. The management accountant has to present the data with his comments and recommendations to the management. Thus, the analysis and interpretations of data are considered as the back-bone of Management Accounting.

v) **Co-ordinating :**

Techniques such as budgeting, financial reporting and analysis and interpretation are commonly used by management accountants to co-ordinate the various activities of the business efficiently. Efficient control contributes to efficiency of organisation which in turn increases the profitability of a concern.

vi) **Communication :**

The management accountant spends his maximum time in communicating to the management. He has to prepare various reports required by the management from time to time to meet the challenges of the business. The publication of the company's annual report is also an important task of a management accountant.

vii) **Establishes Standards of Performance :**

Management Accounting establishes standards of performance in the different realms of activities such that any deviation therefrom can be easily measured, leading to further investigation of the causes and institution of prompt remedial measures for rectifying the same. This is made possible through budgetary control and standard costing which are essential adjuncts of management accounting.

viii) **Undertakes various Special Studies :**

Modern business is operating under such dynamic conditions, where even a minor change in business can have a significant impact on the business results. Therefore, managements is always interested to know the areas of business which can contribute to the stability and profitability of the concern. To meet this objective, management accountant undertakes various special studies such as sales analysis, economic forecasts, price spread analysis etc.

ix) **Tax Administration :**

In modern business organisations, the responsibilities of a management accountant also includes, the tax administration. This task involves submission of necessary documents and return to the tax authorities and supervision of all matters relating to tax administration.

x) **Controlling :**

Management Accounting helps in the controlling by providing performance reports and control reports which highlight variances between expected and actual performances. Such reports serves as a basis for taking necessary corrective action to control operations.

In short, Management Accounting furnishes useful accounting data and analysed statistical information required for the decision-making process in management which vitally affects the survival and the success of every business.

1.2.7 PRINCIPAL SYSTEMS AND TECHNIQUES

Management Accounting is an information system designed to communicate meaningful economic and financial information to the management so that management may discharge its functions efficiently. The Management Accounting system consists of number of tools and techniques which are frequently used by the management accountant to meet the increasing needs of the business. The **Principal Systems and Techniques of Management Accounting** are as follows :

i) **Financial Planning :**

Planning is necessary not only for efficient utilization of available resources but also for better and progressive business results. It is more significant for finance function because finance plays a deciding role in managerial decision. Financial planning is the process of deciding in advance the financial objective by employing financial planning. In the short term, it can help a concern in meeting its obligations by balancing flow of funds. At the same time, its proper application can ensure efficient utilisation of available financial resources in the long period.

ii) **Statistical Analysis :**

Accountants frequently confront masses of data from which they would like to draw systematic and logical conclusions. Statistical Analysis and in particular, statistical sampling theory provides scientific method for drawing reliable and valid conclusions about the properties of an entire population when only a properly chosen sample of the population has been studied in detail.

iii) **Cost Accounting :**

Cost Accounting is a vital part of the total management accounting system. It includes the recording, classifying, analysis and reporting of all cost aspects of company performance. The cost accounting and procedures have to be designed with great care keeping in view the nature and requirement of the firm and the data required at the different levels of management for effective cost control and cost reduction.

iv) **Standard Costing :**

Another major technique for operating control through management accounting is Standard Costing. Under this arrangement, standard costs are used to control the major activities of the business. Standard costs are predetermined targets against which actual result are evaluated. This is the basis for a system of management control, for which a proper monitoring of performance is a key factor. The variances between standard and actual costs are computed and reported to managements.

v) **Marginal Costing :**

Marginal Costing is a managerial technique that considers only variable costs in the additional output decisions. It is a reporting system that values inventory and cost of sales at its manufacturing variable cost. It is frequently used as an internal management reporting system.

vi) **Budgetary Control :**

Budgetary Control refers to a system of business control that uses budgets to control the major activities of business. The budgets for all major activities of the business are prepared in advance. Generally, the budget is prepared by updating the previous year's figures in the light of some forward projections.

vii) **Funds Flow Analysis :**

Funds Flow Analysis attempts to highlight the causes of change in the financial condition of a business enterprise between two dates. Any statement prepared for this purpose is referred to as funds flow statement. A funds flow statement helps management in the efficient planning and control of cash.

viii) **Management Reporting :**

Management Reporting is considered essential component of a well designed planning and control system. Decision-makers frequently require information on various aspects of business. Thus, it is the responsibility of the management accountant to communicate right information to the management at the right time and in a right manner.

ix) **Analysis of Financial Statement :**

Financial Statement Analysis is a growing and ever changing set of system and procedures designed to provide decision makers with relevant information derived from the basic sources of data, such as company financial statements and government and industry publications. Over the years, number of techniques have been devised to analyse financial statements e.g. comparative financial statements, common-size statements, ratio analysis, trend analysis, and fund flow statement.

1.2.8 ADVANTAGES

Management Accounting offers the following **advantages** to the corporate enterprise :

i) It increases the efficiency in the activities of the business.
ii) It ensures efficient regulation of business activities by establishing efficient system of planning and budgeting.
iii) It makes possible the efficient utilisation of the available resources and thereby increases the return on capital employed.
iv) It ensures effective control by comparing actual results with the standards.
v) It maintains a good public relation by providing quality services to the customers of the business.
vi) It provides means to motivate the employees of the organisation.
vii) It keeps management informed about the going operations enabling it to suggest remedial measures in case of deviations.
viii) It helps in evaluating the efficiency and effectiveness of the company's business policies with the incorporation of management audit.
ix) It is one of the "diagnostic techniques" available to the managers and executives for improving economic performance by realisation of the accounting system in use.
x) It helps in development of realistic data in respect of future transactions.
xi) It provides technique for useful interpretation of accounting information.

1.2.9 LIMITATIONS

The important **Limitations of Management Accounting** are as follows :

i) **Psychological Resistance :**

The management accounting system spells a radical change in the management approach towards solving day-to-day problems confronted by it. This calls for a reorganisation of personnel as well as reorientation of their activities. This is bound to attract opposition especially from the labour force misconstruing it as a tool meant for their exploitation. Constant education about the benefits of such a new techniques alone will allay the fears of the labour force by and large. Management accounting, as a new discipline, is no exception to this rule and it encountered psychological resistance at least in the initial stages.

ii) **Expensive Installation :**

For installation of a system of management accounting in a business concern, an elaborate organisation and a large number of manuals are very essential. This in turn escalates the establishment charges such that, only large scale organisations can afford to install it.

iii) **Continuance of Intuitive Decision-making :**

Management accounting eliminates the intuitive decision-making process of management and replaces it with scientific decision-making. Unfortunately, many managements are prone to take the easy and simple path of intuitive decision-making rather than the difficult but reliable scientific decision-making process in the day-to-day management.

iv) **Broad-based Scope :**

The scope of management accounting is wide and broad-based and this creates many difficulties in the implementation process. It is easy to record, analyse, and interpret a historical event converted into monetary terms in a most objective manner. But it will be difficult to perform the same functions in respect of future and unquantifiable situations in the light of the past records.

v) **Comprehensive Coverage :**

The fusion of a number of subjects like financial accounting, statistics, engineering, economics, taxation has culminated in the emergence of management accounting. Under the circumstances, more of these subjects will have its impact on the fixation of standards as well as solutions to the problems connected with the management performance.

vi) **Evolutionary Stage :**

Management Accounting is a new discipline and a growing subject too. It is still in the infancy stage and undergoing evolutionary process. Naturally, it faces certain obstacles and impediments before achieving perfection and finality. This necessitates sharpening of the analytical tools and improving of techniques for removing the air of doubt as regards uncertainty in their applications.

vii) **Persistent Efforts :**

The conclusion drawn by the management accountant may not be readily and willingly implemented. For this purpose, the management accountant has to strive to convince the staff members.

viii) **Basic Records :**

The management accounting collects the data from various sources like Financial Accounting, Cost Accounting, Statistics and other operational records. If such data or information is incorrect or partial, the decisions arrived at on the basis of such data may be incorrect and misleading.

x) **Principle of Objectivity not Followed :**

The principle of objectivity is not followed in its real spirit in management accounting. The collection and analysis is considerably influenced by the personal bias of the management accountant.

x) **No Substitute for Management :**

In fact, Management Accounting is a means to an end, the end being the successful business operations for achievements of business objectives. It cannot replace management as it is simply a tool or a technique in the hands of management and ultimate success in business depends upon the will and dedication of management.

However, number of limitations from which Management Accounting is suffering can be over come if the management is convinced about the importance of, and the necessity for management accounting. As well as these limitations do not undermine the significance of Management Accounting.

1.3 DISTINCTION BETWEEN FINANCIAL ACCOUNTING AND MANAGEMENT ACCOUNTING

Though Management Accounting and Financial Accounting cannot be put in water-tight compartment classification, it should be remembered that the former is only an off-shoot of the latter. Precisely, Management Accounting supplements the functions of Financial Accounting in as much as it provides the necessary accounting data and statistical information needed by the management for improving the efficiency as a whole. Despite the closer inter-relationship that exists, there are certain points of difference between **Financial Accounting** and **Management Accounting** which are discussed below.

Sr. No	Points	Financial Accounting	Management Accounting
i)	Primary Users of Information	The users of Financial Accounting statements are mainly external to the business enterprise. The financial statements prepared under financial accounting show how the resources have been used by a business enterprise during a specific period of time and thus are useful to external users in making sound economic decisions. These financial statements are relevant to management but are not adequate for the purpose of planning, control and decision-making. External users include shareholders, creditors, financial analysts, government authorities, stock exchange, labour unions, etc.	Management Accounting aims at preparing reports and supplying information to management for planning, controlling and decision-making. The information generated under the accounting system is used by members of management at different levels. The nature of internal reports and data varies for different levels of management in conformity with their information requirements for analysing business operations and for planning and control purpose. Thus, different sets of information could be developed under managerial accounting and supplied to different persons responsible for activities in the organisation.
ii)	Nature	The historical nature of Financial Accounting serves a limited purpose of throwing light on the events and results of the past. The forward looking management accounting greatly helps the management in improving the results in future through various tools and techniques of budgeting and budgetary	Management Accounting is mainly concerned with the future plans and policies, whereas financial accounting is concerned with historical records relating to the past. Management rely on the past records for formulation of future plans and hence, the interdependence of management accounting and financial

Sr. No	Points	Financial Accounting	Management Accounting
		control, standard costing, profit planning etc.	accounting cannot be over - emphasised.
iii)	Accounting Method	Financial Accounting follows the double-entry system for recording, classifying and summarising business transactions. This accounting process results in aggregate balances of all accounts maintained in a firm's books.	Management Accounting is not based on the double - entry system. The data under management accounting may be gathered for small or large segments or activities of an organisation and monetary as well as other measures can be used for different activities in the firm. The only constraint regarding managerial accounting principles and methods is that they should be useful for management purpose.
iv)	Accounting Principles	Financial Accounting data is primarily meant for external users. The "generally accepted accounting principles" are important in financial accounting and are used extensively while recording, classifying, summarising and reporting business transactions. The use of GAAP adds credibility and reliability of financial statements and creates confidence among the financial statement users.	Management Accounting is not bound to use the "generally" accepted accounting principles. It can use any accounting technique or practice which generates useful information. Besides, data developed in management accounting may be facts, estimates, projections, analyses etc.
v)	Obligatory	It is more or less obligatory on the part of every business concern to adopt Financial Accounting for disclosing the results of the business to the rightful owners.	In modern time, a business concern is free to install any system of Management Accounting.
vi)	Time Span	Financial Accounting data and statements are developed for a definite period, usually a year or a half-year. It requires that financial statements be developed and presented at regular time intervals. Company annual reports may be prepared semi- annually or quarterly but the important point is that they are prepared on a regular basis.	Management Accounting reports and statements are prepared whenever needed. Reports may be prepared on a monthly, weekly or even daily basis. Frequency of reports is determined by particular planning, controlling and decision-making needs.
vii)	Legal Formalities	Financial Accounting statements are standardized and meant for external use. The preparation and presentation of annual final accounts of companies are governed by the provisions of the Companies and Income Tax Act in force.	Since a business concern is free to install the system of Management Accounting, there is no statutory regulation fixing the norms and standards for preparation and presentation of accounting statements. Needless to state that, these statements can be adapted to the changing needs of the management since they are meant for internal use.

Sr. No	Points	Financial Accounting	Management Accounting
viii)	Unit of Measurement	All information under Financial Accounting is in terms of money. That is, transactions measured in terms of money have already occurred. In comparison managerial accounting applies any measurement unit that is useful in a particular situation.	Besides the monetary units, the Management Accountant may find it necessary to use such measures, as number of labour hours, machine hours and product units for the purpose of analysis and decision-making. The common objective in all measurement, reporting and data analysis in managerial accounting is usefulness for a particular purpose. Historical cost and past transactions are essential to financial accounting but may be secondary to managerial accounting as they are not of much use to management.
ix)	Purpose of Report	Financial Accounting produces information and reports which are general purpose reports in order to serve the informational needs of many external users such as shareholders, creditors, potential investors, customers, supplier, regulatory authorities, employees and the general public. Financial accounting is concerned with overall of a firm performance rather than individual segments or departments.	The reports and data developed in Management Accounting are known as specific purpose reports designed for a particular user (manager) or particular decision. Managerial accounting uses internal reports to evaluate the performance of entities, product lines, departments and managers.
x)	Focus	Financial Accounting focuses on the company as a whole. Sometimes, in financial accounting, some information is given about different products or lines of activity due to financial reporting requirements as provided in the Companies Act or other rules and regulations.	Management Accounting provides detailed and disaggregated information about products, individual activities, divisions, plants, operations, tasks or any other responsibility centers.
xi)	Precision Exactness	In Financial Accounting precision is stressed greatly since the past result of the business are reflected through them.	Management Accounting lays no emphasis on precision as the data and particulars compiled are merely estimates and relate to the future.
xii)	Subject Matter and Scope	Financial Accounting also known as external accounting, produces information and reports for external users.	Managerial Accounting, also known as internal accounting, identifies, collects measures, classifies and reports information that is useful to managers in planning, control and decision-making.

1.4 DISTINCTION BETWEEN COST ACCOUNTING AND MANAGEMENT ACCOUNTING

The term 'management accounting' is of recent origin and is used to describe the modern concept of accounts as a tool of management. It is concerned with all such accounting information that is useful to management. Management Accounting consist of four essential tasks : i) cost determination; ii) cost, control; iii) performance evaluation and; iv) supplying information for planning and decision-making.

It will be seen from the above points that, the scope of management accounting is broader than that of cost accounting. In cost accounting, the main emphasis is on cost determination and cost control whereas management accounting utilises the principles and practices of financial accounting and cost accounting in addition to other modern management techniques for efficient operation of business, The various techniques; employed by management accounting include marginal costing and cost-volume-profit analysis, standard costing, budgetary control, uniform costing and inter-firm comparison, funds flow statements, ratio analysis; and also certain techniques from various branches of knowledge like mathematics, statistics, economics which-so-ever can help management in achieving the business goals. Cost accounting also uses many of these techniques and its objectives are also quite similar to those of management accounting.

Inspite of the above minor differences between the two, both work as complementary. Because, a management accountant will not be in a position to discharge his responsibility in the absence of a sound cost-accounting system. Because, cost accounting provides some of the useful data to the management accountant who in turn utilises them to appraise the management. In the same way, cost accounting would be of not much use to the managerial personnel in the absence of a proper management accounting system. Hence, both are complementary. **Mr. M. N. Arora** in his book, **Cost Accountancy** pointed out that; in fact, management accounting is an extension of the managerial aspects of cost accounting. The scope of management accounting is wide and broad-based and includes financial accounting, cost accounting, budgeting, audit, taxation, etc. However, very few minor differences exist between Cost Accounting and Management Accounting. These are discussed below :

Sr. No	Points	Cost Accounting	Management Accounting
i)	**Prime Objectives**	Cost Accounting aims at ascertaining the cost of goods and services. It lays emphasis on the stage by stage computation of costs. For cost ascertainment, different techniques and system of costing are used under different circumstances.	Management Accounting aims at the presentation of the cost data, to the extent required, wherever and whenever they are required together with other relevant information to the management for taking decisions.
ii)	**Data coverage**	Cost reports deal mainly with the costs incurred or budgeted and standards, variances, savings, etc. Cost reporting is a continuous process and may be daily, weekly, monthly etc.	Cost data forms a part of managerial reports. Report includes both the quantitative and qualitative information.
iii)	**Use of Reports**	Though cost reports are meant for management, they are useful even to the external parties.	Management reports are useful only to the management but not to both internal and external parties.
iv)	**Control of appropriate authority**	Cost accounts and reports are to be prepared as per certain rules, principles, procedures etc, as specified by the appropriate authority (e.g. ICWAI) to the industry to which the company belongs. It has been made obligatory to keep cost records under the Companies Act.	Preparation of reports as per the rules of any appropriate authority etc. No such rigidity is there in the case of managerial reports. The procedure, format etc. can be modified from time to time depending upon convenience and requirements.

Sr. No	Points	Cost Accounting	Management Accounting
v)	Statutory verification	Cost accounts and reports, in many cases, are subject to statutory audit (i.e. cost audit). Hence, they should be prepared, as far as possible, on objective manner.	Management reports are not subject to any statutory audit. Of course, there is a management audit. But, it is voluntary and it evaluates the managerial functions, decisions, etc. However, management reports include both the objective and the subjective data.
vi)	Nature	Cost Accounting is concerned not only with historical costs but also with predetermined costs. This is because cost accounting does not end with what has happened in the past but also extends to plans and policies to improve the performance in the future. Mostly cost accounting helps in determination of selling price.	Management Accounting is mainly concerned with the future plan policies. Management rely on the past records for formulation of future plans and hence, the interdependence of management accounting and cost accounting cannot be over emphasised.
vii)	Subject Matter and Scope	Cost Accounting and Costing are often used interchangeably. Cost Accountancy is the widest of all the terms and embraces not only costing and cost accounting but also cost control and cost audit. Cost accountancy is used to describe the principles, conventions, techniques and systems which are employed in a business to plan and control the utilisation of its resources.	Management Accounting is also known as Managerial Accounting, or Accounting for Management or Management Oriented Accounting etc. It is also known as internal accounting, identifies, collects, measures, classifies, and reports information that is useful to managers in planning, control and decision-making.

As per the above mentioned points of differences, though a few differences can be identified between Cost Accounting and Management accounting, the line of difference is very thin. Because, both these accounting systems are closely linked as they use common basic data and reports to a material degree.

QUESTIONS FOR SELF-STUDY

I. **Theory Questions :**
1) What is Management Accounting ? Discuss the role of management accounting in the area of planning, control and decision making.
2) "Management Accounting is nothing more than use of cost and financial information for management purpose". Explain the statement with suitable illustrations.
3) Discuss the importance of management accounting for managerial decision-making. State briefly the difference between Management Accounting and Financial Accounting.
4) Define Management Accounting and explain its significance.
5) Describe how Management Accounting satisfies the various needs of management for arriving at appropriate business decisions.
6) What are the main limitations of Financial Statements ?
7) Explain the scope of Management Accounting.

8) How does Management Accounting differ from Financial Accounting ?
9) Explain the meaning of the term "Management Accounting" and state how it can be used as an instrument of higher control.
10) What is Management Accounting ? Explain the principal systems and techniques of Management Accounting.
11) Why is Financial Accounting subject to more strict rules and regulations than Management Accounting ?
12) Explain the role of Management Accounting in a fast changing business environment. In what manner can Management Accounting considered to be an extension of Financial Accounting ? Give salient points of distinction between the two.
13) Define 'Management Accounting'. Describe the limitations of Management Accounting.
14) "Management Accounting is often called as a tool for management". Discuss. Explain briefly the functions of Management Accounting.
15) What do you understand by the term "Management Accounting" ? Explain its usefulness in modern business.
16) "Management Accounting is an extension of Financial Accounting". Explain.
17) Discuss the managerial functions in which Management Accounting information can be well utilised.
18) "Management Accounting assists in the corporate planning process". Explain.
19) In what essential respects is Management Accounting different from Financial Accounting ?
20) "Management Accounting is a mid-way between Financial Accounting and Cost Accounting". Elucidate.
21) "Management Accounting is the presentation of accounting information in such a way that, it assists for management in the creation of policy and in the day-to-day operation of an undertaking". Explain.
22) Explain the important phases in the evolution of accounting.
23) What is the use of accounting information ? Explain the purposes of accounting information.
24) What is meant by Financial Accounting ? What are its objectives ?
25) Define the term "Financial Accounting". Explain its functions and limitations.
26) 'Management Accounting plays a vital role in planning, organising, decision-making and controlling functions performed by managers". Discuss.
27) Write short notes on :
    i) Functions of Management Accounting
    ii) Scope of Management Accounting
    iii) Use of Accounting Information
    v) Objectives of Financial Accounting
    v) Cost Accounting
    vi) Limitations of Management Accounting
    vii) Need and Importance of Management Accounting
    viii) Essentials of Management Accounting
    ix) Functions of Management Accounting
    x) Advantages of Management Accounting
28) Differentiate between :
    i) Financial Accounting and Management Accounting
    ii) Cost Accounting and Management Accounting

***

UNIT 2

ANALYSIS AND INTERPRETATION OF FINANCIAL STATEMENTS

SYNOPSIS

2.1 Methods of Analysis

    2.1.1 Comparative Statements

    2.1.2 Common Size Statements

    2.1.3 Trend Percentage or Trend Ratios (Horizontal Analysis)

2.2 Ratio Analysis

    2.2.1 Meaning of Ratio

    2.2.2 Necessity and Advantages of Ratio

- Questions for Self-Study

Financial Statement Analysis

Meaning

Financial Statement Analysis is an analysis which highlights important relationships in the financial statements. It focuses on evaluation of past operations as revealed by the analysis of basic statements. Financial Statement Analysis embraces the methods used in assessing and interpreting the result of past performance and current financial position as they relate to particular factors of interest in investment decisions. It is an important means of assessing past performance and in forecasting and planning future performance.

Definitions

The term 'Financial Statement Analysis' is defined by eminent authorities as follows :

i) **Lev :**

"Financial Statement Analysis is an information processing system designed to provide data for decision making models, such as the portfolio selection model, bank lending decision models, and corporate financial management models".

ii) **Myers :**

"is largely a study of relationship among the various financial factors in a business as disclosed by a single set of statements and a study of the trends of these factors as shown in series of statement".

iii) **W. B. Meig :**

"Financial Statements thus are organised summaries of detailed information and are thus a form of analysis. The type of statements accountants prepare, the way they arrange items on these statements and their standards of disclosure are all influenced by a desire to provide information in a convenient form".

iv) **Metcalf** and **Titard :**

"is a process of evaluating the relationship between component parts of a Financial Statement to obtain a better understanding of a firm's position and performance".

Hence, the focus of **Financial Analysis** is on key figures contained in the Financial Statements and the significant relationship that exists between them.

Objectives

The major **objective of Financial Statement Analysis** is to provide information to decision makers, about a business enterprise for use in decision-making. Users of financial statement information are the decision makers concerned with evaluating the economic situation of the firm and predicting its future course. The major groups of users are management for evaluating the operational and financial efficiency of the enterprise as a whole or of sub-units (e.g. departments); investors for making investment decisions and portfolio decisions, lenders and creditors for determining the creditworthiness and solvency position; employees and labour unions for deciding economic status of the enterprise and making sound decisions in wage and salary negotiations, regulatory authorities for controlling the activities of the firm and making overall corporate policy, economists, researchers and planners for studying firm and specific data behaviour.

Financial Statement Analysis can be used by different users and decision makers to achieve the following basic **objectives** :

i) **Assessment of Past Performance and Current Position :**

Past performance is often considered as a good indicator of future performance. Therefore, an investor or creditors are interested in the trend of past sales, expenses, net income, cash flow and return on investment. These trends offer a means for judging management's past performance and are possible indicators of future performance. Similarly, the analysis of current position indicates where the business stands today. For instance, the current position analysis will show the types of assets owned by a business enterprise and the different liabilities due against the enterprise. It will tell what the cash position is, how much debts the company has in relation to equity and how reasonable the inventories and receivables are.

ii) **Loan Decision by Financial Institutions and Banks :**

Financial statement analysis is used by financial institutions, loaning agencies, banks and others to make sound loan or credit decisions. In this way, they can make proper allocation of credit among the different borrowers. All lenders are primarily concerned with repayment of loan and payment of interest on the due dates. This requires comprehensive investigation and analysis of the financial statements submitted by the borrowers. Financial statement analysis helps in determining credit risk, deciding terms and conditions of loan if sanctioned, interest rate, maturity date etc.

iii) **Prediction of Net Income and Growth Prospects :**

Financial statement analysis helps in predicting the earning prospects and growth rate in the earnings which are used by investors while comparing investment alternatives and other users interested in judging the earning potential of business enterprises. Investors also consider the risk or uncertainty associated with the expected return. The decision makers are futuristic and are always concerned with the future financial statements which contain information on past performances analysed and interpreted as a basis for forecasting future rates of return and for assessing risk. The prediction of future earnings tends to influence and improve the financial decisions made by the investors and financial analysis.

iv) **Prediction of Bankruptcy and Failure :**

Financial statement analysis is a significant tool in predicting the bankruptcy and failure probability of business enterprises. Financial statement analysis accomplishes this through the evaluation of solvency position. After being aware about probable failure, managers and investors both can take preventive measures to avoid or minimise losses. Corporate managements can effect changes in operating policy, reorganise financial structure or even go for voluntary liquidation to shorten the length of time losses.

In accounting and finance area, empirical studies conducted have suggested a set of financial ratios which can give early signal of corporate failure. Such a prediction model based on financial statement analysis is useful to managers, investors and creditors. Managers may use the ratios prediction model to assess the solvency position of their firms and thus can take appropriate corrective action. Investors and shareholders can use the model to make the optimum portfolio selection and to bring changes in the investment strategy in accordance with their investment goals. Similarly, creditors can apply the prediction model while evaluating the creditworthiness of business enterprises.

Interpretation and Criticisms

The Analysis of Financial Statements means a critical examination of statements for better understanding and drawing fruitful conclusions. It is only an analytical study of statements which can help draw dependable conclusions. Therefore, analysis becomes a pre-requisite for interpretation of financial data in the form of annual accounts and statements. The technique of analysis depends upon the objective of analysis.

The type and extent of relationship to be investigated depends upon primarily the objective and purpose of analysis. The purpose of analysis differs among various groups such as creditors, shareholders, potential investors, management, government and so on. For example, the object of short-term creditors is primarily to know about the short-term solvency and the long-term creditors, such as debenture holders and financial institutions aim at knowing the long-term solvency of the enterprises to which they have lent money. There are investors who are interested in the declared rate of dividend; other investors, such as holding companies are interested in the earning capacity and growth and development of the enterprise. Thus, different persons will analyse the financial statements from different objects in mind. Contrary to the above, the management of the business unit looks to the financial statements from different angles. These financial statements are required by the management for the purpose of evaluation and decision-making.

Steps involved in Financial Statement Analysis

Generally, there are three steps involved in financial statement analysis i.e. Selection, Classification and Interpretation. Figure 2.1 shows **Steps involved in Financial Statement Analysis** as follows :

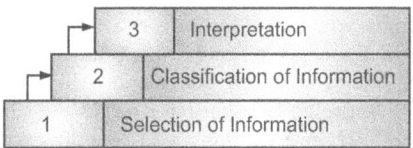

Fig. 2.1 : Steps involved in Financial Statement Analysis

The first step involved refers to the **Selection of Information** relevant to the purpose of evaluation from the total of information contained in the financial statements. The second step involved is the **Classification or grouping of Information** in such a manner so as to to focus on the significant relationships. The final step is **Interpretation** which includes drawing of inferences and conclusions.

Role of Financial Analyst

Joint Stock Companies are required to prepare their published accounts on the prescribed proforma and in accordance with the guidelines provided in the Acts. The **Financial Analyst** should see that the final accounts have been drawn up according to law and nothing has been left out or concealed. Once the analyst is satisfied about the accuracy of published final accounts and statements, he can safely proceed to further analyse them for the purpose of drawing conclusions.

Analysis and interpretation are closely interlinked since interpretation is impossible without a proper analysis and any analysis which is not followed by interpretation becomes a meaningless exercise. Thus, a proper analysis interpretation precedes. For instance, the financial analyst would like to have more detailed information regarding debts due within a month or six months or so from internal sources, since the same cannot be obtained from the financial statements. Further, interpretation requires comparison. This necessitates dissection of financial statements into its constituents in order to measure relative magnitude of the various items contained therein. However, the financial analyst should always keep in mind the limitations of financial statements.

Limitations

The **Financial Statements** (i.e. Profit and Loss Account and Balance Sheet) suffer from certain **limitations**, which are mentioned below :

i) Financial Statements do not show qualitative changes which undoubtedly affect greatly the performance of an undertaking. The financial accounts do not account for events such as change in management, labour strikes, changes in government policies affecting an enterprise etc. The financial analyst should try to assess the impact of qualitative changes on the profitability of the concerning enterprise.

ii) Financial Statements are historical in nature. They tell nothing about the future. Since the financial analyst is concerned with analysis and interpretation for formulation of future business policies, he should restructure the statements in such a manner, that they become more intelligible and useful for projections for the future.

iii) Generally, the audited Profit and Loss Account and Balance Sheet are considered dependable statements. If the analyst is compelled to use the un-audited accounting statements, he should first ascertain their truthfulness. It is very difficult to verify the correctness of the Income Statement and Position Statement without the basic information in the form of ledger accounts and other records.

iv) The concept of accounting period is not technically correct. The Profit and Loss Account is prepared for an accounting year which is generally a period of one year. This gives rise to the problem of cost and income allocation. In fact, real profit or loss can be calculated only at the end when the unit is closed down. The annual accounts can best be considered as interim reports.

v) The profit or loss figure as shown by a Profit and Loss Account is not necessarily a correct figure which is influenced by the personal judgement of the management regarding depreciation, inventory valuation and provisions for various reserves and contingencies. The management can manipulate profit or loss figure to serve their interests. The financial analyst should see that the income has been rightly computed by following consistent accounting policies.

vi) Balance Sheet is a static document, which means, a document showing the economic position of an enterprise on a given date. The Balance Sheet is prepared on the last day of a financial year i.e. on 31st December, 31st, March or 30th June. Generally, the Balance Sheet is prepared and published very late after the close of the accounting year. The Balance Sheet loses much of its significance and practical utility due to a long time gap between the close of an accounting year and the actual publication of the Balance Sheet. A financial analyst should always bear this limitation in mind.

vii) Assets shown in the Balance Sheet might not be shown at their fair or current values. Goodwill is an item which is closely related to profits. If a company suffers loss continuously for the last few years, it clearly means that it no more enjoys the goodwill as shown in the books of the company. But the companies continue to show goodwill at the usual figure despite continuous losses. Similarly, companies in general do not account for the impact of inflation on their fixed assets and liabilities and show them at cost values. The financial analyst should take precautions and give due recognition to the assets valuation as done by a company.

The business house is, generally, not in a position to understand properly the financial statements instantly in their traditional forms. But, when the same statements are presented to the management in an analytical form with brief explanations on critical items, it becomes easier to understand them and to take decisions without inconvenience and loss of time and energy.

2.1 METHODS OF ANALYSIS

A Financial Analyst can adopt the following important tools for **Analysis of the Financial Statements** which are also termed as **Methods of Financial Analysis.** Figure 2.2 shows very clearly the **Methods of Financial Analysis** as follows :

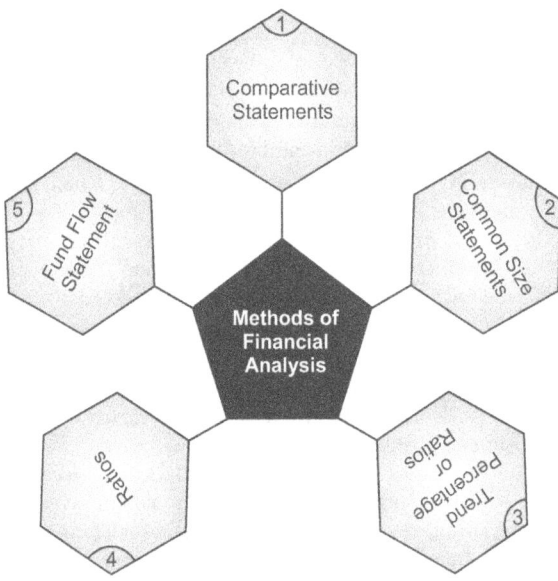

Fig. 2.2 : Methods of Financial Analysis

2.1.1 COMPARATIVE STATEMENTS

Meaning

Joint Stock Companies are required to provide in their annual published accounts the corresponding figures for the year immediately preceding the current financial year so as to provide a comparative picture of their business affairs.

As the very term signifies, **Comparative Statement** is the statement of financial position of a business so formulated as to focus on the elements contained therein and provide the necessary time perspective to it. Normally, it is the Balance Sheet and Profit and Loss Account which alone are prepared in a comparative form, since it is these two statements which are considered as important financial statements. Moreover, it is, through these two statements that the financial position and the operational results of any business can be determined.

Procedure

The decision-makers prefer to study the picture of not only for one or two years but for few more years in the past. The Income Statement and Balance Sheet in their usual form are not much useful from management point of view. Therefore, the analysts re-arrange the information in different groups as the group study along with the individual items is more meaningful for the purpose of interpretation and decision-making. If two or more companies have to be compared i.e. inter-firm comparison, the analyst should take care that the groups are homogeneous. He should also bear in mind the size of the enterprise in terms of capital investment and turnover.

Comparative Financial Statements are designed to disclose the following vital informations :

i) Absolute data in terms of money value or rupee amounts.
ii) Increases or decreases in absolute data in terms of money value.
iii) Increases or decreases in absolute data in terms of percentage.
iv) Comparisons expressed in ratios.
v) Percentage of totals.

It may be noted that the absolute figures, especially when they represent large amounts are not easy to remember; therefore, it is advisable that the figures are expressed as a percentage or ratio.

Necessity

Comparative Financial Statements are very useful to the financial analyst since they contain figures drawn from a single statement and also provide necessary information for the study of financial and operating results over a period of time. They only point out the direction or the trend of the movement as regards financial position and operating results of the business concern.

When financial statements are prepared at periodic intervals of say one month or three months, comparison can be effected with the corresponding month or quarter of preceding accounting year or years. Cumulative totals for the expired portion of the current year to the corresponding totals of the preceding year or years may also be computed by the analyst. The percentage analysis of increase and decrease in corresponding items in comparative financial statement is called horizontal analysis. Comparative financial statement analysis helps in predicting the earning prospects and growth rates in the earning which are used by investors while comparing investment alternatives and other users interested in judging the earning potential of business enterprises. Comparative financial statement analysis is a significant tool in predicting the bankruptcy and failure probability of business enterprises.

Limitations

Comparisons will have significance and will become more effective only if the data compared truly reflect the constancy in the application of generally accepted accounting principles from date to date or period to period. Where there is no change in the accounting principles followed, it should be mentioned as a footnote in the financial statements as well as audited reports.

The analyst should also keep in mind the price level changes that have taken place between the dates of different transactions and that of preparation of financial statements. Where there is a substantial price fluctuation, the analyst must exercise great caution while interpreting the assets revealed by comparative statements. Again absolute comparison of the statements of different business concerns for a certain year is not possible. Some degree of comparison can be achieved by comparing the assets within different companies for a number of years, say at least three years. This is more due to the effect of the choice of certain alternatives that cause considerable difference in one year and tend to even out over several years.

2.1.2 COMMON SIZE STATEMENT

Meaning

Common Size Statements are also known as "**Component Percentage**" or "**100 percent Statement**". Each statement is reduced to the total of 100 and each individual item contained therein is expressed as a percentage to the total 100. Thus, each percentage in the statement shows the relationship of individual item to its representative total.

The Profit and Loss Account and Balance Sheet can also be presented in the form of a **Common-Size Statement**. A statement in which individual items are expressed as a percentage of same common base is termed as a common-size statement. In a common-size Profit and Loss Account, the sale figure is generally taken as the base (sale - 100) to calculate the proportion of other items figuring in the Profit and Loss Account and a common size Balance Sheet expresses individual assets and liabilities as percentage of total assets or liabilities. "When the balance sheet and income statement items are shown in analytical percentages, i.e. the percentages that each item bears to the total of the appropriate item such as total assets, total liabilities, capital and net sales, the common base for comparison is provided. The statements compiled in this form are termed as "**Common-Size Statements**". Common-size comparative statements provide a better historical perspective of an undertaking. Any significant departure from the normal trend needs further investigation to ascertain the reasons for unusual movement in the figures so that due care is taken in the formulation of future plans.

Procedure

Firstly, the total assets, total liabilities, capital and total net sales are reckoned as 100. Secondly, the ratio that each item bears to the total is ascertained by dividing the individual money amounts by the total amount as contained in the statement. For example, if selling and distribution expenses amount to ₹ 80,000 out of a net sales of ₹ 8,00,000 for a company in 2013, then the ratio that this item bears to the total can be calculated as follows :

$$\frac{\text{Selling and Distribution Expenses}}{\text{Net Sales}} \times 100$$

$$= \frac{₹\ 80,000}{₹\ 8,00,000} \times 100$$

$$= 10\%$$

This ratio of 10% denotes that the selling and distribution expenses of the company are 10% of the net sales for 2013. In other words, these expenses amount to ₹ 10 for every ₹ 100 worth of net sales. Common-size statements are usually prepared in the following forms :

i) **Common-Size Income Statement :**

Common-Size Income Statement percentages show the percentage of net sales that has been absorbed by each individual item representing cost or expense in the income statement. The comparison of the **Common-Size Income Statement** ratios is significant since they indicate whether a larger or smaller amount of net sales figure was used in meeting a particular cost or expense item. But it should also be noted that variations in percentages may reflect change in the sales, components of cost of goods sold or both.

ii) **Common-Size Balance Sheet :**

The **Common-Size Balance Sheet** represents the relation of each asset item to total assets and each liability and capital item to total liabilities and capital respectively. As these percentages indicate the relationship to **Balance Sheet** totals, variations from year to year do not necessarily indicate changes in money amounts. The ratios expressed in the **Common-Size Balance Sheet** would reflect a change in the individual item, total or both.

The value of a **Common-Size Balance Sheet** can be further increased by adding one additional column for each year to indicate the percentages of each item within a group to the total of the group.

The **Common-Size Balance Sheet** percentages facilitate a horizontal comparison from year to year and a study of the trends of relationships. They do not throw light on the trends of the individual items from year to year, as the trends of relationship are difficult for interpretation in the value of common-size balance. However, the usefulness of the **Common-Size Balance-Sheet** can be improved by establishing norms of percentage for each item to the relative total.

[EXAMPLE]

Prepare a **Common-Size Income Statement** of Activa Ltd., Aurangabad on the basis of data given below and interpret the results.

Income Statements for the year ended ......

Particulars	2012 ₹	2013 ₹	Particulars	2012 ₹	2013 ₹
To Cost of Goods Sold	2,70,000	2,92,000	By Sales less Returns	3,92,400	4,10,420
To Gross Profit C/D	1,22,400	1,18,420			
	3,92,400	4,10,420		3,92,400	4,10,420
To Administrative Expenses	60,000	63,000	By Gross Profit B/D	1,22,400	1,18,420
To Selling Expenses	30,000	35,000			
To Net Profit C/D	32,400	20,420			
	1,22,400	1,18,420		1,22,400	1,18,420

[ANSWER]

In the books of Activa Ltd., Aurangabad

Common-Size Income Statement for the year ended 31.12.2012 and 31.12.2013

Particulars	2012 ₹	Percentage	2013 ₹	Percentage
Sales	4,00,400	–	4,20,420	–
Less : Returns (–)	8,000	–	10,000	–
∴ Net Sales	3,92,400	100	4,10,420	100
Less : Cost of Goods Sold (–)	2,70,000	68.90	2,92,000	71.20
∴ **Gross Profit**	1,22,400	31.10	1,18,420	28.80
• Administrative Expenses	60,000	15.30	63,000	15.37
• Selling Expenses (+)	30,000	7.70	35,000	8.53
∴ Total Operating Expenses (–)	90,000	23.00	98,000	23.90
∴ Operating Net Profit	32,400	8.10	20,420	4.90

Interpretation

The cost of goods sold and other expenses have increased over the last year. This has resulted in reducing the percentage of net income from 8.10% in 2007 to 4.90% in 2008 to net sales, even though the sales in 2008 have increased by ₹ 18,020. The cost of goods sold has increased from 68.90% to 71.20%, the selling expenses from 7.70% to 8.53%.

2.1.3 TREND PERCENTAGE OR TREND RATIOS (HORIZONTAL ANALYSIS)

Meaning

The financial statements for a series of years may be analysed horizontally to determine the trend of the data contained therein. The **Trend Percentages** are also referred to as **'Trend Ratios'**. This method of analysis is adopted to determine the direction upward or downward. This involves the computation of the percentage relationship that each item in the statement bears to the corresponding items contained in that of the base year. For this purpose, the earliest year involved in comparison or any intervening year may be considered as the base year.

The absolute figure of an activity is not very useful in decision making. Therefore, a set of figures for purposes of comparison is necessary. The accounting figures relating to sales, production, profit, overheads, working capital, etc., for the last few years expressed as a percentage of some figure in a base period, give trends which throw more light on the related problem. Generally, the figures for the last three to five years should be considered for better understanding of an economic phenomenon. The trend percentages emphasise changes in the financial data from year to year and facilitate horizontal comparison and study of the data. These trend ratios can be considered as index numbers showing relative changes in the financial data over a period of years.

Computation

The trend indicates general tendency or direction of change in which management is more interested, but the fact that a trend is more influenced by the base year figure should always be borne in mind. The analysis and interpretation will not be fruitful if the base year figure is usually high or low. Therefore, the selection of the base year should be done carefully. It should be the year of normal conditions. The trend can be rightly interpreted if the effect of inflation on different years figures of money income is neutralised.

Steps involved

The following are the steps involved in the computation of trend percentages or trend ratios. In the first place, the statement probably relating to the earliest year under review is taken as the base, with reference to which all other financial statements are compared and analysed. Secondly, each item in the base statement is taken as 100. Thirdly, if the amount of the corresponding item in the other statement is less than that in the base statement, the trend percentage would be less than 100 and if the amount is more than the base amount, the trend percentage would be more than 100. This trend ratio can be calculated by dividing each amount in the other statement with the corresponding item found in the base statement. It should be remembered that, the trend ratios are generally computed not for all the items in the statement, as the primary objective is only to make comparison between items which are interrelated to one another.

Another method of proper analysis would be to calculate the percentage of physical quantities, wherever possible, by the use of index numbers technique. The percentage of current year may be calculated as under :

$$\% \text{ For Current Year} = \frac{\text{Current year figure}}{\text{Base year figure}} \times 100$$

In short, the calculation of trend percentage involves the following three steps :

i) Selection of base year.

ii) Assigning a weight of 100 to the value of the variable of base year, and

iii) Expressing the percentage change in the value of variable from base year to the study year as shown below with imaginary figures.

In the books of Colgate Ltd., Cochin
Statement showing Trend Percentage as on 31st March, ...

Year	Sales ₹	Percentage (Base Year : 2007-08)
2007-08	2,00,000	100
2008-09	3,50,000	175
2009-10	2,80,000	140
2010-11	3,00,000	150
2011-12	3,50,000	175
2012-13	1,40,000	70
2013-14	2,20,000	110

A trend for a single financial item is seldom very informative. A comparison of trends for related items often help the analyst in perfect understanding of the business facts as is clear from the under mentioned Comparative Balance Sheet with imaginary figures.

In the books of Colgate Ltd., Cochin
Comparative Balance Sheet as on 31st March, ...

Assets	2011-2012 ₹	2012-2013 ₹	2013-2014 ₹	Trend Percentage (Base : year 2011-12)		
				2012	2013	2014
A) Current Assets :						
• Inventory	2,00,000	3,00,000	2,50,000	100	150	125
• Debtors	3,00,000	5,00,000	6,00,000	100	167	200
• Cash Balances (+)	2,00,000	3,50,000	3,00,000	100	175	150
• Total A)	7,00,000	11,50,000	11,50,000	100	164	164
B) Fixed Assets :						
• Buildings	25,00,000	30,00,000	30,00,000	100	120	120
• Plant	12,50,000	15,00,000	16,00,000	100	120	128
• Investment (+)	8,00,000	10,00,000	12,00,000	100	125	150
Total B)	45,50,000	55,00,000	58,00,000	100	121	127
∴ Total Assets (A + B)	52,50,000	66,50,000	69,50,000	100	127	132

The Trend Analysis may be understood by perusing the following Financial Statement based on imaginary figures for few important items of incomes and expenses of Barua Ltd., Vadodra.

Statement showing Trends of various items of Income and Expenses for five years from 2009 to 2013.

Particulars	2009		2010		2011		2012		2013	
	₹	%	₹	%	₹	%	₹	%	₹	%
Sales	20,000	100	22,000	110	30,000	150	25,000	125	32,000	160
Direct Cost	8,000	100	10,000	125	14,000	175	11,000	137	13,000	163
Factory Overheads	1,000	100	1,200	120	1,400	140	1,200	120	1,500	150
Administration Overheads	800	100	800	100	1,000	125	1,000	125	1,000	125
	200	100	250	125	300	150	250	125	350	175
Selling Overheads	12,000	100	12,000	100	16,000	133	14,000	117	19,000	158
Gross Margin	10,000	100	9,750	97	13,300	133	11,550	115	16,150	161
Profit before Tax	40,000	100	45,000	112	45,000	112	50,000	125	80,000	200
Gross Working Capital	20,000	100	25,000	125	25,000	125	30,000	150	35,000	175
Current Liabilities										

Interpretation

The sales shows an increasing trend. The sales in 2013 have increased by 60% as compared to the base year 2009. The direct cost also increased by 63%. In 2013, factory overheads also increased by 50%. The Gross Margin also increased by 58% in 2013. The gross margin is increasing very slowly which is not a good sign. It is necessary to exercise control over the operating expenses to check the rising tendency and to increase the net margin. Gross working capital position is better, it increased by 100% in the year 2013. On the other hand current liabilities position has also increased i.e. 75% in the year 2013 and this current financial position seems to be very bad.

4. Ratios

Ratio Analysis is one of the popular tools of financial statement analysis. In simple words, ratio is the quotient formed when one magnitude is divided by another measured in the same unit. A **Ratio** is defined as **"the indicated quotient of two mathematical expressions" and as "the relationship between two or more things"**. Usually the ratio is stated as a percentage i.e. distribution expenses might be stated as 20.5 percent of sales. Often however, the ratio is expressed in units, thus sales might be expressed as 20 times inventory. Thus, the ratio is a pure quantity or number, independent of the measurement units being used. A financial ratio is defined as a relationship between two variables taken from financial statements of a concern. It is a mathematical yardstick that measures the relationship between two financial figures. It involves the breakdown for the examined financial report into component parts which are then evaluated in relation to each other and to exogenous standards. Financial ratio expedite the analysis by reducing the large number of items involved to a relatively small set of readily comprehended and economically meaningful indicators.

As ratio represents a relationship between figures, number of ratios can be formed by taking any two figures from the financial statements. However, such an approach would not fulfill any purpose unless the figures chosen are significantly correlated with each other. Further more, many of the ratios tend to deal with aspects of the same relationship, and there is little point in calculating several ratios in order to investigate the same point. Experts have identified some ratios as significant and important since they throw considerable light on the financial position of a concern. However, given the large number of ratios available, it is difficult to discern the inter-relationships among them required for a comprehensive understanding of the entity being analysed.

5. Fund Flow Statement

i) **Fund Flow Analysis or Fund Flow Statement :**

The **Fund Flow Statement** is a financial statement which reveals the methods by which the business has been financed and how it has used its funds between the opening and closing Balance Sheet date. Thus, a Fund Flow Statement is a report on movement of funds explaining wherefrom working capital originates and where into the same goes during an accounting period. This statement consists of two parts i.e. i) Sources of Funds and ii) Application of Funds. The difference between the two shows the net change in the working capital during the period.

The transactions which increase working capital are sources of funds and the transactions which decrease working capital are application of funds.

In the words of **Foulke** "A Statement of Sources and Application of funds is a technical device designed to analyse the changes in the financial condition of a business enterprise between two dates".

Fund Flow Statement is called by a variety of names, such as :
- Statement of Sources and Applications of Funds,
- Statement of Funds Supplied and Applied,
- Where Got and Where Gone Statement,
- Statement of Resources Provided and Applied,
- Funds Received and Disbursed Statement,
- Fund Movement Statement,
- Inflow-Outflow of Fund Statement, etc.

The basic object of this statement is to find out increase or decrease in the working capital during a period by showing sources and uses of working capital.

ii) **Cash Flow Analysis or Cash Flow Statement :**

Cash Flow Statement is a statement like Fund Flow Statement. A Cash Flow Statement concentrates on transactions that have a direct impact on cash. It deals with the inflow and outflow of cash between two Balance Sheet dates. That is, it explains the changes in cash position between the two period. Cash Flow means inflow and outflow of cash during an accounting period. From the beginning of the year upto the end of the year cash is received from various sources and spent on various heads. Incoming and outgoing of cash is termed as cash flow. The term cash here stands for cash and bank balances.

Cash plays a very important role in the entire economic life of a business. The technique of preparing a Fund Flow Statement and its utility have been discussed earlier in this chapter. It has also been pointed that this statement summarises the changes in Fund i.e. Working Capital. This statement presents a comprehensive picture of the various compositions of Working Capital and also portrays those financial transactions, which cause a change in Working Capital. But the Working Capital concept of Fund comprises, in addition to Cash and Bank, other current assets and current liabilities too. Hence, Fund Flow Statement fails to convey the quantum of inflow and outflow of cash. A firm needs cash to make payments to its suppliers, to incur day-to-day expenses and to pay salaries, wages, dividends etc.

2.2 RATIO ANALYSIS

2.2.1 MEANING OF RATIO

Ratio is a numerical or an arithmetical relationship between two figures. Those are relationships expressed in mathematical terms between figures which are connected with each other in some manner. Obviously, no purpose will be served by comparing two sets of figures which are not at all connected with each other. Ratios can be expressed in two ways :

i) **Times :**

When one value is divided by another, the unit used to express the quotient is termed as "Times". For example, if out of 100 students in a class, 90 are present, the attendance ratio can be expressed as follows :

$$= 90/100 = .9 \text{ Times}$$

ii) **Percentage :**

If the quotient obtained is multiplied by 100, the unit of expression is termed as "Percentage". For instance, in the above example, the attendance ratio as a percentage of the total number of students is as follows :

$$= .9 \times 100 = 90\%$$

Accounting ratios are, therefore, mathematical relationships expressed between inter-connected accounting figures.

Ratio Analysis – Rationale

One of the most difficult problems confronting the analyst is the interpretation and analysis of financial ratios. An adequate financial analysis involves more than an understanding and interpretation of each of the individual ratios. Further more, the analyst requires an insight into the meaning of the interrelationships among the ratios and financial data in the statements. Gaining such an insight and understanding requires considerable experience in the analysis and interpretation of financial statements. Moreover, even experienced analysts cannot apply their skill equally well to analyse and interpret the financial statements of different concerns. The characteristics may differ from industry to industry and from firm to firm within the same industry. A ratio that is high for one firm at one time may be low for another firm or for the same firm at a different time. Therefore, the analyst must be familiar with the characteristics of the firm whose financial ratios he is interpreting.

The analyst must not undertake the interpretation and analysis of financial ratios in isolation from other information. The following factors must be considered while analysing the financial ratios :

i) General economic condition of the firm.
ii) Risk acceptance.
iii) Future expectations.
iv) Future opportunities.
v) Analysis and interpretation system used by other firms in the industry.
vi) Accounting system of the industry.

The analysis and interpretation of the financial ratios in light of the above listed factors can be useful, but the analyst must still rely on skill, insight and even intention in order to interpret the ratios and arrive at a decision. The interpretation of the ratios can be made by comparing them with :

i) Previous Figures   i.e.   Trend Analysis.
ii) Similar Firms   i.e.   Inter Firm Comparisons.
iii) Targets   i.e.   Individual Ratios are set to meet the objective.

i) Trend Analysis :

Analysts usually use historical standards for evaluating the performance of the firm. The historical standards represent the financial ratio/s computed over a period of time i.e. Trend. The Trend Analysis provides enough clues to the analyst for proper evaluation of the financial ratios. However, the change in firm policies over the period must be considered while interpreting ratios from comparison over time. Furthermore, the average of the ratios, for several years can also be used for this purpose.

ii) Inter-firm Comparisons :

Inter-firm Comparisons may claim the comparisons of similar ratios for a number of different firms in the same industry. Such an attempt would facilitate the comparative study of financial position and performance of the firm in the industry. The published ratios of trade associations or financial institutions can be of great help to the analyst in the interpretation of the financial ratio. However, the variations in the accounting system and changes in the policies and procedures of the firm in comparison with the industry have to be taken care of, while making use of inter-firm comparisons.

iii) Targets :

Under this method, the interpretation of the ratio is made by comparing it with the standard set for this purpose, such a standard ratio, based upon established standard conventions serves as a measuring scale for the evaluation of the ratios. The best example of such standard is the 1 : 1 ratio which is to be considered a good ratio for analysing the acid-test ratio.

Generally speaking, the use of single standard ratio for the interpretation of the ratios is not of much use. Accounting experts usually recommended the use of the group of standard ratios for the evaluation of financial ratios.

Nature of Ratio Analysis

The ratio is calculated by dividing one figure by the other figure. It may be expressed in any of the three ways – 'times', 'proportion' or 'percentage' according to convenience or suitability. A more meaningful financial analysis involves ratios and their comparisons relating to a business concern i) over a period of years, ii) against another unit, iii) against the industry as a whole, iv) against the predetermined standards, v) for one department or division against another department or division of the same unit.

In fact, ratio analysis does not provide an end in itself, but only a means to understand the business concern's financial position. The nature of ratio analysis indicates that quantitative ratio analysis does not provide solutions for all the problems faced by a financial manager, unless several ratios, each of which relates to other, are compiled and analysed in a perfect perspective.

While analysis based on a single set of financial statements is helpful, it may often have to be supplemented with time series analysis which provides insight into a firm's performance and condition over a period of time. In this context, index analysis and analysis of time series of financial ratios are helpful tools.

For tackling any problem initially one should determine what ratios would be helpful in throwing light on the above situation and compute only such ratios.

Several ratios have some common element (Sales, for example, is used in various turnover ratios) and some items tend to move in harmony because of some common underlying factor. Though industry averages and other yardsticks are commonly used in financial ratios, it is somewhat difficult to judge whether a certain ratio is 'good' or 'bad'. Therefore, it is a process which requires proper care, sophistication, experience, etc.

Objectives of Ratio Analysis

Ratio Analysis tries to reduce large figures to an easily understandable relationship. Ratios, as an effective tool of control has to be handled very carefully. Ratios do not make conclusions, but it is a skillful job of the analyst to draw conclusions by making scientific evaluation of the ratio analysis.

Important **Objectives of Ratio Analysis** are as follows :

a) To provide the necessary basis for inter-firm comparison as well as intra-firm comparison.

Inter-firm Comparison :
   i) Between one company and its competitor.
   ii) Between one company and the best company in the industry.
   iii) Between one company and the global average.
   iv) Between one company and the average performance, in the industry.

b) To provide the necessary basis for inter-period comparison.

Inter-period Comparison :
   i) Between two years
   ii) Between two months
   iii) Between two quarters
   iv) Between 'X' months of current year and 'X' month of previous year.

c) To help in providing a part of information needed in the process of decision-making.

d) To focus on facts on a comparative basis and facilitate drawing of conclusions relating to the performance of a firm.

e) To evaluate the performance of a firm in determining the important aspects of a business such as liquidity, solvency, operational efficiency, overall profitability, capital gearing etc.
f) To throw light on the degree of efficiency in the management and the effectiveness in the utilisation of its assets.
g) To provide the way for effective control of the enterprise in the matter of achieving the physical and monetary targets.
h) To help the management in discharging its basic functions like forecasting, planning, co-ordination, communication, control etc.
i) To promote co-ordination among the departments and the staff by a study of performance and efficiency of each department.
j) To point out the financial condition of business whether it is very strong, questionable or poor and enable the management to take necessary steps.
k) To act as an index of the efficiency of an enterprise.

Parties Interested and Applications of Different Ratios

The interrelationship that exists among the different items which appear in the financial statements, are revealed by accounting ratios. Ratio analysis of a firm's financial statements is of interest to a number of parties, mainly, shareholders, creditors, financial executives etc. Different ratios are used to signify different trends in the working of the firm. However, the table given below would help for classification of parties interested and application of ratios.

Sr. No.	Parties Interested	Application of Ratios	To Test
i)	Creditors (Short-term), Investors, Money Lenders and Financial Executives.	a) Current Ratio b) Liquid Ratio c) Absolute Liquid Ratio d) Proprietary Ratio e) Assets to Proprietorship Ratio f) Debt-Equity Ratio g) Capital Gearing Ratio	Liquidity and Solvency
ii)	Shareholders, Creditors (Long-term), Government, Business House, Purchasers and Employees	a) Gross Profit Ratio b) Net Profit Ratio c) Operating Ratio d) Return on Capital Employed e) Dividend Ratio f) Earning per Share g) Dividend per Share	Profitability
iii)	Shareholders and Outsiders	a) Capital Gearing Ratio b) Equity Capital Ratio c) Long-term Loans to Net Worth	Capital Structure
iv)	Management	a) All Types of Ratios	Management Efficiency

2.2.2 NECESSITY AND ADVANTAGES OF RATIO

Necessity of Ratio Analysis

The **Necessity of Ratio Analysis** can be summarised as follows :

i) Ratio Analysis helps in making effective control of the business measuring performance, control of cost etc. Effective control is the key note to better management. Ratio ensures secrecy.

ii) Analysis of Financial Statements enables the analyst to find out the soundness or otherwise of a business. If the analysis reveals financial unsoundness, the factors responsible for such unsoundness can be separated and corrective action taken without loss of time. Figures in their absolute forms, shown in the financial statements are neither significant nor comparable. In fact, they are dumb. But ratios have power to speak.

iii) Ratio Analysis provides inter-firm comparison. They highlight the factors associated with successful and unsuccessful firms. If comparison shows an unfavourable variance, corrective actions can be initiated. Thus, it helps the management to take corrective action.

iv) Intra-firm comparisons are facilitated by Ratio Analysis. It is an instrument for diagnosis of financial health of an enterprise. It facilitates the management to know whether the firm's financial position is improving or deteriorating with the help of ratios by setting a trend.

v) Ratios are effective means of communication and play a vital role in informing the position of and progress made by the business concern to the owners and other interested parties. The communications by the use of simplified and summarised ratios are more easy and understandable.

vi) Ratio Analysis is an effective instrument which, when properly used, is useful to assess important characteristics of business – liquidity, solvency, profitability etc. A study of these aspects may enable conclusions to be drawn relating to capabilities of business.

vii) Ratios enable the mass of accounting data to be summarised and simplified. They act as an index of the efficiency of the enterprise. As such they serve as an instrument of management control.

viii) Ratios are useful tools in the hands of management and others concerned to evaluate the firm's performance over a period of time by comparing the present ratio with the past ones. They point out a firm's liquidity position to meet its short-term obligations and long-term solvency.

ix) Ratio Analysis is an invaluable aid to management in the discharge of its basic function such as planning, forecasting, control etc. The ratios that are derived after analysing and scrutinising the past result, helps the management to prepare budgets to formulate policies and to prepare the future plan of action etc.

x) It throws light on the degree of efficiency of the management and utilisation of the assets and that is why it is called surveyor of efficiency. They help management in decision-making.

Ratio Analysis helps management pinpoint specific areas that reflect improvement or deterioration as well as detect any trouble spots that may prevent the attainment of objectives. The interested parties undertake examination of these three areas frequently to evaluate managements ability to maintain a satisfactory balance among them, and to appraise the efficiency and effectiveness with which the management directs the firm's operations. Thus, the purpose of ratio analysis is to help the reader of asset of accounts to understand the information shown by highlighting a number of key relationships.

Advantage of Ratio Analysis

However, the following are the **Principal Advantages** claimed by **Ratio Analysis** :

i) It guides the management in formulating future financial planning and policies.
ii) It throws light on the efficiency of the business organisation.
iii) It permits comparisons of the firm's figures with data for similar firms and possibly with industry-wise data. And it permits the data to be measured against the yard stick of performance or of sound financial conditions.
iv) It ensures effective cost control.
v) It provides greater clarity, perspective, or meaning to the data and it brings out information not otherwise apparent.
vi) It measures profitability and solvency of a concern.
vii) It permits monetary figures of many digits to be condensed to two or three digits which enhances managerial efficiency.
viii) It helps in investment decisions.

Limitations of Ratio Analysis

In using ratios, the analyst must keep a few general limitations in mind. The main limitations attached to it are as follows :

i) It lacks standard values for the ratio, therefore scientific analysis is not possible.
ii) As there are no standards with which to compare, it fails to throw light on the efficiency of any activity of the business.
iii) It gives only the relationship between different variables and the actual magnitude are not known through ratios.
iv) Ratios are derived from the financial statements and naturally reflect their drawbacks.
v) It fails to indicate immediately where the mistake or error lies.
vi) It does not take into consideration the market and other changes.

QUESTIONS FOR SELF-STUDY

I. **Theory Questions :**

1) What is 'Financial Statement Analysis'? Explain the major objectives of Financial Statement Analysis.

2) Define the term 'Financial Statement Analysis'. Explain in brief the important methods of Financial Analysis.

3) What are 'Comparative Statements'? Explain the necessity of Comparative Financial Statements.

4) Define the term 'Common Size Statements'. State the important procedure followed in preparation of common size statements.

5) What is 'Trend Percentage'? Explain in brief the steps involved in the computation of Trend Percentages?

6) What is 'Ratio Analysis'? Explain the significance of accounting ratio in the analysis of financial statements.

7) Define the term 'Ratio'. Explain the necessity of computation of ratio.

8) What do you understand by the term 'Ratio'? State the advantages of ratio analysis.

9) Write short notes on:

i) Objectives of Financial Statement Analysis, ii) Role of Financial Analyst, iii) Methods of Financial Analysis, iv) Necessity of Comparative Statements, v) Forms of Common Size Statements, vi) Trend Percentage, vii) Fund Flow Statement, viii) Necessity of Ratio Analysis.

✱✱✱

3
UNIT

ANALYSIS AND INTERPRETATION OF RATIOS

SYNOPSIS

3.1 Types of Ratio
    3.1.1 According to the Nature of Items
        3.1.1.1 Balance Sheet Ratios
        3.1.1.2 Revenue Statements or Profit and Loss Account Ratios
        3.1.1.3 Inter Statement or Composite Ratios
    3.1.2 Functional Classification
        3.1.2.1 Liquidity Ratios
        3.1.2.2 Leverage Ratios
        3.1.2.3 Activity Ratios
        3.1.2.4 Profitability Ratios
- Illustrations
- Questions for Self-Study

3.1 TYPES OF RATIO

There are a number of ratios which can be determined on the basis of financial data made available by the company. But the financial analyst is always interested in those ratios which serve his basic purpose. Accordingly, there are certain important ratios which are used very often for analysis and interpretation.

Figure 3.1 summarises various **Types of Ratio** as follows :

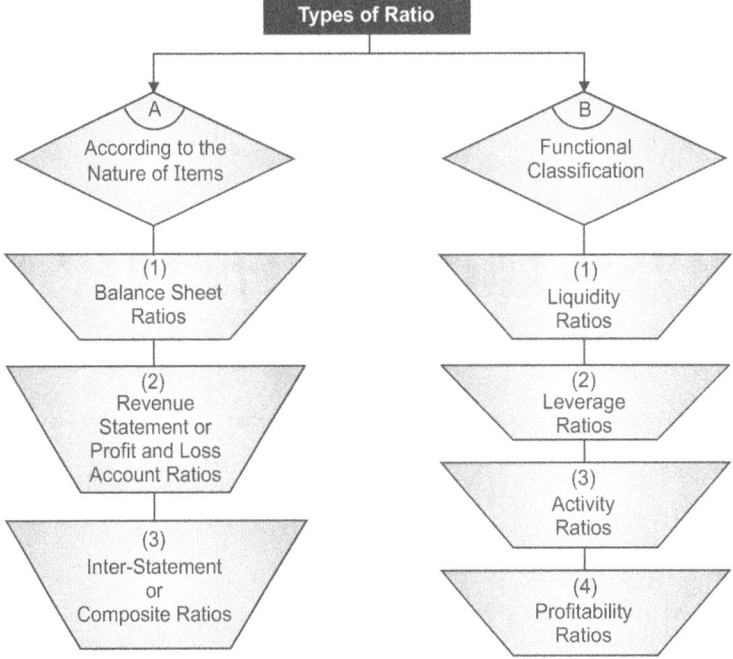

Fig. 3.1 : Types of Ratio

3.1.1 ACCORDING TO THE NATURE OF ITEMS

The traditional classification is based on those statements from which information is obtained for calculating the ratios. The ratios are classified accordingly to the nature of items as follows :

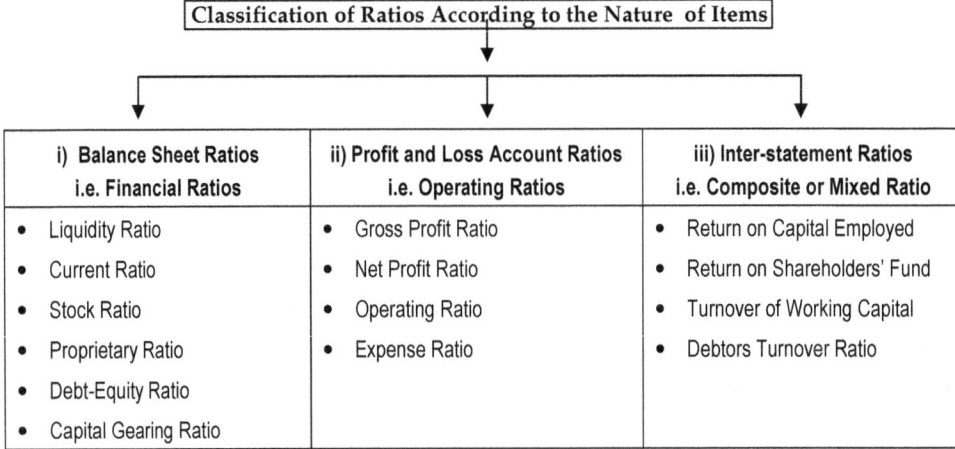

3.1.1.1 Balance Sheet Ratios

Top management will probably want to view the financial structure of the company in terms of basic ratios of assets or liability categories to total assets. These ratios attempt to express the relationship between two Balance Sheet items, e.g. the ratio of stock to debtors or the ratio of owner's equity to total equity.

3.1.1.2 Revenue Statements or Profit and Loss Account Ratios

These ratios indicate the relationship between two such variables which have been taken from the Revenue Statements or Profit and Loss Account. Basically there are two types of such ratios viz.

i) those showing the current year's figure as a percentage of last year, thus facilitating comparison of the changes in the various profit and loss items and

ii) those expressing a relationship among different items for the current year, e.g. the percentage of distribution expenses to sales etc.

3.1.1.3 Inter-Statement or Composite Ratios

The components for computation of these ratios are drawn from both Balance Sheet and Profit and Loss Account. These ratios deal with the relationship between operating and Balance Sheet items. The example of such ratios are debtors turnover ratio, fixed assets turnover ratio, working capital turnover ratio, and stock turnover ratio.

3.1.2 FUNCTIONAL CLASSIFICATION

Ratios can broadly be classified according to functional classification into four major groups viz. Liquidity Ratios, Leverage Ratios, Activity Ratios and Profitability Ratios.

3.1.2.1 Liquidity Ratios

Liquidity Ratios measure the ability of a firm to meet its short-term obligations, and reflect its short-term financial strength or solvency. Important Liquidity Ratios are : i) Current Ratio and ii) Quick or Acid-Test Ratio. Current Ratio is the ratio of total current assets to total current liabilities. A satisfactory current ratio would enable a firm to meet its obligations even if the value of the current assets declines. It is however a quantitative index of liquidity as it does not differentiate between the components of current assets, such as cash and inventory which are not equally liquid. The quick ratio-acid test ratio takes into consideration the different liquidity of the components of current assets. It represents the ratio between quick current assets, and the total current liabilities. It is a rigorous measure and superior to current ratio. However, both these ratios should be used to analyse the liquidity of a firm.

3.1.2.2 Leverage Ratios

The Capital Structure or Leverage Ratios or Solvency Ratios throw light on the long term solvency of a firm. This is reflected in its ability to assure the long-term creditors with regard to periodic payment of interest, and the repayment of a loan on maturity or in pre-determined installments at due date. There are two types of such ratios : i) Debt-equity or Debt assets, and ii) Coverage. The first type is computed from the Balance Sheet and reflects the relative contribution/ stake of owners and creditors in financing the assets of the firm. In other words, such ratios reflect the safety margin to the long-term creditors. The second category of such ratios is based on the income statement and shows the number of times the fixed obligations are covered by earnings before interest and taxes. They indicate, in other words, the extent to which a fall in operating profits is tolerable in that the ability to repay would not be adversely affected.

3.1.2.3 Activity Ratios

The last category of ratios comprises the **Activity Ratios**. They are also known as **Efficiency** or **Turnover Ratios**. Such ratios are concerned with measuring the efficiency in assets management. The efficiency with which assets are managed or used is reflected in the speed and rapidity with which they are converted into sales. Thus, activity ratios are a test of relationship between sales/cost of goods sold and assets. Depending upon the type of asset, activity ratios may be : i) Inventory or Stock turnover ii) Receivables or Debtors turnover, and iii) Total assets turnover. The first of these indicates the number of times inventory is replaced during the year or how quickly the goods are sold. It is a test of efficiency of inventory management. The second category of turnover ratios is indicative of the efficiency of receivables management as it shows how quickly trading goods are sold. It reveals efficiency in managing and utilising the total assets.

3.1.2.4 Profitability Ratios

The profitability of a firm can be measured by the **Profitability Ratios**. Such ratios can be computed either from sales or investments. The profitability ratios based on sales are : i) Profit Margin (gross and net), and ii) Expenses or Operating ratios. They indicate the proportion of sales consumed by operating costs, and the proportion available to meet financial and other expenses. The profitability related to investments includes : i) Return on assets, ii) Return on capital employed and iii) Return on shareholders equity, including earning per share, dividend payout ratio, earning and dividend yield. The overall profitability (earning power) is measured by the return on investment, which is computed as a combined product of net profit margin and investment turnover it is a central measure of the earning power and operating efficiency of a firm.

Interpretation of Ratios

The following tabular representation of **Types of Ratios** and their **Significance** helps to interpret the financial data with the help of Ratio Analysis to exercise managerial control.

INTERPRETATION OF RATIOS

I. Balance Sheet Ratios

Sr. No.	Name of the Ratio	Formula for Calculation of Ratio	Types of Ratio according to		Significance	Precautions
			Nature	Function		
1)	Current Ratio or Working Capital Ratio or '2 : 1 Ratio'	$\dfrac{\text{Current Assets}}{\text{Current Liabilities}}$ Current Assets include : Cash in hand / bank, marketable securities, other short-term high quality investment, bills receivables, prepaid expenses, work-in progress, sundry debtors and inventories etc. Current Liabilities include : Sundry Creditors, bills payables, outstanding and accrued expenses, overdraft, proposed dividend etc.	Balance Sheet	Liquidity Short-Term Solvency	This ratio indicates the solvency of the business i.e. ability to meet the liabilities of the business as and when they fall due. This ratio also indicates how much Current Assets are there as against each rupee of Current Liabilities. The Current Assets are the sources from which the liabilities have to be met. It is also the measure of the margin of safety that management maintains in order to allow for the inevitable unevenness in the flow of funds through the Current Assets and Liabilities account. Certain authorities have recommended that in order to ensure solvency of a concern, Current Assets should be at least twice the Current Liabilities and therefore this ratio is known as "2:1. Ratio". This ratios, also named as, Working Capital, being the excess of the Current Assets over Current Liabilities. Though 2 : 1 is considered desirable, it is not a must. It depends upon the nature of the business. What is important is not the size of the Current Ratio but the allocation and characteristics of Current Assets and Current Liabilities and their relation to the prospective turnover.	This ratio is sensitive to a number of factors which must be taken into account for accurate results such as : i) It must be ascertained whether the Current Assets and Current Liabilities are properly valued. ii) For proper inference the composition of Current Assets should not be over looked. If majority of Current Assets are in the form of inventory, even a 2 : 1 ratio will not result into favourable condition because inventory is considered to be the least Liquid Asset out of all Current Assets of a firm. iii) A very high Current Ratio may not indicate a very favourable position because it means that excessive investments in Current Assets is made. This will result in decrease in profitability because of long funds blocked in working capital. iv) For studying the solvency of the concern from the Current Ratio, still another factor must not be lost sight of i.e. shrinkage in the value of current assets on a forced liquidation.

Sr. No.	Name of the Ratio	Formula for Calculation of Ratio	Types of Ratio according to		Significance	Precautions
			Nature	Function		
2)	**Liquid Ratio** or **Quick Ratio** or **Acid Test Ratio**	$\dfrac{\text{Quick or Liquid Assets}}{\text{Quick or Liquid Liabilities}}$ **Quick Assets include** : All Current Assets except inventory (stock) and prepaid expenses. **Quick Liabilities include** : All Current Liabilites except overdraft and accrued expenses. Some experts advocate that only stock from Current Assets and overdraft from Current Liabilities should be excluded.	Balance Sheet	Liquidity short-term solvency	As regards the ability to honour day to day commitment, Liquid Ratio is a better tool. It is the ratio between Liquid Assets and Liquid Liabilities. An ideal Liquid Ratio is considered as 1 : 1. It signifies a very short term liquidity of a business concern and is, therefore, also called a still stiffer and rigorous test of solvency. The application of Acid-test Ratio is suitable. The Acid-test Ratio assumes that stock may not be realised immediately and therefore, this item is excluded in the computation of this ratio. The logic for exclusion of bank overdraft is based on the fact that bank overdraft is generally a permanent way of financing. Too low a ratio suggests not only liability to meet current claims but also inability to take advantages of cash discounts and other rewards for prompt payment. On the other hand, an excessive amount of Quick Assets could indicate that these assets should be put to more productive or profitable use elsewhere in the enterprise.	The adequacy of this ratio depends on the industry in which the firm operates. **Precautions** : Same as Current Ratio. Care must be exercised in placing too much reliance on 100% Acid-test Ratio without further investigation. E.g. a seasonal business which seeks to stabilise production will tend to have a weak Acid-test Ratio during its period of slack sales, but probably a powerful one in its period of highest selling, so that the earlier weak or downward position would have to be judged in relation to the market prospects for the firm's products in the latter period. An Acid-test Ratio of 1 : 1 is usually considered as ideal and satisfactory. However, this is rule of thumb and should be applied with care.

Sr. No.	Name	Formula	Types of Ratio according to Nature	Types of Ratio according to Function	Significance	Precautions
3.	Proprietory Ratio or Tangible Net Worth to Total Assets Ratio or Capital to Total Assets Ratio or Equity Ratio	$= \frac{\text{Proprietor's Fund}}{\text{Total Assets/Total Capital}}$ **Proprietor's Fund or Owners Equity includes** : Share Capital*, Reserves and Surplus. * : both Preferential and Equity **Total Assets includes** : Fixed and Current Assets. Some experts are of the opinion that Total Assets includes only Tangible Assets. It means "Goodwill" shall be excluded from the total assets.	Balance Sheet	Leverage	It is primarily, the ratio between Proprietor's Funds and Total Assets. It indicates the strength of the funding of the company. As a very rough measure, it may be suggested that 2/3 to 3/4th of the Total Assets should be financed by proprietor's funds. However, the optimum ratio is different in different lines of business. A high proprietary ratio is however frequently indicative of over capitalisation and an excessive investment in Fixed Assets in relation to actual needs. A ratio nearing 100% often gives low earnings per share and consequently a low rate of dividend to shareholders. On the other hand, a low Proprietory Ratio is a symptom of under capitalisation and an excessive use of creditor's fund to finance the business. This ratio is normally a test of strength of credit-worthiness of the business.	This ratio, should be considered alongwith the Current Ratio while observing the solvency of the business. Recall that the owner's equity is the residual interest in the firm's assets after allowance had been made for the claims of creditors against assets.

Sr. No.	Name	Formula	Types of Ratio according to		Significance	Precautions
			Nature	Function		
4.	Capital Gearing Ratio	Equity Share Capital + Reserves and Surplus / Pref. Share Capital* + Loan Capital (*Fixed interest bearing securities)	Balance Sheet	Leverage	It is used to express the relationship between Equity Share Capital and Fixed interest bearing securities of company. Whether fluctuation in profit of a company are followed by a disproportionately large increase or decrease in return to equity shareholders, a company is considered to be highly geared. If the proportion of preferred share and loan capital is high or where the proportion of ordinary share capital to the total capital is low, capital is said to be highly geared and reserve is the position in low gearing. Low gearing indicates that the Equity Share Capital is not paid an adequate return because the profits are swallowed up by the high fixed charges in the form of interest and dividends. Capital gearing signifies the process of maintaining a desired and appropriate gear ratio in a enterprise. While inflationary conditions are expected high gearing is to be employed and in the period marked by trade depression, low gearing should be employed.	As it affects the company's capacity to maintain a stable dividend distribution policy during the difficult trading periods, it must be carefully planned.

Sr. No.	Name	Formula	Types of Ratio according to		Significance	Precautions
			Nature	Function		
5.	Debt Equity Ratio or Total Liabilities to Proprietor's Fund Ratio	Total Debt = (i.e. Long + Short-term) / Net Worth/Owner's Equity **Total Debts includes** : All debts i.e. long-term, short-term, mortages, bills, debentures, etc. **Networth** means Equity Share Capital, Preference Share Capital, Reserves and Surplus i.e. Proprietor's Funds or Equity. (There is difference of opinion regards to Preference Share Capital as to whether is to be included in creditors or in ownership claims).	Balance Sheet	Leverage	The ratio establishes the relationship between Owner's Fund and External Debts, or there relationship between Proprietor's Fund and Borrower's Capital. The long-term solvency of the firm can be assessed from this ratio. Here "Debt" refers to the external or borrowed capital and the equity refers to the shareholder's funds or internal capital. This Ratio reveals the claims of shareholder's and creditor's against the assets of the firm. The normal and safe ratio is 2 : 1. If the ratio is higher, it indicates that the firm is depending heavily on creditors. If the ratio is low, it means that the firm is depending mainly on internal source and owner's funds. The purpose of Debt to Equity Ratio is to derive an idea of the amount of capital supplied to the firm by the owners and of asset "Cushion" available to the creditors on liquidation.	The interpretation of the ratio, however depends almost entirely on the financial and business policy of the enterprise. From this point of view, the importance of the ratio lies in highlighting the seemingly irreconcilable view points of the owners and creditors regarding the method of financing the business : the former having always the temptation of doing business with other people's fund and the latter insisting on that the owners should at least have as large an investment as creditors. Therefore on the average Debt to Equity Ratio 1 : 1 is also acceptable. Too much reliance on external equities may indicate under capitalisation where as too much reliance on internal equity may lead to over capitalisation.

Sr. No.	Name	Formula	Types of Ratio according to		Significance	Precautions
			Nature	Function		
6.	Stock Working Capital Ratio or Inventory to Working Capital Ratio	$= \dfrac{\text{Closing Stock}}{\text{Working Capital}}$	Balance Sheet	Liquidity Short-term solvency	The ratio is an index of the position of over stocking. It shows what part of working capital is represented by the closing stocks. The size of closing stocks must bear a proper proportion of the quantum of working capital. The higher is the cover given by working capital the lower is the risk of loss by the likely fall in the value of inventories in future. There is a need to supplement the ratio of Net Sales to Inventory by another ratio to confirm the position shown by the "Inventory" and the Net Working Capital and provides a relatively more stable basis for comparison than is supplied by the Inventory Turnover Ratio. Inventory Ratio should be calculated as under: $= \dfrac{\text{Cost of goods sold}}{\text{Average Inventory* at cost}}$ * Average Inventory $= \dfrac{\text{Opening Stock + Closing Stock}}{2}$ or $= \dfrac{\text{Net Sales}}{\text{Average Inventory at selling price}}$	The ratio should be interpreted with maximum care. It should not be treated as conclusive proof of overstocking. This ratio should be considered alongwith Stock Turnover Ratio to arrive at correct decision.

II. Revenue Statement or Profit and Loss Account Ratios

Sr. No.	Name of the Ratio	Formula for Calculation of Ratio	Types of Ratio according to		Significance	Precautions
			Nature	Function		
1)	Gross Profit Ratio	$\dfrac{\text{Gross Profit}}{\text{Net Sales}} \times 100$	Revenue	Profitability	The Gross Profit Ratio represents the gross margin. It expresses the relationship of Gross Profit on Sales to Net Sales in terms of percentage. It is the ratio which is most commonly employed by accountants for comparing the earnings of business for one period with those of other or earning of one concern with those of another in the same industry. It indicates the degree to which selling prices of goods per unit may decline without resulting in losses on operations for the firm. A high Gross Profit Ratio as compared with that of the other firm in the same industry implies that the firm in question produces its products of lower cost. It is a sign of good management. On the other hand, a low Gross Profit Ratio may indicate unfavourable purchasing and mark-up policies, the liability of management to develop sales volume, theft, damage, bad maintenance, marked reduction in selling prices not accompanied by proportionate decrease in cost of goods sold.	Gross Profit is the ultimate result of interaction between prices, sales volume and costs. A change in the Gross Profit can be effected by changes in any of these factors. Thus Gross Profit indicates the limit beyond which the sale price of goods cannot be allowed to fall. Some times a high Gross Profit Ratio may also be due to unsatisfactory basis of valuation of stock. i.e. overvaluation of closing stock or undervaluation of opening stock. A detailed analysis of various factors alone give a proper clue for the increased gross profit ratio.

Sr. No.	Name of the Ratio	Formula for Calculation of Ratio	Types of Ratio according to		Significance	Precautions
			Nature	Function		
2)	Expenses Ratio	Specific Operating Expenses / Sales a) **Fixed Expenses to Total Cost Ratio** = $\dfrac{\text{Fixed Expenses}}{\text{Total Cost}}$ b) **Material Consumption to Sales Ratio** = $\dfrac{\text{Material Consumption}}{\text{Sales}} \times 100$ c) **Wages to Sales Ratio** = $\dfrac{\text{Wages}}{\text{Sales}}$ d) **Office Administrative Expenses to Sales Ratio** = $\dfrac{\text{Office Admin. Expenses}}{\text{Sales}}$ e) **Selling and Distribution to Sales Ratio** = $\dfrac{\text{Selling and Distribution Expenses}}{\text{Sales}}$	Revenue	Profitability	These supplement the information given by the Revenue Ratios. As there is a very important relationship existing between Operating Expenses and Volume of Sales, Expense Ratios are calculated by dividing Net Sales into each individual Operating Expenses. (Selling, Administrative and General Expenses). These ratios represent a summation of changes in Net Sales and in the expense items. These ratios are valuable in comparing two similar businesses or operating data from year to year of the same business. a) **Fixed Expenses to Total Cost Ratio**: This ratio shows the idle capacity in the organisation. Sometimes this ratio increases without corresponding increase in Fixed Assets. In such circumstance, the matter should be properly examined. b) **Material consumption to Sales Ratio**: This ratio shows as to how much material is consumed and what is its percentage share in total sales. If the share is high, the profit of the firm declines. c) **Wages to Sales Ratio**: This ratio indicates the percentage of wages to sales. If the ratio is higher, the profit margin will come down.	While interpreting the Expense Ratios it should be remembered that certain Fixed Expenses e.g. Insurance premium, Rates and Taxes would decrease as the sales increase. But Variable Expenses like commission of sales would remain constant.

Sr. No.	Name	Formula	Types of Ratio according to		Significance	Precautions
			Nature	Function		
					iv) **Office and Administration Expenses to Sales Ratio :** This ratio indicates the impact of indirect expenses on sales or profit. Higher the ratio lesser will be the margin of profit. v) **Selling and Distribution Expenses to Sales Ratio :** Thus ratio indicates the impact of selling expenses particularly expenses on (Advertisement) on sales. Higher the ratio lower will be the margin of profit.	
3.	Operating Ratio	$= \dfrac{\text{Cost of goods sold} + \text{Operating Expenses}}{\text{Net Sales}} \times 100$ Operating Expenses consist of Factory Expenses, Administrative Expenses and Selling and Distribution Expenses	Revenue	Profitability	The ratio indicates the percentage of Net Sales that is absorbed by the cost of goods sold and Operating Expenses. Naturally, higher the Ratio the less favourable it is, because it would have a smaller margin to meet interest, dividends, and other corporate needs. It can also be used as a partial index of overall profitability but cannot be used as test of financial condition without taking into account financial and extraordinary items.	In interpreting Operating Ratio full recognition must be given to the possibility of variations in expenses from year to year or company to company, due to changes or differences in policies involving expenses that are subject to managerial decisions.

Sr. No.	Name	Formula	Types of Ratio according to		Significance	Precautions
			Nature	Function		
4.	Net Operating Profit Ratio or Operating Profit Ratio	$= \dfrac{\text{Operating Net Profit}}{\text{Net Sales}} \times 100$ Operating Net Profit is the Net Profit minus income from external securities and other such as interest, dividend, profit on sale of securities, etc.	Revenue	Profitability	This ratio is mainly concerned with Operating Profit or profit obtained from the main line of activity. Non-business income is also included in the profit and when a ratio has to be obtained from business profit this ratio has to be computed. The profitability of a firm can be easily measured by this ratio. The operating efficiency of a firm is ultimately adjusted by the profits earned by it. The Operating Profit Ratio is a tool in the hands of management to control the cost of production and other expenses like administrative and selling expenses. It shows the amount of profit earned for each rupee of sales. If the amount earned is more, it means that there is a low cost operation and if the profit is low the cost of production and other expenses are on the increase.	Non-operating incomes and expenses are strictly excluded when this ratio is calculated. This ratio indicates the firm's capacity to withstand adverse economic conditions.
5.	Net Profit Ratio	$= \dfrac{\text{Net Profit after Taxes}}{\text{Net Sales}} \times 100$	Revenue	Profitability	Net Profit is that proportion of Net Sales which remains with the owners or the shareholders after all costs, charges, and expenses including income-tax have been deducted. The relationship of Net Profit to Net Sales is established by this ratio and is expressed in percentage.	To get a meaningful interpretation of profitability of the firm, a financial analyst must evaluate both the Gross Profit Ratio and Net Profit Ratio jointly.

Sr. No.	Name	Formula	Types of Ratio according to		Significance	Precautions
			Nature	Function		
					This ratio shows the balance of profit left to proprietor, after all expenses are met with. This ratio normally ranges between 5% and 10%. Higher the ratio, higher will be the profit left to the shareholders. This ratio assist the management in controlling costs and in increasing the turnover. A firm with high Net Profit Ratio would be in an advantageous position to survive in the face of falling sales prices, rising costs of production or declining demand for the product. A firm with a low Net Profit Ratio may find it difficult to withstand these adversities. A high Net Profit Ratio can enable the firm to reap the benefits of favourable conditions, such as rising sales prices, falling costs of production or increasing demand for the product. Such a firm can accelerate its profit at a faster rate than a firm with a low Net Profit Ratio.	

III. Inter Statement or Composite Ratios

Sr. No.	Name of the Ratio	Formula for Calculation of Ratio	Types of Ratio according to		Significance	Precautions
			Nature	Function		
1)	Return on Capital Employed or Net Profit to Assets Ratio or Return on Total Assets	$\dfrac{\text{Net Profit before Tax \& Interest}}{\text{Capital Employed}} \times 100$ **Capital Employed means**: either non-current Liabilities plus Shareholder's Funds. or Working Capital plus Non-Current Assets. (If the term Capital Employed is taken as Gross Capital Employed then it means Total Assets.) or Capital Employed = Share Capital + Reserves and Surplus + Long Term Loan – (Non-business Assets + Fictitious Assets) Variations of the ROCE (Return on Capital Employed) a) ROCE = $\dfrac{\text{Net Profit after Taxes}}{\text{Capital Employed}} \times 100$ b) ROCE = $\dfrac{\text{Net Profit after Taxes + Interest}}{\text{Capital Employed}} \times 100$	Composite	Profitability	The ratio shows how well the firm has used the resources of the owners. This ratio is a measure of the profitability of an enterprise. It is also used as basis for various managerial decisions. There is difference of opinion regarding the calculation of Capital Employed. Some of the financial managers are of the view that the amount of Capital Employed must be such that it may fairly represent capital investment throughout the year and therefore they bring in the **Concept of Average Capital Employed**. Alternatively it is equal to Working Capital plus Non-current Assets. **The term Operating Profit means profit before interest and tax.** In fact, the starting point of business budgeting should be the determination of minimum rate of Profit on Capital Investment which is then worked backwards for planning the details of business operations. This is the minimum return expected on Capital Employed and in order to attract capital to particular business, a fair return has to be paid. There is hardly any criterion for determining the	Following points are important regarding calculation of Capital Employed: i) Fictitious Assets like preliminary expenses, accounts of deferred revenue expenditure are excluded. ii) Intangible Assets like goodwill are generally excluded. iii) Though idle assets are excluded from Capital Employed, standby plant and equipment essential to normal running of machinery should not be excluded. iv) Investments made outside business are to be excluded but those made for bonafide purposes of the business are included. v) All stocks are included, valuating them on a consistent basis, generally at cost. vi) Trade debtors are included after taking into account provision for bad debts. vii) Any balance at bank in excess of the normal requirements of business may be excluded.

Sr. No.	Name	Formula	Types of Ratio according to Nature	Types of Ratio according to Function	Significance	Precautions
		iii) ROCE = $\dfrac{\text{Net Profit after Taxes + Interest}}{\text{Capital Employed} - \text{Intangible Assets}} \times 100$ iv) ROCE = $\dfrac{\text{Operating Profit}}{\text{Capital Employed}} \times 100$ **Average Capital Employed** = $\dfrac{\text{Capital Employed at the beginning of the year + Capital Employed at the end of the year.}}{2}$			minimum return with reference to which Return on Capital Investment may be judged. Return on Capital Employed is the only measure which can be said to show satisfactory, the overall performance of an undertaking from the standpoint of profitability. It enables the management to show whether the funds entrusted to it have been properly used or not. Thus, it can become an integral part of budgetary control system in order that management may able to follow the progress being made and to take corrective action, if necessary.	
2.	Return on Proprietor's Fund or Return on Shareholder's Investments or Return of Total Shareholder's Equity	$\dfrac{\text{Net Profit after Interest and Taxes}}{\text{Shareholder's Funds}} \times 100$ The term 'Net Profit' here means, Net Income after Interest and Taxes. It is different from 'Net Operating Profit'. The Shareholder's Funds will includes Equity Share Capital, Preference Share Capital, Share Premium and Reserves and Surplus less Accumulated Losses.	Composite	Profitability	This ratio shows how well the firm has used the resources of the owners. This ratio is a measure of the profitableness of an enterprise. The realisation of satisfactory Net Income is the major objective of a business and the ratio shows the extent to which this objective is being achieved. This ratio should be compared with the ratio of similar companies. The Shareholder's Equity also refer to the Net Worth of a firm.	Alongwith this ratio i) Return on Assets and ii) Return on Capital Employed should also be useful for meaningful financial analysis.

Sr. No.	Name	Formula	Types of Ratio according to Nature	Types of Ratio according to Function	Significance	Precautions
3.	Return on Equity Capital or Common Equity	$\dfrac{\text{Net Profit (after taxes and preferential dividend)}}{\text{Equity Share Capital}} \times 100$ Equity Shareholder's Funds will include: Paid-up Share Capital (Equity) + Share Premium + Reserve and Surplus Less Accumulated Losses.	Composite	Profitability	The profitability from the point of view of the Equity Shareholders will be judged after taking into account the amount of dividend payable to Preference Shareholders. This is one of the most important relationship in Ratio Analysis. Obtaining a satisfactory return is the most desirable objective of a business. The ratio of Net Profit to Owner's Equity reflects the extent to which this objective has been accomplished. This ratio is thus, of great interest to present as well as prospective shareholders and also of great concern to management, which has the responsibility of maximising the owner's welfare. The Return of Owner's Equity of the company should be compared to the ratio of other similar companies and the industry average. This will indicate the relative performance and strength of the company in attracting the prospective investors.	Actually this ratio is very useful to the investors. It helps the investors to take buying decisions.
4.	Earning per Equity Share or Earning per Share Ratio (EPS Ratio)	$\dfrac{\text{Net Profit (after taxes and preferential dividend)}}{\text{Number of Equity Shares}} \times 100$	Composite	Profitability	This ratio shows percentage of profit available to Equity Shareholders or how much return they earn per share. It is used to compare the performance of a company with higher rate of return, will have greater demand in the market resulting	While adopting EPS Ratio, it should also be remembered that if there is any increase in EPS ratio it should not be taken to mean an increase in the profitability of a firm, since retained earnings might have been utilised for payment of dividend. Another

Sr. No.	Name	Formula	Types of Ratio according to Nature	Types of Ratio according to Function	Significance	Precautions
					in increase in the market value. This ratio is adopted to known the Return to shareholders on the Capital Employed. According to this, the Earning Net Profit (after tax and pref. dividend) as numerator and number held by the shareholders as denominator. EPS is a popular ratio, as it measures the profitability of a firm from the owner's stand point. Like other profitability ratios, this ratio should also be compared with that of similar firms, industry average and also over a period of time.	demerit of EPS ratio is that it does not clearly discloses as to what portion of profits have been paid to the owners as a dividend and what portion has been retained in the business. This only represents how much of the profit belong to the Equity Shareholders rather theoretically.
5.	Price Earning Ratio or PER Ratio or P/E Ratio	$= \dfrac{\text{Market Price per Equity Share}}{\text{Earning Per Equity Share}}$	Composite	Profitability	The Price Earning Ratio is widely used by the security analyst to evaluate the firm's performance as expected by the investors. It indicates investor's judgement or expectation of the firm's performance. Management is also interested in this method of market appraisal of the firm's performance and would like to find the causes if the P/E Ratio declines. As a rule, higher the P/E Ratio, the better it is for the Equity Shareholders.	While estimating the earnings, only normal earnings associates with the existing assets alone are considered.

Sr. No.	Name	Formula	Types of Ratio according to Nature	Types of Ratio according to Function	Significance	Precautions
6.	**Earning Price Ratio** or **EP Ratio** or **Earning Yield Ratio**	$= \dfrac{\text{Earning Per Equity Share}}{\text{Market Price per Equity Share}} \times 100$	Composite	Profitability	This ratio is reciprocal or complementary of P/E Ratio. As low percentage may reflect a high rate of growth in the past.	
7.	**Dividend Payout Ratio** or **Payout Ratio** or **D/P Ratio**	$= \dfrac{\text{Total Dividend Paid to Equity holders}}{\text{Total Net profits belonging to Equity holders}} \times 100$ or $= \dfrac{\text{Dividend Per Share (DPS)}}{\text{Earning Per Share (EPS)}} \times 100$	Composite	Profitability	This ratio is also known as Payout Ratio. It measures the relationship between the earnings belonging to the Equity holders and dividends actually paid to them. Precisely the D/P ratio expresses what percentage share of Net profits after taxes and Preference Dividend is paid out as dividend to the Equity Shareholders. This ratio is computed by dividing the Total Dividends paid to Equity holders by the Total Profits belonging to them. The D/P Ratio is popular ratio. A comparison of this ratio with that of similar firms, industry average and over years, would reflect on the adequacy or otherwise of dividend paid to the equity holders. This ratio also indicate another important aspect. It throws light on the aspect of Retained Earning. When the dividend payout is high the Retained Earning will be less and this means less internal finance. The finance decision of the companies vary.	Many companies after attaining a stage would like to utilise the Self-Generated Funds or Self Reliance Funds (i.e. Retained Earnings) for expansion by capitalising these funds. The Retained Earning can be built up over a period, if company follows a conservative dividend policy. Hence the less payout of the shareholders. Besides indicating the general level of market dividend yield reflects the market estimates of future dividend growth and risk. The higher the dividend growth expeditions for given share the lower the current - yield, the higher the markets estimate of risk the higher the current yield.

Sr. No.	Name of the Ratio	Formula for Calculation of Ratio	Types of Ratio according to		Significance	Precautions
			Nature	Function		
					The Payout Ratio indicates whether the dividend paid is high or low and on this basis the firm can decide whether it has to change its dividend payout decision with a view to increasing the Retained Earnings.	
8)	Dividend Yield Ratio	$\dfrac{\text{Dividend per Equity Share}}{\text{Market Price per Equity Share}} \times 100$	Composite	Profitability	As the market price is different from face value and paid up value of equity share, the rate of return of the investor cannot be equal to the rate of dividend declared by the company. Suppose, the company had declared 50% dividend on its Equity Shares of ₹ 100 each and if the market price of the share is ₹ 200, the purchaser of the share will have to pay ₹ 200 and on ₹ 200 he will get dividend of ₹ 50. It means he will get the dividend @ 25% on his investment. The dividend yield is calculated by dividing the Cash Dividends per Equity Share by the market value per share.	Besides indicating the general level of market, dividend yield reflects the market estimates of future dividend growth and risk. The higher the dividend growth expectations for given share, the lower the current yield, the higher the market's estimate of risk, the higher the current yield.

Sr. No.	Name	Formula	Types of Ratio according to		Significance	Precautions
			Nature	Function		
9.			Composite	Activity	Debtors contribute an important elements of Current Assets and therefore, the quality of debtors to a great extent determines the liquidity of a firm. Two ratios are used by a Financial Analyst to judge the liquidity of a firm : i) Debtors Turnover Ratio. ii) Debts collection period or Average collection period. i) Debtors Turnover Ratio indicates the efficiency of the staff in-charge of the collection of back debts. The higher the value of the debtors turnover, the more efficient is the management of receivables. The ratio should be compared with ratios of similar firms and industry average to get a better picture of the quality of debtors. The ratio also helps in Cash Budgeting since the flow of cash from customers can be estimated on the basis of estimated sales. ii) This ratio indicates the number of times the debtors turn each year. It also indicates the collection period of debtors. A high turnover is considered to be good as there will be better cash flow. If the collection period is shorter, the quality of debtors	The collection period, however, has to be compared with the standards and the standard being the industry turnover. When compared to the industry turnover, if the ratio is low, it means that the firm is not collecting the debts regularly. However hard and fast rules cannot be adopted as far as credit sales policy is concerned. The firm should strike a balance between rigidity and liberalization. Then only a normal collection period prevails. Many other factors, such as business environment, outlook of the management, the pricing policy, the nature of the product sold etc. also decide the credit sales policy and credit sales policy decides the Debtors Turnover Ratio.
a)	**Debtors Turnover Ratio** or **Receivable Turnover Ratio** or **Debtors Velocity**	$= \dfrac{\text{Accounts Receivables}}{\text{Average Daily Sales}}$ or $= \dfrac{\text{Accounts Receivables}}{\text{Net Sales}} \times 365$ $= \dfrac{\text{Credit Sales (Net)}}{\text{Average Debtors}}$ Accounts Receivables includes Trade Debtors and Bills Receivables				
b)	**Debt Collection Period Ratio** or **Average Collection Period Ratio**	$= \dfrac{\text{Months (or days) in a year}}{\text{Debtors Turnover}}$ OR $= \dfrac{\text{Average Accounts Receivable}}{\text{Net Credit Sales for the year}}$ $\times$ Months (or days) in a year or $= \dfrac{\text{Accounts Receivable}}{\text{Credit Sales (Net)}}$ Average (monthly or daily)				

Sr. No.	Name	Formula	Types of Ratio according to Nature	Types of Ratio according to Function	Significance	Precautions
		Note : In case credit sales figure is not given, total sales figure can be used to compute Receivable Turnover.			will be good and this means the debtors promptly pay their dues. The scope of bad debts will be less. 40 to 60 days are usually considered as normal ratio and the quality of the debt will be good. If the turnover is low the cash in flows will be slow and the quality of debts will not be good. Change in the ratio indicates changes in the company's credit policy or changes in its ability to collect its receivables. The main objective of the comparison implied in the Debtors Turnover Ratio, is to learn how old the accounts are and partly to learn how fast cash will flow from their collections.	
10.	Stock Turnover Ratio or Inventory Turnover Ratio	$= \dfrac{\text{Cost of goods sold}}{\text{Average Inventory at Cost}}$ or $= \dfrac{\text{Net Sales}}{\text{Average Inventory at Selling Price*}}$ (where cost of goods sold is not available, Net Sales are taken). * Average Inventory of Stock = $\dfrac{\text{Opening Stock + Closing Stock}}{2}$	Composite	Activity	This ratio relates the cost of goods sold during a given period to the average inventory; This ratio helps in determining the liquidity of a business concern in as much as it indicates the rate at which the inventory are converted into sales and into cash ultimately This ratio also throw light on the inventory policy pursued by any unit and the reasonableness of the same.	The relation is between variables. If both items (Net Sales and Stock) increase in the same proportion the ratio remain unchanged and a situation may develops that may inadveantly lead to bad financial condition. For Example Sales : ₹ 1,00,000 1,50,000 2,50,000 Stock ₹ 10,000 15,000 25,000 Ratio 10 : 1 10 : 1 10 : 1 Working Capital ₹ 12,500 12,500 12,500

Sr. No.	Name	Formula	Types of Ratio according to		Significance	Precautions
			Nature	Function		
		(If opening stock is not available, closing stock is to be taken as average stock). (The cost of goods sold refers to goods sold-gross profit).			A high Inventory Turnover Ratio is good from the liquidity point of view. On the other hand, a low ratio would indicate that the inventory does not move fast and remains in warehouse for a longer time. A too high inventory turnover may be the result of a very low level of inventory which results frequent stock outs. The turnover will be very high if the firm replenishes its inventory in too many small lot sizes. The situations of frequent stock-outs and too many small inventory ratios need to be investigated into further. The computation of the Inventory Turnover Ratios for the individual components of inventory may help the management in detecting the imbalance investments in various inventory components. An **Inventory Turnover Ratio**, standing by itself, means absolutely nothing because there is no fixed norm for turnover. To give meaning to turnover figure one must compare it with other such figures so that a comparative analysis with industry or over a time is possible.	Though the ratio is constant for 3 years, inventory may prove excessive for size of business and could ultimately result in bankruptcy. In order to discern this danger point this ratio must be supplemented by the Ratio of Inventory to Working Capital. While employing Inventory Turnover Ratio, the following factors must be kept in mind: • Seasonal conditions • Supply conditions • Price trends and • Trend of volume of business. This ratio is combination of several factors. The figures down from financial statements are subject to change as time passes the time value concept will notice considered at the time of computing ratio.

Sr. No.	Name	Formula	Types of Ratio according to		Significance	Precautions
			Nature	Function		
11.	Creditors Turnover Ratio	= $\dfrac{\text{Credit Purchases}}{\text{Average Creditors*}}$ (* Average Creditors are obtained by adding closing creditors to opening creditors and dividing the same by two). In absence of detailed information the following formula can be adopted : = $\dfrac{\text{Total Credit Purchases}}{\text{Closing Creditors}}$ Alternative Method : = $\dfrac{\text{Creditors}}{\text{Credit Purchases}} \times 365$ (or 360 days)	Composite	Activity	This ratio reveals the number of times the creditors turn on the average each year. This tells at what speed the creditors are paid. If the payment to creditors is delayed the firm sometimes may have to bear burden of debt service charges. This ratio can be computed as per first method, when the information regarding Credit Purchases, Opening and Closing balances of creditors are available. In absence of the detailed information as said earlier, the alternative formula can be adopted to compute the ratio. From the stand point of liquidity and solvency if longer credit period is allowed by the creditors the firm will be in an advantageous position the safety period is 60 to 90 days. The creditworthiness of the firm is also established by the ratio. The firm can pay promptly to its creditors if the payment time is properly adjusted. The ratio will tell whether the time period is normal or not.	This ratio is combination of several factors. The figures drawn from financial statements are subject to change as time passes. The 'time value concept' will not be considered at the time of computing ratio.

Sr. No.	Name of the Ratio	Formula for Calculation of Ratio	Types of Ratio according to		Significance	Precautions
			Nature	Function		
12)						
a)	Fixed Assets Turnover Ratio	$\dfrac{\text{Sales}}{\text{Net Fixed Assets}} \times$ Number of times	Composite	Activity	The ratio indicates the efficiency in the utilisation of Fixed Assets. This ratio also indicates whether the Fixed Assets are being fully utilised. It is an important measure of efficiency and profit earning capacity of the business. A high ratio is an index of the efficiency, a low ratio suggests idle capacity and excessive investment in Fixed Assets. Generally, a standard ratio is taken as five times.	The analyst should be cautious in deriving conclusions from the Fixed Assets Turnover Ratio. To obtain Fixed Assets Turnover Ratio, sales are divided by depreciated value of Fixed Assets. Hence, as with the Fixed Assets Turnover Ratio, the Total Assets Turnover Ratio should be cautiously used. In the denominator of this ratio assets are net of depreciation. Therefore, older assets with lower book value may create a misleading impression of high turnover.
b)	Total Assets Turnover Ratio	$\dfrac{\text{Sales}}{\text{Total Assets}}$* * Some analysts exclude intangible assets. In such case, ratio should be: $\dfrac{\text{Sales}}{\text{Total Tangible Assets}}$	Composite	Activity	Not only Fixed Assets are directly concern with the generation of sales, but other assets also contribute to the production and sales activity of the firm. The firm must manage its Total Assets efficiently and should generate maximum sales through their proper utilisation.	

FORMULAE TO REMEMBER

	Ratios	Formulae
1)	Current Ratio	$\dfrac{\text{Current Assets}}{\text{Current Liabilities}}$
2)	Net Working Capital Ratio	$\dfrac{\text{Net Working Capital}}{\text{Net Assets}}$
3)	Quick Ratio	$\dfrac{\text{Quick Assets}}{\text{Liquid Liabilities}}$
4)	Cash Position Ratio	$\dfrac{\text{Cash (+) Marketable Securities}}{\text{Liquid Liabilities}}$
5)	Proprietary Ratio	$\dfrac{\text{Shareholders' Fund}}{\text{Total Asset (or) Total Resources}}$
6)	Solvency Ratio	$\dfrac{\text{Outside Liabilities}}{\text{Total Assets}}$
7)	Fixed Assets to Proprietors Fund Ratio	$\dfrac{\text{Fixed Assets}}{\text{Proprietors' Fund}}$
8)	Current Assets to Proprietors' Fund Ratio	$\dfrac{\text{Current Assets}}{\text{Proprietors' Funds}}$
9)	Capital Gearing Ratio	$\dfrac{\text{Fixed Interest Bearing Funds}}{\text{Equity Share Capital}}$
10)	Debt-Equity Ratio	$\dfrac{\text{External Equities}}{\text{Internal Equities}}$ or $\dfrac{\text{Outsiders Fund}}{\text{Shareholders Fund}}$
11)	Fixed Assets to Current Assets	$\dfrac{\text{Fixed Assets}}{\text{Current Assets}}$
12)	Reserves to Equity Capital Ratio	$\dfrac{\text{Revenue Reserve}}{\text{Equity Capital}}$
13)	Gross Profit Ratio	$\dfrac{\text{Gross Profit}}{\text{Net Sales}} \times 100$
14)	Operating Ratio	$\dfrac{\text{Cost of Goods Sold (+) Operating Exp.}}{\text{Net Sales}} \times 100$
15)	Material Consumed Ratio	$\dfrac{\text{Material Consumed}}{\text{Net Sales}} \times 100$
16)	Conversion Cost Ratio	$\dfrac{\text{Manufacturing Exp. (--) Material Cost}}{\text{Net Sales}} \times 100$
17)	Particular Expense Ratio	$\dfrac{\text{Particular Expense}}{\text{Net Sales}} \times 100$
18)	Net Profit Ratio	$\dfrac{\text{Net Profit}}{\text{Net Sales}} \times 100$
19)	Return on Assets	$\dfrac{\text{Net Profit}}{\text{Total Assets}} \times 100$

20)	Return on Capital Employed	$\dfrac{\text{Operating Profits}}{\text{Capital Employed}}$
21)	Return on Shareholders' Equity	$\dfrac{\text{Net Profit}}{\text{Shareholders' Fund}} \times 100$
22)	Stock Turnover Ratio	$\dfrac{\text{Cost of Goods Sold (or) Net Sales}}{\text{Average Inventory}}$
23)	Debtors Turnover Ratio	$\dfrac{\text{Credit Sales}}{\text{Average Debtors}}$ (or) $\dfrac{\text{Total Sales}}{\text{Closing Debtors}}$
24)	Debt Collection Period	$\dfrac{\text{Months (or) days in a year}}{\text{Debtors Turnover}}$
25)	Creditors Turnover Ratio	$\dfrac{\text{Net Credit Purchases}}{\text{Average Accounts Payable}}$
26)	Average Payment Period	$\dfrac{\text{Accounts Payable}}{\text{Net Credit Purchases}} \times 365$
27)	Working Capital Turnover Ratio	$\dfrac{\text{Cost of Sales}}{\text{Net Working Capital}}$
28)	Fixed Assets Turnover	$\dfrac{\text{Cost of Sales}}{\text{Net Fixed Assets}}$
29)	Total Capital Turnover	$\dfrac{\text{Cost of Sales}}{\text{Total Capital Employed}}$
30)	Capital Turnover	$\dfrac{\text{Cost of Sales}}{\text{Capital Employed}}$
31)	Interest Coverage	$\dfrac{\text{EBIT}}{\text{Fixed Interest Charges}}$
32)	Dividend Coverage	$\dfrac{\text{Net Profit after Tax and Interest}}{\text{Preference Dividend}}$
33)	Equity Shareholders' Coverage	$\dfrac{\text{Net Profit (after Interest, Tax and Pref. Dividend)}}{\text{Equity Dividend}}$
34)	Earning per Equity Shares	$\dfrac{\text{Profits available for Equity Shares}}{\text{Number of Equity Shares}}$
35)	Dividend Yield	$\dfrac{\text{Dividend Per Share}}{\text{Market Price per Share}}$
36)	Price Earning Ratio	$\dfrac{\text{Market Price of a Share}}{\text{Earning per Share}}$
37)	Fixed Interest Coverage	$\dfrac{\text{Operating Income}}{\text{Annual Interest Expenses}}$
38)	Dividend Per Share	$\dfrac{\text{Dividend Paid to Equity Shareholders}}{\text{Number of Equity Shares}}$
39)	Dividend Payout Ratio	$\dfrac{\text{Dividend Per Share}}{\text{Earning Per Share}}$

ILLUSTRATIONS

ILLUSTRATION 1

From the following Balance-Sheet of Ashoka Ltd., Akola calculate the following ratios :

i) Current Ratio
ii) Liquid Ratio
iii) Absolute Liquidity Ratio
iv) Current Assets to Fixed Assets Ratio
v) Debt to Equity Ratio
vi) Proprietary Ratio
vii) Capital Gearing Ratio and
viii) Fixed Assets Ratio

Balance Sheet as on 31st March, 2014

Liabilities	₹	Assets	₹
Equity Share Capital	10,00,000	Goodwill (At cost)	5,00,000
6% Preference Share Capital	5,00,000	Plant and Machinery	6,00,000
General Reserve	1,00,000	Land and Buildings	7,00,000
Profit and Loss	4,00,000	Furniture	1,00,000
Provision for Taxation	1,76,000	Inventories	6,00,000
Bills Payable	1,24,000	Bills Receivable	30,000
Bank Overdraft	20,000	Sundry Debtors	1,50,000
Sundry Creditors	80,000	Bank	2,00,000
12% Debenture	5,00,000	Investment (Short-Term)	20,000
Total	29,00,000	Total	29,00,000

SOLUTION

i) **Current Ratio** $= \dfrac{\text{Current Assets}}{\text{Current Liabilities}}$

$= \dfrac{₹\,10,00,000}{₹\,4,00,000}$

$= 2.5 : 1$

Note : Current assets include inventories, sundry debtors, bills receivable, bank balance and short-term investments. Current liabilities include sundry creditors, bills payable, bank overdraft, provision for taxation etc.

ii) **Liquid Ratio** $= \dfrac{\text{Liquid Assets}}{\text{Liquid Liabilities}}$

where,

Liquid Assets = Current Assets (–) Stock
Liquid Liabilities = Current Liabilities (–) Bank Overdraft

$= \dfrac{₹\,10,00,000\,(-)\,₹\,6,00,000}{₹\,4,00,000\,(-)\,₹\,20,000}$

$= \dfrac{₹\,4,00,000}{₹\,3,80,000}$

$= 1.05 : 1$

iii) Absolute Liquidity Ratio = $\dfrac{\text{Cash at Bank (+) Short-Term Investments}}{\text{Current Liabilities}}$

= $\dfrac{₹\,2,20,000}{₹\,4,00,000}$

= 0.55 : 1

iv) Current Assets to Fixed Assets = $\dfrac{\text{Current Assets}}{\text{Fixed Assets}}$

= $\dfrac{₹\,10,00,000}{₹\,19,00,000}$

= 0.526 : 1

Note : Fixed assets include Goodwill, Plant and Machinery, Furniture and Land and Buildings.

v) Debt to Equity Ratio = i) $\dfrac{\text{Long-term Debt}}{\text{Shareholders Fund}}$

= $\dfrac{₹\,5,00,000}{₹\,10,00,000\ (+)\ ₹\,5,00,000\ (+)\ ₹\,1,00,000\ (+)\ ₹\,4,00,000}$
$\quad\quad\quad\text{Equity Sh.}\quad\text{Pref. Sh.}\quad\text{General}\quad\text{Profit and}$
$\quad\quad\quad\text{Capital}\quad\quad\text{Capital}\quad\text{Reserve}\quad\text{Loss}$

= $\dfrac{₹\,5,00,000}{₹\,20,00,000}$

= 0.25 : 1

ii) $\dfrac{\text{Long-term Debt}}{\text{Long-term Debt (+) Shareholders Funds}}$

= $\dfrac{₹\,5,00,000}{₹\,5,00,000\ (+)\ ₹\,20,00,000}$

= $\dfrac{₹\,5,00,000}{₹\,25,00,000}$

= 0.20 : 1

vi) Proprietary Ratio = $\dfrac{\text{Shareholders Funds}}{\text{Total Assets}}$

= $\dfrac{₹\,20,00,000}{₹\,29,00,000}$

= 0.69 : 1

vii) Capital Gearing Ratio = $\dfrac{\text{Fixed Interest bearing securities}}{\text{Equity Sh. Capital (+) Reserves and Surplus}}$

= $\dfrac{₹\,10,00,000\ \text{i.e.}\ [₹\,5,00,000\ \text{Pref.} + ₹\,5,00,000\ \text{Deb.}]}{₹\,10,00,000 + ₹\,5,00,000}$

= $\dfrac{₹\,10,00,000}{₹\,15,00,000}$

= 0.66 : 1

viii) Fixed Assets Ratio = $\dfrac{\text{Fixed Assets}}{\text{Capital Employed}}$

= $\dfrac{₹\,19,00,000}{₹\,25,00,000}$

= 0.76 : 1

Management Accounting | Analysis and Interpretation of Ratios

ILLUSTRATION 2

Bharat Machines Ltd., Banarus submits the following Profit and Loss Account for the year ended 31st March, 2014.

Dr. Profit and Loss Account for the year ended on 31st March, 2014 Cr.

Particulars	₹	Particulars	₹
To Opening Stock	52,00,000	By Sales	3,20,00,000
To Purchases	1,60,00,000	By Closing Stock	76,00,000
To Wages	48,00,000		
To Manufacturing Expenses	32,00,000		
To Gross Profit C/D	1,04,00,000		
	3,96,00,000		3,96,00,000
To Selling Expenses	8,00,000	By Gross Profit B/D	1,04,00,000
To Office Expenses	45,60,000	By Profit on Sale of Shares	9,60,000
To Loss by Fire	2,40,000		
To Loss on Sale of Furniture	1,60,000		
To Net Profit C/D	56,00,000		
	1,13,60,000		1,13,60,000

Calculate : i) Gross Profit Ratio ii) Net Profit Ratio iii) Operating Profit Ratio iv) Operating Net Profit Ratio.

SOLUTION

i) **Gross Profit Ratio** $= \dfrac{\text{Gross Profit}}{\text{Sales}} \times 100$

$= \dfrac{₹ 1,04,00,000}{₹ 3,20,00,000} \times 100$

$= 32.5\%$

ii) **Net Profit Ratio** $= \dfrac{\text{Net Profit}}{\text{Sales}} \times 100$

$= \dfrac{₹ 56,00,000}{₹ 3,20,00,000} \times 100$

$= 17.5\%$

iii) **Operating Profit Ratio** $= \dfrac{\text{Cost of Goods Sold (+) Operating Expenses}}{\text{Sales}} \times 100$

$= \dfrac{₹ 2,16,00,000 (+) ₹ 53,60,000}{₹ 3,20,00,000} \times 100$

$= 84.25\%$

iv) **Operating Net Profit Ratio** $= \dfrac{\text{Operating Net Profit}}{\text{Sales}} \times 100$

$= \dfrac{₹ 56,00,000 (+) ₹ 1,60,000 (-) ₹ 9,60,000}{₹ 3,20,00,000} \times 100$

$= 15\%$

ILLUSTRATION 3

The following is the summarised Profit and Loss Account for the year ending 31st March, 2014 and the Balance-Sheet as on that date of Cifco Ltd., Chennai.

Dr.   Profit and Loss Account for the year ended 31st March, 2014   Cr.

Particulars	₹	Particulars	₹
To Opening Stock	10,000	By Sales	1,00,000
To Purchases	55,000	By Closing Stock	15,000
To Gross Profit C/D	50,000		
	1,15,000		1,15,000
To Office Expenses	15,000	By Gross Profit B/D	50,000
To Interest	3,000		
To Selling Expenses	12,000		
To Net Profit C/D	20,000		
	50,000		50,000

Balance Sheet as on 31st March, 2014

Liabilities	₹	Assets	₹
Share Capital	1,00,000	Land and Buildings	50,000
• Equity Shares of ₹ 10 each		Plant and Machinery	30,000
Profit and Loss	20,000	Stock	15,000
Creditors	25,000	Debtors	15,000
Bills Payable	15,000	Bills Receivable	12,500
		Cash and Bank	17,500
		Furniture	20,000
Total	1,60,000	Total	1,60,000

Additional Information :   ₹

- Average Debtors   12,500
- Credit Purchases   40,000
- Credit Sales   80,000
- Calculate : i) Stock Turnover Ratio, ii) Debtors Turnover Ratio, iii) Creditors Turnover Ratio, iv) Working Capital Turnover Ratio, v) Sales to Capital Employed, vi) Return on Shareholders Funds, vii) Gross Profit Ratio, viii) Net Profit Ratio, ix) Earning Per Share, x) Operating Ratio.

SOLUTION

i) **Stock Turnover Ratio** $= \dfrac{\text{Cost of Goods Sold}}{\text{Average Stock}}$

$= \dfrac{₹\,50,000 \text{ i.e. (Sales (–) Gross Profit)}}{₹\,10,000\,(+)\,₹\,15,000/2}$

$= \dfrac{₹\,50,000}{₹\,12,500}$

= 4 times

ii) **Debtors Turnover Ratio** $= \dfrac{\text{Credit Sales}}{\text{Average Debtors}}$

$= \dfrac{₹\,80,000}{₹\,12,500}$

$= 6.4 \text{ times}$

iii) **Creditors Turnover Ratio** $= \dfrac{\text{Credit Purchases}}{\text{Average Accounts Payable}}$

$= \dfrac{₹\,40,000}{₹\,40,000 \text{ i.e. } \left(\substack{\text{Creditors} \\ ₹\,25,000}\right) (+) \left(\substack{\text{Bills Payable} \\ ₹\,15,000}\right)}$

$= 1 \text{ time}$

iv) **Working Capital Turnover Ratio** $= \dfrac{\text{Sales}}{\left(\substack{\text{Working} \\ \text{Capital}}\right) (+) \left(\substack{\text{Current} \\ \text{Assets}}\right) (-) \left(\substack{\text{Current} \\ \text{Liabilities}}\right)}$

$= \dfrac{₹\,1,00,000}{₹\,20,000}$

$= 5 \text{ times}$

v) **Sales to Capital Employed** $= \dfrac{\text{Sales}}{\text{Capital Employed}} \times 100$

$= \dfrac{₹\,1,00,000}{\substack{₹\,1,00,000 \\ \text{Equity Share Capital}} (+) \substack{₹\,20,000 \\ \text{Profit and Loss}}}$

$= \dfrac{₹\,1,00,000}{₹\,1,20,000}$

$= 0.83 : 1$

vi) **Returns on Shareholders Funds** $= \dfrac{\text{Net Profit}}{\text{Shareholders Funds}} \times 100$

$= \dfrac{₹\,20,000}{₹\,1,20,000} \times 100$

$= 16.67\%$

vii) **Gross Profit Ratio** $= \dfrac{\text{Gross Profit}}{\text{Sales}} \times 100$

$= \dfrac{₹\,50,000}{₹\,1,00,000} \times 100$

$= 50\%$

viii) **Net Profit Ratio** $= \dfrac{\text{Net Profit}}{\text{Sales}} \times 100$

$= \dfrac{₹\,20,000}{₹\,1,00,000} \times 100$

$= 20\%$

ix) **Earning per Share** $= \dfrac{\text{Net Profit}}{\text{Number of Equity Shares}}$

$= \dfrac{₹\,20,000}{10,000 \text{ Shares}}$

$= ₹\,2$

x) **Operating Ratio** $= \dfrac{\text{Cost of Goods Sold} (+) \text{Operation Expenses}}{\text{Sales}} \times 100$

$= \dfrac{₹\,50{,}000\,(+)\,₹\,27{,}000}{₹\,1{,}00{,}000} \times 100$

$= 77\%$

ILLUSTRATION 4

The summarised Balance Sheet of David Green Ltd., Dombivali as on 31st March, 2012, 2013 and 2014 are given below :

Balance Sheet as on 31st March ...... (₹ in Crores)

Liabilities		2012	2013	2014
Paid-up Capital		194	194	194
Long-Term Borrowings				
i) from Banks		68	97	127
ii) from Others		281	343	376
Current Liabilities	(+)	52	54	99
		595	688	796

Assets		2012	2013	2014
Net Block		286	261	239
Current Assets		143	199	234
Profit and Loss	(+)	166	228	323
		595	688	796

Calculate the following ratios for three years :

i) Debt Equity Ratio
ii) Current Ratio
iii) Fixed Asset Ratio
iv) Proprietary Ratio

SOLUTION (₹ in crores)

Particulars		31-3-2012	31-3-2013	31-3-2014
i) Debt Equity Ratio = $\dfrac{\text{Long-term debt}}{\text{Shareholders equity funds}}$	=	$\dfrac{349}{194 - ₹\,166}$	Negative	Negative
	=	$\dfrac{349}{28}$		
	=	12.46		
ii) Current Ratio = $\dfrac{\text{Current Assets}}{\text{Current Liabilities}}$	=	$\dfrac{143}{52}$	= $\dfrac{199}{54}$	= $\dfrac{234}{99}$
	=	2.75 : 1	= 3.685 : 1	= 2.36 : 1
iii) Fixed Asset Ratio = $\dfrac{\text{Fixed Assets}}{\text{*Capital Employed}}$	=	$\dfrac{286}{377}$	= $\dfrac{261}{406}$	= $\dfrac{239}{374}$
	=	0.76 : 1	= 0.64 : 1	= 0.639 : 1
iv) Proprietary Ratio = $\dfrac{\text{Shareholders Funds}}{\text{Total Assets}}$	=	$\dfrac{28}{429}$	Negative	Negative
	=	0.0652 : 1		

* Capital Employed = Paid-up capital + Long-term borrowing − Profit and Loss (Debit balance)

ILLUSTRATION 5

Abstract of financial information of Elite Ltd., Edlabad for three years are given below :

Particulars	31-3-2012	31-3-2013	31-3-2014
Gross Profit	36%	$33\frac{1}{3}\%$	30%
Stock Turnover	20 Times	25 Times	14 Times
Average Stock	₹ 38,400	₹ 36,000	₹ 70,000
Average Debtors	₹ 87,500	₹ 1,68,750	₹ 2,00,000
Income Tax Rate	50%	50%	50%
Net Income after tax as % sales	6%	7%	12%
Maximum credit period allowed to the customers	60 Days	60 Days	30 Days

Required :
i) A statement of profits in comparative form for three years.
ii) Evaluate the position of the company regarding profitability and liquidity on the basis of information available.
iii) What additional information will you require to evaluate fully the position of company on the liquidity front ?

SOLUTION

i) Income Statement for the year ended ......

	Particulars		31-3-2012 ₹	31-3-2013 ₹	31-3-2014 ₹
	Sales		12,00,000	13,50,000	14,00,000
Less :	Cost of Goods Sold	(−)	7,68,000	9,00,000	9,80,000
∴	**Gross Profit**		4,32,000	4,50,000	4,20,000
Less :	Operating Expenses	(−)	2,88,000	2,61,000	84,000
∴	**Profit Before Tax**		1,44,000	1,89,000	3,36,000
Less :	Taxes	(−)	72,000	94,500	1,68,000
∴	**Profit After Tax**		72,000	94,500	1,68,000

Working Notes :

Particulars	31-3-2012	31-3-2013	31-3-2014
• Cost of Goods Sold • Stock Turnover × Average stock	20 × ₹ 38,400 = ₹ 7,68,000	25 × ₹ 36,000 = ₹ 9,00,000	14 × ₹ 70,000 = ₹ 9,80,000
• Cost of goods sold as % of Sales	64%	$66\frac{2}{3}\%$	70%
• Sales	₹ 12,00,000	₹ 13,50,000	₹ 14,00,000
• Net Income as % to Sales (given)	6%	7%	12%
• Net Income / PAT	₹ 72,000	₹ 94,500	₹ 1,68,000
• Profit Before Tax	₹ 1,44,000	₹ 1,89,000	₹ 3,36,000
• Operating Expenses (Gross Profit (−) Profit Before Tax)	₹ 2,88,000	₹ 2,61,000	₹ 84,000

ii) From the above statements it is quite clear that the profitability of the company is increasing quite consistently. From 6% in the year 2011-12 it has gone up to 7% in 2012-13 and upto 12% in 2013-14. However, stock turnover ratio which was 20 times in 2011-12 has slumped to 14 times in 2013-14 after going upto 25% in 2012-13. This needs improvement for better liquidity position.

The debtors turnover ratio was 13.7 times in first year and 8 and 7 times respectively in the second and third year (Sales ÷ Average Debtors) which has also gone down and needs to be improved. It should also be noted that debtors turnover ratio is decreasing inspite of reducing credit allowed to debtors in the third year which indicates that collection policy needs to be tightened.

iii) In order to evaluate the position of the company regarding liquidity fully, current liabilities and current assets should also be made available.

ILLUSTRATION 6

From the following information, prepare Balance-Sheet of Finolex Ltd., Faizpur as on 31st March, 2014 with as many details as possible.

i) Current Ratio = 2.5 : 1.
ii) Liquid Ratio = 1.5 : 1.
iii) Working Capital = ₹ 60,000.
iv) Reserves and Surplus = ₹ 20,000.
v) Bank Overdraft = ₹ 10,000.
vi) Fixed Assets to Proprietor's Funds = 0.75.
vii) There are no long term liabilities or fictitious assets.

SOLUTION

The Balance Sheet can be prepared with the help of the following working notes :

a) **Working Capital** = ₹ 60,000 i.e. Current Assets (–) Current Liabilities

Therefore, Current Assets (–) Current Liabilities = ₹ 60,000

or 2.5 (–) 1 = ₹ 60,000

(Current Ratio is 2.5 which means Current Assets are 2.5 times of Current Liabilities).

or 1.5 = ₹ 60,000
    1 = ₹ 40,000

Therefore, Current Liabilities = ₹ 40,000
Current Assets are 2.5 × ₹ 40,000 = ₹ 1,00,000.

b) To find out **Liquid Current Assets**, the following calculations can be made :

$$\text{Liquid Ratio} = 1.5 : 1 = \frac{\text{Liquid Current Assets}}{\text{Current Liabilities (–) Bank Overdraft}}$$

$$1.5 = \frac{\text{Liquid Current Assets}}{₹ 40,000 (–) ₹ 10,000}$$

= 1.5 × ₹ 30,000 = Liquid Current Assets

Liquid Current Assets = ₹ 45,000

But, Current Assets (−) Stock = Liquid Assets
∴   ₹ 1,00,000 (−) Stock = ₹ 45,000
           Stock = ₹ 55,000

c) Fixed Assets to Proprietor's Funds = 0.75 : 1 which means that out of proprietor's funds, 75% amount is invested in Fixed Assets. This suggests that remaining 25% of Proprietor's Funds are invested in the Working Capital.

∴   25% = ₹ 60,000 i.e. Working Capital
∴   100% = ₹ 2,40,000 (−) Proprietor's Funds
     Fixed Assets = 75% = ₹ 1,80,000
     Proprietor's Funds = Share Capital (+) Reserves
                       = ₹ 2,00,000 (+) ₹ 40,000
                       = ₹ 2,40,000

Balance Sheet of Finolex Ltd., Faizpur as on 31st March 2014

Liabilities		₹	Assets	₹
Share Capital		2,00,000	Fixed Assets	1,80,000
Reserves and Surplus		40,000	Current Assets :	
Current Liabilities :			• Stock 55,000	
• Creditors	30,000		• Other Current Assets (+) 45,000	1,00,000
• Bank Overdraft	(+) 10,000	40,000		
	Total	2,80,000	Total	2,80,000

ILLUSTRATION 7

Using the following data, complete the Balance Sheet of Godrej Ltd., Gauhati in the format given below :

Gross Profit : 20% of Sales	₹ 60,000
Shareholders Funds	₹ 50,000
Credit Sales	80% of Total Sales
Total Assets Turnover	3 times
Inventory Turnover to Cost of Sales	8 times
Average collection period (360 days a year)	18 days
Current Ratio	1.6
Long-Term Debt to Equity	40%

Format of Balance Sheet of Godrej Co., Gauhati as on ....

Liabilities	₹	Assets	₹
Creditors	−	Cash	−
Long-Term Debt	−	Debtors	−
Shareholders Equity	−	Inventory	−
		Fixed Assets	
Total	−	Total	−

SOLUTION

a) Gross Profit is 20% of Sales = ₹ 60,000
   Therefore,   Sales = ₹ 3,00,000
   But Cost of Sales = Total Sales (−) Gross Profit
       Cost of Sales = ₹ 3,00,000 (−) ₹ 60,000
                    = ₹ 2,40,000

b) Inventory Turnover Ratio = 8 times

$$8 \text{ times} = \frac{\text{Cost of Goods Sold}}{\text{Average Inventory}}$$

$$8 \text{ times} = \frac{₹2,40,000}{\text{Average Inventory}}$$

∴ Average Inventory $= \dfrac{₹2,40,000}{8}$

∴ Average Inventory = ₹ 30,000

Since Opening Stock is given, **₹ 30,000** is taken as Closing Stock i.e. Inventory

c) Total Assets Turnover = 3 times

∴ $3 \text{ times} = \dfrac{\text{Sales}}{\text{Total Assets}}$

$3 \text{ times} = \dfrac{₹3,00,000}{\text{Total Assets}}$

∴ Total Assets $= \dfrac{₹3,00,000}{3}$

∴ **Total Assets** = ₹ 1,00,000
∴ **Total Liabilities** = ₹ 1,00,000

d) Average collection period = 18 days

∴ Debtors Turnover Ratio $= \dfrac{360 \text{ days}}{18 \text{ days}}$

= 20 times

∴ Debtors $= \dfrac{\text{Cost of Sales}}{\text{Debtors Turnover Ratio}}$

Debtors $= \dfrac{₹2,40,000}{20 \text{ times}}$

∴ Debtors = **₹ 12,000**

e) Debt-equity Ratio (long-term) = 40%
   Shareholders Funds = ₹ 50,000
   Debt 40% of ₹ 50,000 = ₹ 20,000

f) Creditors = Total Liabilities (–) Equity (–) Long-Term Debt
   = ₹ 1,00,000 (–) ₹ 50,000 (–) ₹ 20,000
   = **₹ 30,000**

g) Current Ratio $= \dfrac{\text{Current Assets}}{\text{Current Liabilities i.e. (Creditors)}}$

$1.6 = \dfrac{\text{Current Assets}}{₹30,000}$

∴ 1.6 × ₹ 30,000 = Current Assets
∴ **Current Assets** = **₹ 48,000**
Currents Assets = Inventory + Debtors + Cash
₹ 48,000 = ₹ 30,000 + ₹ 12,000 + ?
∴ Cash = ₹ 48,000 – ₹ 42,000
∴ **Cash** = **₹ 6,000**

h) Fixed Assets = Total Assets (–) Current Assets
   = ₹ 1,00,000 (–) ₹ 48,000
   = ₹ 52,000

Balance Sheet of Godrej Ltd., Gauhati as on ....

Liabilities	₹	Assets	₹
Creditors	30,000	Cash	6,000
Long-Term Debt	20,000	Debtors	12,000
Shareholders Equity	50,000	Inventory	30,000
		Fixed Assets	52,000
Total	1,00,000	Total	1,00,000

ILLUSTRATION 8

The following is the Balance Sheet of Hindustan Tool Ltd., Himmatpur, as on 31st March, 2014.

Balance Sheet as on 31st March, 2014

Liabilities	₹	Assets	₹
Share Capital	2,00,000	Land and Buildings	1,40,000
Profit and Loss	30,000	Plant and Machinery	3,50,000
General Reserve	40,000	Stock-in-Trade	2,00,000
12% Debentures	4,20,000	Debtors	1,00,000
Creditors	1,00,000	Bills Receivable	10,000
Bills Payable	50,000	Bank Balance	40,000
Total	8,40,000	Total	8,40,000

Calculate :
i) Current Ratio,   ii) Quick Ratio   iii) Inventory to Working Capital
iv) Debt to Equity   v) Proprietary Ratio   vi) Capital Gearing Ratio
vii) Current Assets to Fixed Assets

SOLUTION

i) **Current Ratio** $= \dfrac{\text{Current Assets}}{\text{Current Liabilities}}$

$= \dfrac{₹\,3,50,000}{₹\,1,50,000}$

$= 2.33 : 1$

Working Note :   Current Assets = Stock (+) Debtors (+) Bills Receivable (+) Bank Balance
Current Liabilities = Creditors (+) Bills Payable

ii) **Quick Ratio** $= \dfrac{\text{Liquid Current Assets}}{\text{Liquid Current Liabilities}}$

$= \dfrac{₹\,1,50,000}{₹\,1,50,000}$

$= 1 : 1$

Working Note : Liquid Current Assets = Debtors + Bills Receivables + Bank Balance

iii) **Inventory to Working Capital** $= \dfrac{\text{Inventory}}{\text{Working Capital}}$

$= \dfrac{₹\,2,00,000}{₹\,2,00,000}$

$= 1 : 1$

Working Note :   Working Capital = Current Assets (−) Current Liabilities

iv)	**Debt to Equity**	=	$\dfrac{\text{Long-Term Debt}}{\text{Shareholders Fund}}$
		=	$\dfrac{₹\,4{,}20{,}000}{₹\,2{,}70{,}000}$
		=	1.55 : 1

Working Note: Long-term Debt = 12% Debentures
Shareholder's Funds = Share Capital (+) Reserves (+) Profit and Loss Account

v)	**Proprietory Ratio**	=	$\dfrac{\text{Proprietor's Fund}}{\text{Total Assets}}$
		=	$\dfrac{₹\,2{,}70{,}000}{₹\,8{,}40{,}000}$
		=	0.32 : 1

Working Note: Proprietor's Funds = Share Capital (+) Reserve (+) Profit and Loss Account

vi)	**Capital Gearing Ratio**	=	Fixed Income Bearing $\dfrac{\text{Securities *}}{\text{Share Capital}}$
		=	$\dfrac{₹\,4{,}20{,}000}{₹\,2{,}00{,}000}$
		=	2.1 : 1

(* 12% Debentures)

vii)	**Current Assets to Fixed Assets**	=	$\dfrac{\text{Current Assets}}{\text{Fixed Assets}}$
		=	$\dfrac{₹\,3{,}50{,}000}{₹\,4{,}90{,}000}$
		=	0.71 : 1

ILLUSTRATION 9

The following figures are extracted from the books of India Cable Ltd., Igatpuri as on 31st March, 2014.

	Particulars		₹
	Sales		24,00,000
Less :	Operating Expenses	(–)	**18,00,000**
	∴ **Gross Profit**		**6,00,000**
Less :	Non-Operating Expenses	(–)	2,40,000
	∴ **Net Profit**		**3,60,000**
	Current Assets		7,60,000
	Inventories		8,00,000
	Fixed Assets	(+)	**14,40,000**
			30,00,000
	Net Worth		15,00,000
	Debt		9,00,000
	Current Liabilities	(+)	6,00,000
	Total Liabilities		**30,00,000**
	∴ Working Capital		**9,60,000**
(Current Assets (+) Inventories (–) Current Liabilities)			

Calculate :

i) Gross Profit Ratio   ii) Net Profit Ratio   iii) Return on Assets
iv) Inventory Turnover v) Working Capital Turnover vi) Net Worth to Debt

SOLUTION

i) **Gross Profit Ratio** $= \dfrac{\text{Gross Profit}}{\text{Sales}} \times 100$

$= \dfrac{₹\,6,00,000}{₹\,24,00,000} \times 100$

$= 25\%$

ii) **Net Profit Ratio** $= \dfrac{\text{Net Profit}}{\text{Sales}} \times 100$

$= \dfrac{₹\,3,60,000}{₹\,24,00,000} \times 100$

$= 15\%$

iii) **Return on Assets** $= \dfrac{\text{Net Profit}}{\text{Total Assets}} \times 100$

$= \dfrac{₹\,3,60,000}{₹\,30,00,000} \times 100$

$= 12\%$

iv) **Inventory Turnover** $= \dfrac{\text{Sales}}{\text{Average Inventory}}$

$= \dfrac{₹\,24,00,000}{₹\,8,00,000}$

$= 3 \text{ times}$

Working Notes :

a) In the absence of 'Cost of goods sold', Sales are taken for calculation of this ratio.
b) Opening stock is not given in the example and therefore closing stock is taken as Average inventory.

v) **Working Capital Turnover** $= \dfrac{\text{Sales}}{\text{Net Working Capital}}$

$= \dfrac{₹\,24,00,000}{₹\,9,60,000}$

$= 2.5 \text{ times}$

Note : Net Working Capital = Current Assets (–) Current Liabilities

vi) **Net Worth to Debt** $= \dfrac{\text{Net Worth}}{\text{Debt}}$

$= \dfrac{₹\,15,00,000}{₹\,9,00,000}$

$= 1.66 : 1$

Management Accounting   Analysis and Interpretation of Ratios

ILLUSTRATION 10

The following are the summarised Profit and Loss Account and Balance-Sheet of Jindal Ltd., Jabalpur for the year ended 31st March, 2014.

Dr.   Profit and Loss Account for the year ended 31st March, 2014   Cr.

Particulars	₹	Particulars	₹
To Opening Stock	99,500	By Sales	9,50,000
To Purchases	5,45,000	By Closing Stock	1,50,000
To Carriage Inward	15,500		
To Gross Profit C/D	4,40,000		
	11,00,000		11,00,000
To Operating Expenses	2,00,000	By Gross Profit B/D	4,40,000
To Non-Operating Expenses	40,000	By Non-operating Income	60,000
To Net Profit C/D	2,60,000		
	5,00,000		5,00,000

Balance Sheet as on 31st March, 2014

Liabilities	₹	Assets	₹
Equity Share Capital	2,00,000	Land and Buildings	1,50,000
• Equity Share of ₹ 10 each		Plant and Machinery	1,80,000
Reserves	2,00,000	Stock-in-Trade	50,000
Profit and Loss	60,000	Debtors	45,000
Other Current Liabilities	90,000	Cash and Bank	60,000
Bills Payable	40,000	Bills Receivable	1,05,000
Total	5,90,000	Total	5,90,000

Calculate :

    i)   Gross Profit Ratio   ii)   Net Profit Ratio
    iii) Operating Profit Ratio   iv) Operating Ratio
    v)   Return on Capital Employed   vi) Net Profit to Fixed Assets
    vii) Stock Turnover Ratio   viii) Debtors Turnover Ratio
    ix) Creditors Turnover Ratio   x)   Sales to Working Capital
    xi) Sales to Fixed Assets   xii) Sales to Capital Employed
    xiii) Return on Total Resources   xiv) Turnover of Total Assets

SOLUTION

i) **Gross Profit Ratio** $= \dfrac{\text{Gross Profit}}{\text{Sales}} \times 100$

                                              $= \dfrac{₹\,4,40,000}{₹\,9,50,000} \times 100$

                                              $= 46.31\%$

ii) **Net Profit Ratio** $= \dfrac{\text{Net Profit}}{\text{Sales}} \times 100$

                                              $= \dfrac{₹\,2,60,000}{₹\,9,50,000} \times 100$

                                              $= 27.36\%$

iii) Operating Profit Ratio $= \dfrac{\text{Operating Profit}}{\text{Sales}} \times 100$

$= \dfrac{₹\,2,40,000}{₹\,9,50,000} \times 100$

$= 25.26\%$

Working Note : Operating Profit = Net Profit (+) Non-Operating Expenses (−) Non-Operating Income

$= ₹\,2,60,000\ (+)\ ₹\,40,000\ (−)\ ₹\,60,000$

$= ₹\,2,40,000$

iv) Operating Ratio $= \dfrac{\text{Cost of Goods Sold (+) Operating Expenses}}{\text{Sales}} \times 100$

$= \dfrac{₹\,5,10,000\ (+)\ ₹\,2,00,000}{₹\,9,50,000} \times 100$

$= 74.74\%$

v) Return on Capital Employed $= \dfrac{\text{Net Profit}}{\text{*Capital Employed}} \times 100$

$= \dfrac{₹\,2,60,000}{₹\,4,60,000} \times 100$

$= 56.52\%$

Capital Employed = *Share capital (+) Reserves (+) Profit and Loss Account

vi) Net Profit to Fixed Assets $= \dfrac{\text{Net Profit}}{\text{Fixed Assets}} \times 100$

$= \dfrac{₹\,2,60,000}{₹\,3,30,000} \times 100$

$= 78.78\%$

vii) Stock Turnover Ratio $= \dfrac{\text{Cost of goods sold}}{\text{Average Stock*}}$

$= \dfrac{₹\,5,10,000}{₹\,1,24,750}$

$= 4.088 \text{ times}$

*Average Stock $= \dfrac{\text{Opening Stock (+) Closing Stock}}{2}$

$= \dfrac{₹\,99,500\ (+)\ ₹\,1,50,000}{2}$

$= ₹\,1,24,750$

viii) Debtors Turnover Ratio $= \dfrac{\text{Credit Sales}}{\text{Average Debtors + Average Bills Receivables}}$

$= \dfrac{₹\,9,50,000}{₹\,45,000\ +\ ₹\,1,05,000}$

$= 6.33$

Working Note:

a) It is assumed that all sales are on credit.

b) In the absence of information Closing Debtors and Bills Receivable are assumed to Average Debtors and Bills Receivable.

ix) **Creditors Turnover Ratio** $= \dfrac{\text{Credit Purchases}}{\text{Average Creditors (+) Average Bills Payable}}$

$= \dfrac{₹ 5,45,250}{₹ 50,000 + ₹ 40,000}$

$= 6.05$ times

Working Note:

a) All purchases are assumed to be on credit.

b) Creditors are not given clearly in the example and therefore they are assumed to be ₹ 50,000 out of Other Current Liabilities.

c) Closing balances of Bills Payable and Creditors are assumed to be average balances.

x) **Sales to Working Capital** $= \dfrac{\text{Sales}}{\text{Working Capital}}$

$= \dfrac{₹ 9,50,000}{₹ 1,25,000}$

$= 7.6$ times

*Working Capital = Stock (+) Debtors (+) Cash and Bank (+) Bills Receivable (−) Other Current Liabilities (+) Bills Payable

$= ₹ 50,000 (+) ₹ 45,000 (+) ₹ 60,000 (+) ₹ 1,05,000 (−)$

$₹ 90,000 (+) ₹ 45,000$

$= ₹ 2,60,000 (−) ₹ 1,35,000$

$= ₹ 1,25,000$

xi) **Sales to Fixed Assets** $= \dfrac{\text{Sales}}{\text{Fixed Assets}}$

$= \dfrac{₹ 9,50,000}{₹ 3,30,000}$

$= 2.87$ times

xii) **Sales to Capital Employed** $= \dfrac{\text{Sales}}{\text{Capital Employed}}$

$= \dfrac{₹ 9,50,000}{₹ 4,60,000}$

$= 2.06$ times

xiii) Return on Total Resources $= \dfrac{\text{Net Profit}}{\text{Total Assets}} \times 100$

$= \dfrac{₹\,2,60,000}{₹\,5,90,000} \times 100$

$= 44.06\%$

xiv) Turnover of Total Assets $= \dfrac{\text{Sales}}{\text{Total Assets}}$

$= \dfrac{₹\,9,50,000}{₹\,5,90,000}$

$= 1.61 \text{ times}$

ILLUSTRATION 11

The following is the condensed Balance-Sheet of Kismat Ltd., Kanpur for 3 years ended on 31st March, 2012, 31st March, 2013 and 31st March, 2014.

(₹ in lacs)

Particulars		31-3-2012 ₹	31-3-2013 ₹	31-3-2014 ₹
Current Assets :				
Stock : • Raw Materials		12	18	20
• Finished Goods		30	35	25
• Stores and Spares		3	4	5
Debtors		40	50	50
Cash and Bank		5	10	20
Fixed Assets	(+)	90	110	120
Total Assets		**180**	**227**	**240**
Current Liabilities		20	32	30
Debenture-Secured		60	60	60
Unsecured Loans - Bank		15	40	45
Reserve and Surplus		30	32.5	38.75
Profit and Loss Account before providing for taxation and dividends		15	22.5	26.25
Equity Shares of ₹ 100 each		20	20	20
10% Preference shares of ₹ 100 each	(+)	20	20	20
Total Liabilities		**180**	**227**	**240**
Sales		300	360	400
Gross Profit		15%	18%	20%

The company earned the net profits before providing for income-tax @ 50%. Equity Shareholders to get dividends 50% more than Preference Shareholders. Show the Appropriation Account and work out the following ratios after reworking the Balance-sheet.

  i) Acid-Test ratio ii) Stock turnover ratio iii) Earning per share

  iv) Ratio of fixed assets to shareholders funds v) Return on capital employed

SOLUTION

Profit and Loss Appropriation Account of Kismat Ltd., Kanpur

Particulars		31-3-2012 ₹	31-3-2013 ₹	31-3-2014 ₹
Profit before tax and dividend		15,00,000	22,50,000	26,25,000
Less : Income-tax @ 50%	(−)	7,50,000	11,25,000	13,12,500
∴ **Profit after Tax**		7,50,000	11,25,000	13,12,500
Less : Preference Dividends (10%)	(−)	2,00,000	2,00,000	2,00,000
∴ Earnings for Equity shareholders		5,50,000	9,25,000	11,12,500
Less : Equity Dividends (15%)	(−)	3,00,000	3,00,000	3,00,000
∴ **Balance of Profits**		2,50,000	6,25,000	8,12,500

Balance Sheet of Kismat Ltd., Kanpur as on ......

Particulars		31-3-2012 ₹	31-3-2013 ₹	31-3-2014 ₹
Current Liabilities		20,00,000	32,00,000	30,00,000
Add : Provision for Tax	(+)	7,50,000	11,25,000	13,12,500
Total Current Liabilities		27,50,000	43,25,000	43,12,500
Current Assets *		90,00,000	1,17,00,000	1,20,00,000
Working Capital (CA − CL)		62,50,000	73,75,000	76,87,500
Add : Fixed Assets	(+)	90,00,000	1,10,00,000	1,20,00,000
∴ Capital Employed		1,52,50,000	1,83,75,000	1,96,87,500
Shareholder's Funds-Equity		20,00,000	20,00,000	20,00,000
Share Capital-Preference		20,00,000	20,00,000	20,00,000
Reserves and Surplus		30,00,000	32,50,000	38,75,000
Profit and Loss Appropriation Account Balance	(+)	2,50,000	6,25,000	8,12,500
Shareholder's Funds		72,50,000	78,75,000	86,87,500

(**N.B. :** Current Assets = Total Assets (−) Fixed Assets).

Calculation of Ratio :

Particulars	31-3-2012 ₹	31-3-2013 ₹	31-3-2014 ₹
i) **Acid Test Ratio :** $\dfrac{\text{Liquid Current Assets}}{\text{Current Liabilities}}$	$\dfrac{45,00,000}{27,50,000}$ = 1.64 : 1	$\dfrac{60,00,000}{43,25,000}$ = 1.39 : 1	$\dfrac{70,00,000}{43,12,500}$ = 1.62 : 1
ii) **Stock Turnover Ratio :** $\dfrac{\text{Cost of goods sold}}{\text{Average Stock}}$	$\dfrac{2,55,00,000}{45,00,000}$ = 5.67 times	$\dfrac{2,95,00,000}{51,00,000}$ = 5.78 times	$\dfrac{3,20,00,000}{53,50,000}$ = 5.98 times

Management Accounting 3.47 Analysis and Interpretation of Ratios

iii) **Earnings per Share :** $\dfrac{\text{Earnings for Equity shareholders}}{\text{Number of equity shares}}$	$\dfrac{5,50,000}{20,000}$ = ₹ 27.5	$\dfrac{9,25,000}{20,000}$ = 46.25	$\dfrac{11,12,500}{20,000}$ = ₹ 55.62
iv) **Fixed Assets to Shareholder's Funds :** $= \dfrac{\text{Fixed Assets}}{\text{Shareholder's funds}}$	$\dfrac{90,00,000}{72,50,000}$ = 1.24 times	$\dfrac{1,10,00,000}{78,75,000}$ = 1.4 times	$\dfrac{1,20,00,000}{86,87,500}$ = 1.38 times
v) **Return on Capital Employed :** $= \dfrac{\text{Profit after tax}}{\text{Capital employed}}$	$= \dfrac{7,50,000}{1,52,50,000}$ $\times 100$ = 4.92%	$= \dfrac{11,25,000}{1,83,75,000}$ $\times 100$ = 6.12%	$= \dfrac{13,12,500}{1,96,87,500}$ $\times 100$ = 6.67%

ILLUSTRATION 12

From the following annual accounts of Laxmi Cable Ltd., Lasalgaon for the year ended on 31st March, 2013 and 31st March, 2014 you are requested to calculate important ratios which will help the management in assessing overall performance of the company.

Particulars		31-3-2013 ₹	31-3-2014 ₹
Sales		12,00,000	14,96,000
Less : Cost of Sales	(−)	9,44,000	11,92,000
∴ **Gross Profit**		2,56,000	3,04,000
Less : Expenses :	(−)		
• Warehousing and Transport		76,000	96,000
• Administration		76,000	76,000
• Selling		44,000	56,000
• Debenture Interest	(−)	−	8,000
∴ **Net Profit**		60,000	68,000
Fixed Assets Less : Depreciation		1,20,000	1,60,000
Current Assets :			
• Stock		2,40,000	3,76,000
• Debtors		2,00,000	3,28,000
• Cash	(+)	40,000	28,000
∴ **Total Assets**		**6,00,000**	**8,92,000**
Share Capital		3,00,000	3,00,000
Reserves		60,000	1,20,000
Profit and Loss Account		40,000	48,000
Debentures		−	1,20,000
Current Liabilities	(+)	2,00,000	3,04,000
∴ **Total Liabilities**		**6,00,000**	**8,92,000**

SOLUTION

In order to comment on overall performance of the company, it is necessary to calculate the following ratio.

1. Profitability Ratio

Particulars	31-3-2013 ₹	31-3-2014 ₹
i) Gross Profit Ratio = $\dfrac{\text{Gross Profit}}{\text{Sales}} \times 100$	$= \dfrac{2{,}56{,}000}{12{,}00{,}000} \times 100$ = 21.33%	$= \dfrac{3{,}04{,}000}{14{,}96{,}000} \times 100$ = 20.32%
ii) Net Profit Ratio = $\dfrac{\text{Net Profit}}{\text{Sales}} \times 100$	$= \dfrac{60{,}000}{12{,}00{,}000} \times 100$ = 5%	$= \dfrac{68{,}000}{14{,}96{,}000} \times 100$ = 4.54%
iii) Operating Net Profit Ratio $= \dfrac{\text{Operating Net Profit}}{\text{Sales}} \times 100$	$= \dfrac{60{,}000}{12{,}00{,}000} \times 100$ = 5%	$= \dfrac{68{,}000 \, (+) \, 8{,}000}{14{,}96{,}000} \times 100$ = 5.08%
*₹ 8,000 = Interest on Debentures.		
iv) Operating Ratio $= \dfrac{\text{Cost of Goods Sold + Operating Expenses}}{\text{Sales}} \times 100$	$= \dfrac{9{,}44{,}000 \, (+) \, 1{,}96{,}000}{12{,}00{,}000} \times 100$ = 95%	$= \dfrac{11{,}92{,}000 \, (+) \, 2{,}28{,}000}{14{,}96{,}000} \times 100$ = 94.92%
Note : Operating expenses are the expenses excluding interest on debentures		
v) Return on Capital Employed $\dfrac{\text{Net Profit}}{\text{Capital Employed}} \times 100$	$= \dfrac{60{,}000}{12{,}00{,}000} \times 100$ = 15%	$= \dfrac{76{,}000}{5{,}88{,}000} \times 100$ = 12.93%

Note : Capital Employed = Share Capital + Reserves + Profit and Loss Account + Debentures.

2. Financial Ratio

Particulars	31-3-2013 ₹	31-3-2014 ₹
i) Current Ratio = $\dfrac{\text{Current Assets}}{\text{Current Liabilities}}$	$= \dfrac{4{,}80{,}000}{2{,}00{,}000}$ = 2.4 : 1	$= \dfrac{7{,}32{,}000}{3{,}04{,}000}$ = 2.40 : 1
ii) Quick Ratio = $\dfrac{\text{Quick Assets}}{\text{Current Liabilities}}$ * Stock	$= \dfrac{4{,}80{,}000 \, (-) \, 2{,}40{,}000}{2{,}00{,}000}$ = 1.2 : 1	$= \dfrac{7{,}32{,}000 \, (-) \, 3{,}76{,}000}{3{,}04{,}000}$ = 1.17 : 1
iii) Debt-Equity Ratio = $\dfrac{\text{Long-Term Debt}}{\text{Proprietor's Funds}}$ (Share Capital = Profit and Loss A/c + Reserves)	Nil	$= \dfrac{1{,}20{,}000}{4{,}68{,}000}$ = 0.256 : 1
iv) Proprietary Ratio = $\dfrac{\text{Total Assets}}{\text{Proprietor's Funds}}$	$= \dfrac{6{,}00{,}000}{4{,}00{,}000}$ = 1.5 : 1	$= \dfrac{8{,}92{,}000}{4{,}68{,}000}$ = 1.90 : 1

3. Turnover Ratios

Particulars	31-3-2013 ₹	31-3-2014 ₹
i) Fixed Assets Turnover = $\dfrac{\text{Sales}}{\text{Fixed Assets}}$	$= \dfrac{12,00,000}{1,20,000}$ = 10 times	$= \dfrac{14,96,000}{1,60,000}$ = 9.35 times
ii) Working Capital Turnover $\dfrac{\text{Sales}}{\text{*Working Capital}}$ (*Current Assets – Current Liabilities)	$= \dfrac{12,00,000}{2,80,000}$ = 4.28 times	$= \dfrac{14,96,000}{4,28,000}$ = 3.49 times
iv) Debtors Turnover = $\dfrac{\text{Credit Sales}}{\text{Average Debtors}}$ (Closing Debtors)	$= \dfrac{12,00,000}{2,00,000}$ = 6 times	$= \dfrac{14,96,000}{3,28,000}$ = 4.56 times
iv) Stock Turnover Ratio = $\dfrac{\text{Cost of Goods Sold}}{\text{Average Stock}}$	$= \dfrac{9,44,000}{2,40,000}$ = 3.93 times	$= \dfrac{11,92,000}{3,76,000}$ = 3.17 times

Conclusion :

If we have a glance at the above mentioned ratios, it is clearly seen that most of the ratios in profitability group are declining in 2013-14 as compared to 2012-13. The only exception to this is the ratio of operating net profit to sales which has increased marginally from 5% to 5.08% in the year 2013-14.

The turnover ratios are also showing a declining trend. There is an increase in fixed assets as well as working capital in the year 2012-13 but this increase has not resulted in increase in sales. As a result of this the various turnover ratios are declining in 2013-14 as compared to 2012-13.

The financial ratios are more or less stable in both the years. However, Debt-equity ratio in 2013-14 is 0.256 : 1 against a nil ratio in 2012-13 because the company has issued debentures in the year 2012-13.

In conclusion it can be said that the overall position of the company seems to be on the decline and therefore an urgent action is required to rectify the situation.

ILLUSTRATION 13

The Capital of Morvi Tiles Ltd., Muradabad is as follows :

Particulars		
Equity Shares of ₹100 each	₹	10,00,000
12% Preference Shares of ₹10 each	₹	5,00,000
Profit after tax	₹	4,00,000
Equity Dividend paid		20%
Market price of Equity Share	₹	120

Calculate the following ratios :
i) Dividend yield on Equity Shares.
ii) Cover for Preference and Equity Dividend.
iii) Earnings per Equity Shares.
iv) Price-Earning Ratio

SOLUTION

Working Notes: ₹

  Profit after tax   =   4,00,000
  Less: Preference Dividend @ 12% on ₹ 5,00,000   =   (−) 60,000
  - Profit available for Equity Shareholders   =   3,40,000
  - Equity Dividend 20% on ₹ 10,00,000   =   2,00,000
  - Dividend per Equity Share   = $\dfrac{₹\,2,00,000}{\text{Shares }10,000}$
                                                                =   ₹ 20

i) Dividend yield on Equity Shares = $\dfrac{\text{Dividend per Equity Share}}{\text{Market Price per Equity}}$

  = $\dfrac{₹\,20}{₹\,120} \times 100$

  = 16.67%

ii) **Cover for Preference and Equity Dividend**

  = $\dfrac{\text{Profit Available for Dividend}}{\text{Total Dividend}}$

  = $\dfrac{₹\,4,00,000}{₹\,2,60,000}$

  = 1.53 times

iii) Earnings per Equity Share = $\dfrac{\text{Profit for Equity Shareholder's}}{\text{Number of Equity Shares}}$

  = $\dfrac{₹\,3,40,000}{\text{Shares }10,000}$

  = ₹ 34

iv) Price Earnings Ratio = $\dfrac{\text{Market Price of an Equity}}{\text{Earnings per Share}}$

  = $\dfrac{₹\,120}{₹\,34}$

  = 3.52 times

ILLUSTRATION 14

Assume that Nevil India Ltd., Nainital has Owner's Equity of ₹ 1,00,000. The ratios for the firm are,

  Short-Term Debt to Total Debt = 0.4
  Total Debt to Owner's Equity = 0.6
  Fixed Assets to Owner's Equity = 0.6
  Total Assets Turnover = 2 times
  Inventory Turnover = 8 times

Complete the following Balance-Sheet from the information given above :

Balance Sheet of Nevil India Ltd., Nainital as on ......

Liabilities	₹	Assets	₹
Short-Term Debt		Cash	
Long Term Debt (+)		Inventory	
Total Debt		Total Current Assets	
Owner's Equity		Fixed Assets	
Total		Total	

SOLUTION

$$\text{Owner's Equity} = ₹1,00,000$$
$$\text{Total Debt to Owner's Equity} = 6$$

Therefore, Total Debt = ₹ 60,000

Short-Term Debt is 0.4 of ₹ 60,000

∴ Short-Term Debt = ₹ 24,000

Therefore, Long-Term Debt = ₹ 60,000 (−) ₹ 24,000
$$= ₹ 36,000$$

Fixed Assets are 6 of Owner's Equity

∴ Fixed Assets = ₹ 60,000

Total Assets = Total of Liabilities of Balance-Sheet
= ₹ 1,00,000 (+) ₹ 36,000 (+) ₹ 24,000
Equity Long-Term Debt (+) Short-Term Debt
= ₹ 1,60,000

$$\text{Total Assets Turnover} = \frac{\text{Cost of Goods Sold}}{\text{Total Assets}}$$

$$2 = \frac{\text{Cost of Goods Sold}}{₹1,60,000}$$

Cost of Goods Sold = 2 × ₹ 1,60,000
Cost of Goods Sold = ₹ 3,20,000

Note : The numerator for the above ratio is taken as cost of goods sold instead of sales in the absence of information.

$$\text{Inventory Turnover Ratio} = \frac{\text{Cost of Goods Sold}}{\text{Average Inventory}}$$

$$8 = \frac{₹3,20,000}{\text{Average Inventory}}$$

∴ $\text{Average Inventory} = \frac{₹3,20,000}{8}$

Therefore, Average Inventory i.e.

Closing Inventory = ₹ 40,000
Cash = Total Assets (−) Fixed Assets (−) Inventory
= 1,60,000 (−) ₹ 60,000 (−) ₹ 40,000
= ₹ 60,000

Balance Sheet of Nevil India Ltd., Nainital as on ......

Liabilities		₹	Assets		₹
Short-Term Debt	24,000		Cash	60,000	
Long-Term Debt	(+) 36,000		Inventory	(+) 40,000	
∴ Total Debts		60,000	∴ Total Current Assets		1,00,000
Owner's Equity		1,00,000	Fixed Assets		60,000
	Total	1,60,000		Total	1,60,000

ILLUSTRATION 15

From the following figures and ratios, make out the Balance Sheet of Onil Oil Ltd., Otur in the following format.

Balance Sheet of Onil Oil Ltd., Otur as on ......

Liabilities	₹	Assets	₹
Equity Capital	3,00,000	Fixed Assets	6,00,000
Retained Earnings	2,00,000	Inventory	–
Debentures	1,25,000	Debtors	–
Other Long-Term Loans	–	Cash	–
Accounts Payable	1,00,000		
Total		Total	

Gross Profit Margin = 20%
Quick Ratio = 1.5 : 1
Stock Turnover Ratio = 12 times
Average collection period = 30 days
Total Assets Turnover = 3 times
Other long-term debts (excluding debentures) to proprietor's funds = 0.75 : 1

SOLUTION

i) **Long-Term Debt to Proprietor's Funds :**

$$0.75 = \frac{\text{Other Long-Term Debt}}{\text{Proprietor's Funds}}$$

$$0.75 = \frac{\text{Long-Term Debt}}{₹3,00,000 + ₹2,00,000 \text{ (Share Capital + Retained Earnings)}}$$

∴ Other Long-Term Debt = ₹ 3,75,000

ii) **Sales :**

$$\text{Total Assets Turnover Ratio} = \frac{\text{Sales}}{\text{Total Assets}}$$

∴ $3 = \frac{\text{Sales}}{₹11,00,000}$

∴ Sales = ₹ 11,00,000 × 3
∴ Sales = ₹ 33,00,000

Management Accounting   3.53   Analysis and Interpretation of Ratios

Notes:

Total Assets = Total Liabilities

Total Liabilities = Share Capital (+) Retained earnings (+) Debentures (+) Other long-term debt (+) Account Payable

= ₹ 3,00,000 (+) ₹ 2,00,000 (+) ₹ 1,25,000 (+) ₹ 3,75,000 (+) ₹ 1,00,000

= ₹ 11,00,000.

∴ Total Assets = ₹ 11,00,000

iii) Debtors:

Average collection period = 30 days

Sales = ₹ 33,00,000

$$\text{Debtors turnover} = \frac{360 \text{ days}}{30 \text{ days}} = 12 \text{ times}$$

$$\text{Debtors turnover} = \frac{\text{Credit Sales}}{\text{Average Debtors (Closing Balance)}}$$

$$12 = \frac{₹ 33,00,000}{\text{Debtors}}$$

Therefore, Debtors = ₹ 2,75,000

Note:
a) It is assumed that there are 360 days in a year.
b) All sales are assumed to be on credit in the absence of information.

iv) Inventory:

$$\text{Inventory Turnover Ratio} = \frac{\text{Cost of goods sold}}{\text{Average Inventory}}$$

$$12 = \frac{26,40,000}{\text{Average Inventory}}$$

Therefore, Average Inventory (Closing) = ₹ 2,20,000.

Note:
a) Cost of goods sold = Sales – Gross Profit.
b) In the absence of information, Closing Inventory is taken as Average Inventory.

*Cash

Total Assets	= ₹	11,00,000
Fixed Assets	= ₹	6,00,000
Debtors (As per iii)	= ₹	2,75,000
Inventory (As per iv)	= ₹	2,20,000
Cash (Balancing figure)*	= ₹	5,00,000
Total	=	₹ 11,00,000

Balance Sheet of Onil Oil Ltd., Otur as on ......

Liabilities	₹	Assets	₹
Equity Capital	3,00,000	Fixed Assets	6,00,000
Retained Earning	2,00,000	Debtors	2,75,000
Debentures	1,25,000	Inventory	2,20,000
Long Term Loans	3,75,000	Cash	5,000
Accounts Payable	1,00,000		
Total	11,00,000	Total	11,00,000

ILLUSTRATION 16

The following data represents the ratios pertaining Popicon Ltd, Pune for the year ending 31st March, 2014.

Annual Sales	₹ 40,00,000
Sales to net worth	4 times
Current Liabilities to Net Worth	50%
Total Debt to Net Worth	80%
Current Ratio	2.2
Sales to Inventory	8 times
Average collection period	40 days
Fixed Assets to Net Worth	70%

From the above information, prepare the Balance Sheet as on 31st March, 2014 with as many details as possible. Assume that all sales are on credit basis.

SOLUTION

i) Sales to Net Worth = 4 times
   Sales = ₹ 40,00,000

Therefore, $4 = \dfrac{₹ 40,00,000}{\text{Net Worth}}$

∴ Net Worth = $\dfrac{₹ 40,00,000}{4}$

   Net Worth = ₹ 10,00,000

ii) Current Liabilities to Net Worth = 50%
    This means that total debt are 50% net worth.
    Current Liabilities = ₹ 10,00,000 × 50%
    Therefore, Current Liabilities = ₹ 5,00,000
    Total Debt to Net Worth = 80%

iii) This means the total debt is 80% of net worth.
     Therefore, Total Debt = ₹ 8,00,000

iv) Current Ratio = $\dfrac{\text{Current Assets}}{\text{Current Liabilities}}$

Therefore, $\dfrac{\text{Current Assets}}{₹ 5,00,000} = 2.2$

∴ Current Assets = 2.2 × ₹ 5,00,000
   Current Assets = ₹ 11,00,000

v) Sales to Inventory = 8 times
   Sales = ₹ 40,00,000
   Inventory = $\dfrac{₹ 40,00,000}{8}$
   = ₹ 5,00,000

vi) Average collection period = 40 days
    Sales = ₹ 40,00,000
    Debtors Turnover = $\dfrac{360 \text{ days}}{40 \text{ days}}$
    = 9 times

Therefore, Debtors = $\dfrac{₹ 40,00,000}{9}$
    = ₹ 4,44,444

vii) Therefore,
$$\text{Fixed Assets to Net Worth} = 70\%$$
$$\text{Fixed Assets} = 70\% \text{ of } ₹ 10,00,000$$
$$= ₹ 7,00,000$$

Balance Sheet of Popicon Ltd., Pune as on 31st March, 2014

Liabilities	₹	Assets		₹
Net Worth	10,00,000	Fixed Assets		7,00,000
Long Term Debt	3,00,000	Current Assets :		
Current Liabilities	5,00,000	• Stock	5,00,000	
		• Debtors	4,44,444	
		• Cash	(+) 1,55,556	11,00,000
Total	18,00,000		Total	18,00,000

Note :
a) Total Debt is ₹ 8,00,000/- and Current Liabilities are ₹ 5,00,000.
    Therefore, Long-term debt = ₹ 3,00,000
b) Total Current Assets = ₹ 11,00,000
Out of these stock and debtors together are ₹ 9,44,444. Therefore cash ₹ 1,55,556 is the balancing figure.

ILLUSTRATION 17

The standard ratios for the industry and the ratios of a company are given below. Determine the efficiency of the working of the company.

Particulars	Standard Ratios	Ratios of 'X' Co.
Current Ratio	2.50	1.90
Gross Profit Ratio	0.30	0.35
Fixed Expenses to Sales	0.15	0.20
Variable Expenses to Sales	0.10	0.08
Sales/Capital	3.00	4.00
Fixed Assets/Long-term funds	1.00	0.90
Rate of Return on capital	15%	22%

SOLUTION

i) The profitability of Co. X is better than the industry standard. The gross profit ratio as well as fixed and variable expenses to sales and rate of return on capital is better for Co. X than the industry standard.

ii) Current ratio for Co. X is however not satisfactory as compared to industry standard. There is a scope for improvement for Co. X in this respect.

QUESTIONS FOR SELF-STUDY

I. **Theory Questions :**

1) What is an Accounting Ratios ? Explain the significance of Accounting Ratio technique in financial analysis of a company.

2) How do you classify Accounting Ratios ? Which basis of classification do you consider more appropriate ?

3) The success of accounting ratio technique depends upon many things. What precautions will you take in the analysis and interpretation of financial statements?

4) "Current ratio should always be 2 : 1 to represent adequate short period solvency". Comments on this statement.

5) How do you apply the accounting ratio technique in the measurement of profitability of a business concerned? Do you think that an increase in Gross Profit is always an enhancement of profitability.

6) Explain the following accounting ratio.

i) Acid Test Ratio, ii) Current Ratio, iii) Debit Equity Ratio, iv) Gross Profit Ratio, v) Operating Ratio, vi) Balance Sheet Ratios, vii) Combined Ratios, h) Return on Capital Employed.

II. Practical Problems:

1) The following are the summarised Profit and Loss Account for the year ended 31st March, 2014 and Balance Sheet on that date.

Profit and Loss Account for the year ended 31st March, 2014

Particulars	₹	Particulars	₹
To Opening Stock	9,950	By Sales	85,000
To Purchases	54,525	By Closing Stock	14,900
To Incidental Expenses	1,425		
To Gross Profit C/D	34,000		
	99,900		99,900
To Operating Expenses :		By Gross Profit B/D	34,000
i) Selling and Distribution	3,000	By Non-Operating Incomes :	
ii) Administration	15,000	• Interest 300	
iii) Finance	1,500	• Profit on sale of shares (+) 600	900
To Non-Operating Expenses :			
i) Loss on sale of Assets	400		
To Net Profit C/D	15,000		
	34,900		34,900

Balance Sheet as on 31st March, 2014

Liabilities	₹	Assets	₹
Issued Share Capital :		Land and Buildings	15,000
• 2,000 Equity Shares of ₹ 10 each	20,000	Plant and Machinery	8,000
Reserve	9,000	Stock in Trade	14,900
Profit and Loss Account	6,000	Sundry Debtors	7,100
Current Liabilities	13,000	Cash at Bank	3,000
Total	48,000	Total	48,000

Compute : i) Current Ratio, ii) Operating Ratio, iii) Stock Turnover Ratio and iv) Return on total resources.

2) With the help of the following ratios regarding Tata Ltd., Tatanagar draw the Balance-Sheet of the company for the year 2014.

Current Ratio	2.5	Net Working Capital ₹ 3,00,000	
Liquid Ratio	1.5	Stock Turnover Ratio = 6 times (Cost of Sales/ Closing Stock)	
Gross Profit Ratio	20%	Fixed Assets Turnover Ratio (on Cost of Sales) 2 times	
Debt Collection Period	2 months	Fixed Assets to Shareholders Net Worth = 0.80	
Reserves and Surplus to Capital	0.50		

3) The following is the Balance Sheet of ABC Ltd. Aurangabad as on 31st March, 2014.

Liabilities	₹	Assets	₹
Equity Share Capital	2,00,000	Goodwill	1,20,000
Capital Reserve	40,000	Fixed Assets	2,80,000
8% Loan on Mortgage	1,60,000	Stock	60,000
Trade Creditors	80,000	Debtors	60,000
Bank Overdraft	20,000	Investments	20,000
Taxation – Current	20,000	Cash in Hand	60,000
Profit and Loss Account Profit 31-3-2014 for the year ending (After taxation and interest on fixed deposit) 1,20,000 **Less :** Transfer to Reserve (–) 40,000	80,000		
Total	6,00,000	Total	6,00,000

Sales amounted to ₹ 12,00,000

You are required to calculate the following ratios : i) Current Ratio, ii) Quick Ratio, iii) Equity Ratio, iv) Debt to Equity Ratio, v) Net Profit Ratio

4) From the following ratios and additional information prepare the Balance Sheet as on 31st March, 2014.
   a) Current Ratio : 2.5 to 1
   b) Liquid Ratio : 1.5 to 1
   c) Working Capital : ₹ 60,000
   d) Bank Overdraft : ₹ 10,000
   e) Fixed Assets to Proprietor's Fund : 0.75
   f) Reserve and Surplus : ₹ 40,000
   There were no fictitious or long-term loans.

5) Following is the Balance Sheet of Warren Tea Ltd., Walchandnagar as on 31st March, 2014 together with additional information as on that date.

Balance Sheet as on 31st March, 2014

Liabilities	₹	Assets	₹
Paid-up Capital	2,00,000	Goodwill	30,000
Reserve Fund	50,000	Building	1,20,000
Profit and Loss	12,750	Machinery	29,000
Bank Overdraft	11,250	Stock in Trade	66,000
Creditors	36,000	Debtors	85,000
Taxation Provision	20,000		
Total	3,30,000	Total	3,30,000

Additional Information :

Gross Profit – ₹ 2,10,000, Average Stock on hand – ₹ 63,000, Turnover for the year 2013-2014 – ₹ 8,40,000.

You are required to calculate the following accounting ratios –
a) Current Ratio,
b) Liquid Ratio,
c) Proprietary Ratio,
d) Stock Turnover Ratio
e) Gross Profit Ratio.

6) Following is the Balance Sheet of Binaca Ltd., Bandra as on 31st March, 2014

Liabilities	₹	Assets	₹
Paid-up Capital	12,00,000	Goodwill	2,00,000
Reserve	2,00,000	Land	6,00,000
Profit and Loss Account	4,30,000	Plant	4,30,000
Sundry Creditors	5,00,000	Sundry Debtors	8,20,000
Bank Overdraft	1,00,000	Stock of Goods	2,50,000
		Bank Balance	1,30,000
Total	24,30,000	Total	24,30,000

Additional Information :

	₹
Gross Profit for the year 2013-14	9,00,000
Sales for the year 2013-2014	30,00,000
Stock of goods on 1st April, 2013	2,00,000

From the above information calculate the following accounting ratios –
a) Current Ratio, b) Liquid Ratio,
c) Gross Profit Ratio, d) Stock Turnover Ratio,
e) Proprietary Ratio

7) From the following information relating to Charminar Ltd., Chennai, calculate the following ratios.
a) Current Ratio, b) Liquidity Ratio,
c) Debt Equity Ratio, d) Proprietary Ratio
e) Fixed Assets to Proprietary Fund Ratio

Assets and Liabilities	₹	₹
Fixed Assets :		85,00,000
Current Assets :		85,00,000
• Stock in Trade	30,00,000	
• Stores and Spares	14,00,000	
• Sundry Debtors	35,00,000	
• Advances and Deposits (+)	6,00,000	
	(+)	1,70,00,000
Share Capital and Reserves		1,00,00,000
Long-Term Borrowings – Debentures		50,00,000
Bank Overdraft – Cash Credit		20,00,000
		1,70,00,000

***

UNIT 4

FUND FLOW STATEMENT AND CASH FLOW STATEMENT

SYNOPSIS

- 4.1 Meaning of Funds
- 4.2 Flow of Funds
- 4.3 Fund Flow Statement
- 4.4 Working Capital
- 4.5 Causes of Changes in Working Capital
- 4.6 Proforma of Sources and Application of Funds
- 4.7 Proforma of Adjusted Profit and Loss Account
- 4.8 Proforma of Cash Flow Statement
- Questions for Self-Study

Under the Companies Act, a company is required to include the figures of previous year in the financial statements, so that the interested parties may compare individual figures for better understanding of the corporate performance and economic position. The schedules attached to published accounts explain important items for the knowledge of the concerning parties. No doubt the annual accounts in their traditional forms are very important but they suffer from certain limitations. The serious limitation of a Balance Sheet is that it is a static document as it shows the economic position at a point of time and fails to show fully the movements or changes in the assets, liabilities and owners equity. From the financial accounts in their usual form, it is not clear as to **how the funds were generated** and **how they were utilised** between the closing dates of two Balance Sheets. In order to provide such information's, another document known as

Statement of Changes in Financial Position is prepared. This document shows the changes in financial position between two closing dates of the Balance Sheets.

4.1 MEANING OF FUNDS

The concept **'fund'** is used in three different dimensions, which is shown in Figure 4.1 as follows :

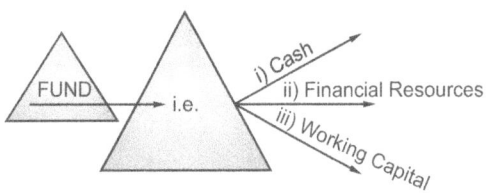

i) In a narrow sense, **Fund** means '**cash**', and the statement based on this concept is known as cash flow statement.

ii) In a broader sense, **Fund** means '**all financial resources**' which flows through working capital accounts and fixed capital accounts.

iii) In a broadcast sense, **Fund** means, '**working capital**' i.e. current assets minus current liabilities.

Fig. 4.1 : Meaning of Funds

In this connection, it is important to understand clearly the meaning of the word **'Fund'** which is used in three different senses. In a narrow sense, fund means **cash** and the statement based on this concept is known as **Cash Flow Statement**. In a broader sense, fund means **all financial resources** which flows through working capital accounts and fixed capital accounts and a **Fund Flow Statement** based on this concept is almost a new form of Balance Sheet. The Accounting Principles Board U.S.A. has recommended the preparation and presentation of statement of changes in financial position according to the broadest sense of the term 'Fund'. However, the meaning of 'Fund' in both the narrow as well as broader senses do not find favour with many academicians and practitioners, who prefer to consider **'Fund'** in the sense of Working Capital i.e. Current assets minus Current liabilities.

4.2 FLOW OF FUNDS

The term **'Flow'** means change. The **Flow of Fund** means change in fund or change in Working Capital. Flow of Fund is said to have taken place when a business transaction makes a change in the amount of fund which existed just before the happening of the transaction. The flow of funds refers to transfer of economic values from one asset to another, from one equity to another, form an asset to an equity or vice-versa or a combination of any of these. **Fund Flow Statement** essentially studies the movements to and from working capital area.

The term fund flow indicates the inflows and outflows of funds during a particular accounting period, generally a year. The flow exhibits the movements of funds in both the directions inside the business and outside the business. However, the flow of funds must arise due to external and not internal transactions of the business. For instance, the capitalization of reserves by the issue of bonus shares is an internal transaction. Such transaction are not included in the statement as there is no real addition to the funds of the company. When the term funds is used in the sense of working capital, funds flow will mean inflow and outflow of working capital.

4.3 FUND FLOW STATEMENT

Balance Sheet is a static statement showing financial position of a business on any particular day, but it is unable to throw any light on the changes in the position of assets and liabilities that have taken place over a certain period. For this purpose it is necessary to compare the two Balance Sheets. The changes in the financial position does not result from operating profit. The success or the failure of any business depends upon the availability of funds for better utilisation. The **Fund Flow Statement** reveals the sources from which the funds are made available and how they are utilised or applied. In other words, the Funds Flow Statement explains in brief the changes occurred in the items in two Balance Sheet. The Funds Flow Statement describes the sources from which additional funds were derived and the uses to which these funds were put.

Meaning

The term funds is used in different ways. It also includes cash as well as non-cash funds like depreciation. All receipt of cash form the sources of funds, whereas all payments in cash form the application of funds. When the term fund is used in broader sense it covers all assets and the liabilities which shows the sources of funds. In simple words, it means movement of funds i.e. incoming of funds from different sources and their outgoing i.e. use for different purposes like as purchase of assets or repayment of liabilities etc.

A **Fund Flow Statement** is also known by different names such as :
i) Where Got Where Gone Statement,
ii) Statement of Sources and Application of Funds,
iii) Statement of changes in Working Capital,
iv) Statement showing Summary of Financial Operations.
v) Statement of Sources and Application of Working Capital.
vi) Statement of changes in Financial Position, etc.

It may be noted that there is no official name of the statement as its preparation is still obligatory. Only few enlightened firms in India publish this statement for the guidance of their members and creditors. However, it is advisable that the title of the statement reflects the concept of fund on which it is based. Following are various **Sources and Applications of Funds** :

Sources of Funds	₹	Applications of Funds	₹
Funds from Operations	–	Loss from Operations	–
Issues of new Share Capital	–	Payment of Dividend	–
Issue of Debentures	–	Purchase of Fixed Assets	–
Long term Borrowings	–	Payment of Tax	–
Sales of Investments	–	Redemption of Shares	–
Sale of Fixed Assets	–	Redemption of Debentures	–
Dividend Received	–	Payment of Long Term Debt.	–
• Decrease in Working Capital (If application of funds is more than the sources)	–	• Increase in Working Capital (If sources of funds is more than the application)	–

Uses of Funds Flow Statement

Funds Flow Statement helps the financial analyst in having a more detailed analysis and understanding of changes in the distribution of resources between two Balance Sheet dates. In case such study is required regarding the future working capital position of the company, a projected funds flow statement can be prepared. The **Uses of Funds Flow Statement** are shown in Figure 4.2 as follows :

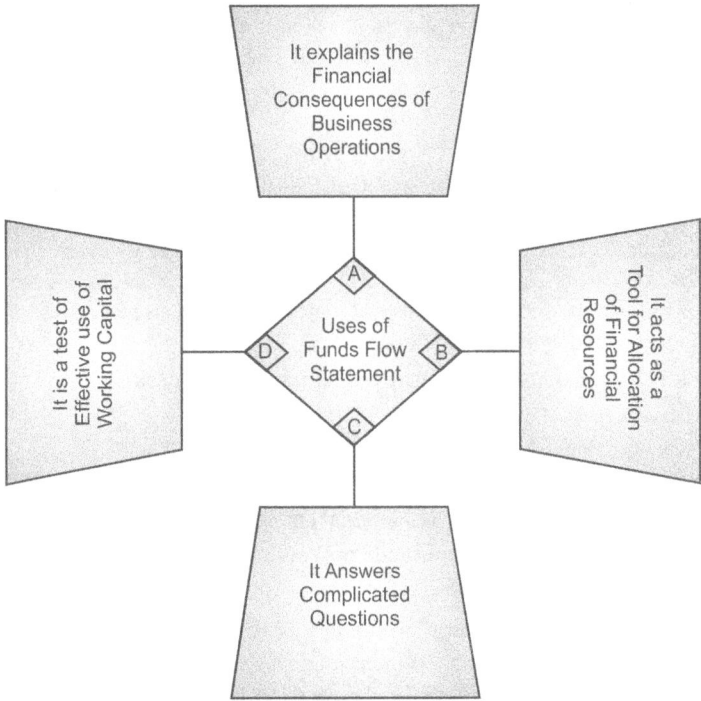

Fig. 4.2 : Uses of Funds Flow Statement

A)   It explains the Financial Consequences of Business Operations :

Funds flow statement provides a solution to so many conflicting situations such as,
   i)   While financing various types of investment which plan and policy is to be implemented.
   ii) Why the liquid position of the business is becoming more and more unbalanced in spite of business making more and more profits ?
   iii) How was it possible to distribute dividends in excess of current earnings or in the presence of a net loss for the period ?
   iv) How the business could have good liquid position in spite of business making losses or acquisition of fixed assets ?
   v)   Where have the profits gone ?
   vi) How the funds generated are to be utilise for the different purposes ?
   vii) Why were dividends not larger ?

B) It acts as a Tool for Allocation of Financial Resources :

A projected funds flow statement will help the analyst in finding out how the management is going to allocate the scarce resources for meeting the productive requirements of the business. The use of funds should be phased in such an order that the available resources are put to the best use of the enterprise. The funds should be managed in such a way that the business is in a position to make payment of interest and loan installments as per the agreed schedule. The fund flow statement is being used as a tool of financial analysis by the management and other parties interested in understanding the changes in financial position of an undertaking.

C) It Answers Complicated Questions :

With the help of fund flow statement the financial analyst can find out answers to a number of complicated questions; such as :

i) What should be the liquid position ? What should be the credit policy in the light of the liquidity position indicated by the fund flow statement ?
ii) What is the overall creditworthiness of the enterprise ?
iii) What are the sources of repayment of the loans taken ?
iv) How much funds are generated through normal business operations.
v) In what way the management has utilised the funds in the past and what are going to be likely uses of funds ?

D) It is a Test of Effective use of Working Capital :

Funds flow statement is a test of effective use of working capital by the management during a particular period. The adequacy or inadequacy of working capital will tell the financial analyst about the possible steps that the management should take for effective use of surplus working capital or make arrangement in case of inadequacy of working capital. In practice, the financial requirements of industry for term loans are met by the specialised financial institutions and working capital needs are generally satisfied by commercial banks, which ask for a copy of funds flow statement from the borrowing party.

The National Association of Accountants states the following Uses of Funds Statement :

i) Estimating the amount of funds needed for growth.
ii) Improving the rate of income on assets.
iii) Planning the temporary investment of idle funds.
iv) Securing additional working capital when needed.
v) Securing economies in the centralised management of cash in organisations whose management is decentralised.
vi) Planning the payment of dividends to shareholders and interest to creditors.
vii) Easing the effects of an insufficient cash balance.

Advantages of Funds Flow Statement

Following are the main **Advantages of Funds Flow Statement** :

i) The Funds Flow Statement is increasingly being used as a tool of financial analysis by the management, bankers, financial institutions, investors and other parties interested in understanding the changes in financial position of an undertaking.
ii) A funds flow statement can be used as a control device to make the financial planning more effective.
iii) The financial requirements of industry for term loans are met by the specialised financial institutions and working capital needs are generally satisfied by commercial banks which ask for a copy of Funds Flow Statement from the borrowing party.

iv) The potential shareholder can also form an idea about the financial health of an organisation from the study of its funds flow statement and take decision about his investment plan.

v) A study of funds flow statement clearly tells about the liquid position and the supplier of raw materials can review its own credit policy in the light of the liquidity position indicated by the funds flow statement.

vi) Fund flow statement is a test of effective use of working capital by the management in a particular period of time.

vii) It gives an insight into the financial operations of the concern which helps in analysing past and future expansion plans.

viii) With the help of funds statement, a finance manager can ensure that the business will have funds when required.

ix) This is an important and useful tool of management which can throw light on many financial problems.

x) It shows liquid position of business more accurately.

xi) It also indicates what is the overall creditworthiness of the enterprise

Limitations of Funds Flow Statement

The **Funds Flow Statement** suffers from certain **limitations**, which are as under :

i) It is based on the information's contained in the traditional final accounts. Therefore, it also suffers from the same limitations with which the usual published accounts suffer.

ii) A funds flow statement cannot replace the traditional financial statements. Infact, a funds flow statement is prepared from the balance sheets and other important information's pertaining to sources and uses of funds.

iii) A funds flow statement is not as much revealing as a balance sheet. It simply fills the gaps where a balance sheet fails to reflect the changes in financial position.

iv) It is argued that the component of cash is more important than the working capital because it is the cash and not the other components i.e. stock and receivables, which is required to pay off the liabilities of a concern.

v) It is also argued that a balance sheet is itself in the nature of a fund flow statement as the liability side depicts the sources from which the funds generate and the assets side show the application of the funds and as such a funds flow statement is not significant.

4.4 WORKING CAPITAL

Working Capital is ordinarily understood as excess of Current Assets over Current Liabilities. Some persons call Total Current Assets as **Gross Working Capital** and Current Assets minus Current Liabilities as **Net Working Capital** or Net Current Assets. In other words, the term Funds stands for Net Working Capital or Net Current Assets or Free Current Assets. The important components of **Current Assets** are, Cash in Hand, Cash at Bank, Bills Receivable, Stocks, Debtors, Income Outstanding, Prepaid Expenses etc.

Similarly, the important components of **Current Liabilities** are, Creditors, Bills Payable, Expenses Outstanding, Debts due within a year, Provision for Bad Debts etc.

4.5 CAUSES OF CHANGES IN WORKING CAPITAL

Changes in Working Capital position of a business unit are significant considerations in the analysis of operating results and financial condition. The sources of working capital, the disposition of working capital and the composition of the working capital at the end of the period, are all important factors in evaluating past activities and in judging a company's ability to prosper in the future. The flow of funds occurs when a transaction changes on one hand a non-current account, and on the other a current account and vice-versa. When a change in a non-current account, for example, fixed assets, long-term liabilities, reserves and surplus, fictitious assets etc. is followed by a change in another non-current account, it does not amount to flow of funds. This is because of the fact that in such cases neither the working capital increases nor decreases. In the same way, when a change in one current account results in a change in another current account, it does not affect funds. Funds move from non-current to current transactions.

There are four possibilities viz.

i) **Increase** in the value of **Current Assets** which **increases** the **Working Capital**.

ii) **Decrease** in the value of **Current Assets** which **decreases** the **Working Capital**.

iii) **Increase** in the value of **Current Liabilities** which **decreases** the **Working Capital**.

iv) **Decrease** in the value of **Current Liabilities** which **increases** the **Working Capital**.

In case of flow of fund, only the following type of transactions may cause the flow of fund directly.

i) Transactions between **Current Assets and Fixed Assets.**

ii) Transactions between **Current Assets and Capital and Long-term Liabilities**.

iii) Transactions between **Current Liabilities and Fixed Assets**.

iv) Transactions between **Current Liabilities and Capital and Long-term Liabilities**.

Thus, at the end of the year, it is possible to measure,

i) the **inflows into Working Capital** for the whole year as a consequence of raising of capital, raising of loans, sale of fixed assets, sale of investments and operational inflow due to profits. Funds from operation have to be adjusted. Depreciation on Fixed Assets, amortisation of Fictitious Assets, Loss on sale of Fixed Assets, Provision and Reserves are added and gain on sale of Fixed Assets is to be deducted.

ii) the **outflows from Working Capital** as a consequence of Purchase of Fixed Assets, Payment of Dividends, Payment of Taxes, Payment of Preference Capital and Long-term Debts, Payment of Debentures etc.

Funds Flow Statement and Income Statement

A **Funds Flow Statement differs from an Income Statement** (i.e., Profit and Loss Account) in several respects which are as follows :

i) Flow of funds is said to have taken place when a business transactions makes a change in the amount of fund which existed just before the happening of transaction. If the changes results in the increase of fund then the transaction responsible for such a change is said to be a **source of fund**. If the change results in the decrease of fund then the transaction responsible for such a change is said to be application or a **use of fund**. On the other hand, **income statement** or profit and loss account is a very important part of financial statements in as much as the determination of net profit of a business enterprise is the central feature of accounting. Business is conducted primarily to earn profit. This statement matches revenues and costs incurred in the process of earning revenues.

ii) **Sources of funds** are many besides operations such as share capital, debentures, sale of fixed assets, etc. An **Income Statement** which discloses the results of operations cannot even accurately tell about the funds from operations alone because of non-fund items (such as depreciation, writing off of fictitious assets, etc.) being included therein.

iii) A **Funds Flow Statement** matches the "funds raised" and "funds applied" during a particular period. The sources and applications of funds may be of capital as well as of revenue nature. An **Income Statement** matches the incomes of a period with the expenditures of that period which are both of a revenue nature. For example, where shares are issued for cash, it becomes a source of funds while preparing a funds flow statement but it is not an item of income for an Income Statement.

iv) A **Funds Flow Statement** deals with the financial resources required for running the business activities. It explains how were the funds obtained and how were they used, whereas an **Income Statement** discloses the results of the business activities, i.e., how much has been earned and how it has been spent.

v) The **Funds Flow Statement** simply tells about the working capital position of the business. It does not explain how much profit the business has really earned. This can be found out only by an income statement.

Preparation of Funds Flow Statement

The preparation of a Funds Flow Statement (Based on Working Capital Concept) is not difficult, if we could identify the various sources of funds and the items for which these sources are used. The main **sources of funds** are : i) Issue of equity capital and debentures : ii) Sale of any assets for cash, iii) Sale of investments, iv) Raising of additional loans, v) Non trading receipts, vi) Business operations. The **funds** so generated may be **utilised** for the following purpose :

i) Repayment of preference share capital, ii) Redemption of debentures, iii) Purchase of fixed assets, iv) Purchase of long-term investments v) Non-trading payments, vii) Operational losses etc.

Fund from Business Operations :

The business operations results in profit or loss. In case of profit the fund is changed positively. Therefore, the **profit** becomes a **source of fund**. To find the real fund from business operations, the Trading and Profit and Loss Account has to be prepared.

4.6 PROFORMA OF SOURCES AND APPLICATION OF FUNDS (i.e. Funds Flow Statement)

The Income Statement and Balance Sheet are prepared in accordance with the proforma as prescribed under the Indian Companies Act but there in no prescribed proforma for a **Funds Flow Statement** because the law does not require its preparation and publication. Therefore, a firm can prepare a Funds Flow Statement in any manner it deem fit. A specimen proforma of the statement in an account form is given below :

Sources and Application of Funds (i.e. Funds Flow Statement)

for the year ended 31st March ………

	Sources	₹		Application	₹
i)	Funds from Business Operations		i)	Loss of Funds due to Business Operations	
ii)	Issue of Shares		ii)	Redemption of Preference Shares	
iii)	Issue of Debentures		iii)	Redemption of Debentures	
iv)	Sale of Investments		iv)	Purchase of Investments	
v)	Sale of Assets		v)	Purchase of Assets	
vi)	Loans Raised		vi)	Payment of Loans	
vii)	Non-trading Receipts		vii)	Tax Paid	
viii)	• Decrease in Working Capital		viii)	Dividend Paid	
			ix)	Non-trading Payments	
			x)	• Increase in Working Capital	
	Total			Total	

A Funds Flow Statement can also be prepared in a horizontal statement form which is as under :

Funds Flow Statement for the year ended 31st March, ...

Sources of Funds		₹
i) Funds from Business Operations		–
ii) Issue of Shares		–
iii) Issue of Debentures		–
iv) Sale of Investment		–
v) Sale of Fixed Assets		–
vi) Loans Raised		–
vii) Non-Trading Receipt	(+)	–
Total Funds Generated		–

Application of Funds		₹
i) Loss of Funds due to Business Operations		–
ii) Redemption of Preference Shares		–
iii) Redemption of Debentures		–
iv) Purchase of Investments		–
v) Purchase of Fixed Assets		–
vi) Payment of Loan		–
vii) Non-Trading Payments	(+)	–
Total Funds Used		–

Requirements for preparation of Funds Flow Statement :

For the preparation of a **Funds Flow Statement**, we need Balance Sheets and Income Statements for the last two years and other information's which are not revealed by the annual accounts but which have otherwise affected the movements of fund during the financial year. In case only the Balance Sheets are available, then other information affecting the funds from business operations and the financial position should be collected. The other information's needed for the preparation of a Funds Flow Statement are the depreciation charged on assets, provision made for taxation and dividend, capital expenditure written off, asset discarded without any recovery, loss on sale of assets, profit on sale of any capital asset, transfer from one account to another account, taxes and dividend paid during the year, interim dividend paid, non-trading incomes and expenditure or losses debited to Profit and Loss Account, etc. With such an information in hand, we can proceed to prepare the Funds Flow Statement in the following manner :

Steps in preparation of Funds Flow Statement :

Following steps are required in preparation of Funds Flow Statement.

    Step I   : Preparation of Adjusted Profit and Loss Account to find out funds from business operations.

    Step II : Preparation of Statement of Changes in Working Capital.

    Step III : Determination of Other Sources and Application of Fund.

Step I : Preparation of Adjusted Profit and Loss Account :

To calculate the net operational flow of fund, the profit as shown by the traditional Income Statement need to be recast as it contains certain items of non-fund and non-operating nature. For example, depreciation is a non-fund item which does not result in the outflow of cash or it does not require any current expenditure to be incurred during the financial year. Therefore, the amount of depreciation charge should be added back to the profit in the calculation of Funds from Business Operations. Similarly writing-off of goodwill, patents, trade marks, preliminary expenses, discount on issue of shares and debentures, etc. are the items which figure on the debit side of Income Statement but they are also in the nature of depreciation not affecting the flow of funds. Such items, therefore, should be added back to profit. All appropriations of profits such as transfers to different reserves, provisions for taxation, proposed dividend, etc. not being operating costs should be added back to the profit figures. From the total so arrived at, the non-operating incomes like dividend received income tax refund, compensation received, profit on sale of asset, etc. should be deducted to arrive at the figure of total operational inflow.

4.7 PROFORMA OF ADJUSTED PROFIT AND LOSS ACCOUNT

The funds from business operations for the financial year can be calculated by deducting the profit at the beginning of the year from the total operational inflow for the year. A specimen proforma of Adjusted Profit and Loss Account in an account form is given below :

Dr.　　　　　Adjusted Profit and Loss Account for the year ended 31st March ......　　　　　Cr.

Particulars	₹	Particulars	₹
To Depreciation		By Opening Balance of Profit and Loss Account	
To Amount Written off on account of :		By Rent received and receivables	
i) Discount on issue of shares/debentures		By Dividend received and receivables	
ii) Preliminary Expenses		By Profit on Sale or Appropriation of Fixed Assets	
iii) Goodwill/Trade Marks/ Patents/Copyrights		By Income Tax Refund	
iv) Other deferred expenses		By Savings in excess provision made or	
To amount transferred out of profit of current year to :		By Decrease in Revenue Reserve caused by transfer to Profit and Loss Account.	
i) General Reserve		• By Funds from Business Operation (Balancing Figure)	
ii) Capital Reserve			
iii) Dividend Equilisation Reserve			
iv) Depreciation Sinking Fund			
v) Provision for Taxation			
vi) Proposed Dividend			
vii) Contingency Reserve			
viii) Any other Revenue Reserve			
To Loss on Sale of Fixed Assets (Buildings, Land, Plant and Machinery)			
To any other expenditure charged to Profit and Loss Account but not affecting cash			
To Closing Balance of Profit and Loss Account			

A Funds from Business Operation Statement can also be prepared in horizontal statement form as under:

Particulars	₹	₹
Profit / Loss as per Income Statement. (at the end of the year)		
Add : • Depreciation		
• Preliminary Expenses		
• Discount on issue of Shares and Debentures written off		
• Goodwill, Trade Mark, Patents, Copyrights Written off		
• Loss on Sale of Machine		
• Loss on Investment Sold		
• Interim Dividend Paid		
• Provision for Taxation		
• Proposed Dividend		
• Machine Lost		
• Transfer to Reserves (+)		
Less : • Profit on Sale of Machine, Investment or any other Fixed Assets		
• Dividend Received		
• Tax Refund (−)		
Less : Profit / Loss at the beginning of the year (−)		
∴ Funds from Business Operations		

Step II : Preparation of Schedule or Statement of Changes in Working Capital.

After bringing in all the items of sources and application of fund, the Funds Flow Statement should be balanced. In case the 'Sources' exceed the 'Application', there is an increase of working capital which means an use of Fund. On the other hand, if the Applications are more than the Sources, the difference will represents the Decrease in working capital or source of fund.

The Schedule of changes in Working Capital is not considered as a part of Funds Flow Statement but it is generally accompanied with the Funds Flow Statement. All current assets and current liabilities are brought into the Schedule of Changes in Working Capital. The increase or decrease in individual items of current assets and current liabilities affecting the net change in working capital are depicted in the Schedule. The net increase or decrease in working capital is the same as shown in the Funds Flow Statement. If there is any variation between the two figures of increase/decrease of working capital as per Fund Flow Statement and schedule of changes in working capital, then it is an indication that some mistake has been committed somewhere in the calculation of funds from business operations in the determination of other sources and application of funds.

The Schedule of Changes in Working Capital may be prepared as per the proforma given below.

Schedule of Changes in Working Capital

Assets and Liabilities	Previous Year ₹	Current Year ₹	Changes in Working Capital	
			Increase ₹	Decrease ₹
Current Assets :				
• Stock in Trade				
• Sundry Debtors				
• Cash Balance				
• Outstanding Income				
• Bank Balance				
• Prepaid Expenses				
Total (A)				
Current Liabilities :				
• Sundry Creditors				
• Outstanding Expenses				
• Bills Payable				
• Pre-received Incomes				
• Bank Overdraft				
Total (B)				
Net Working Capital (A – B)				
∴ Increase / Decrease in Working Capital				
Total				

Step III : Determination of Other Sources and Application of Funds

After having calculated the funds from business operations, the next step should be to find out the other sources and application of fund. For this purpose the Balance Sheet items should be carefully compared. For example, an increase in the current year's debentures amount generally means a source of fund and a decrease in application of fund or increase in the value of current year investment implies application and decrease means a source of fund.

CASH FLOW STATEMENT

Meaning

Cash Flow Statement as its name suggests takes into consideration only those transactions which are related with movement of cash and all those dealings which affects the cash position of the concern. With the help of **cash flow statement**, a finance manager can ensure that business will have liquid assets for meeting day to day expenses.

Fund flow statement indicates movement of funds or change in working capital but **Cash Flow Statement** shows movement of cash only. The statement of changes in financial position can also be prepared on the basis of the cash concept of the word 'Fund'. It is known as **Cash Flow Statement** if fund is considered in the sense of cash. The preparation of **Cash Flow Statement** is important to understand the paradoxical situation in which a firm finds difficulty in honouring its short-period business commitments despite the existence of sufficient working capital as indicated by the Fund Flow Statement based on working capital. This happens when a large proportion of working capital is tied up in the form of inventories and other working assets. The Fund Flow Statement based on working capital concept does not take into account the qualitative structure of working capital. Cash is a peculiar component of working capital. It should be distinguished from other components in any scheme of short-period financial planning. The **Cash Flow Statement** enables a firm to know the availability of cash from different sources and the manner of its utilisation.

A projected **Cash Flow Statement** tells the management about the cash position at different timings. The management can arrange for additional necessary cash in case cash outflow exceeds the cash inflow in any particular period of time. Similarly surplus cash, if any, can be invested for effective utilisation of cash balances. When all transactions such as sales, purchases, incomes and expenses are in cash, net profit is equivalent to net cash from operations. In actual practice we never come across as stated above. Most of the transactions of the business are on credit basis so that net profit can be equal to net cash from operations.

DIFFERENCE BETWEEN FUND FLOW STATEMENT AND CASH FLOW STATEMENT

The basic difference between Funds Flow Statement and Cash Flow Statement can be summarised as follows :

	Fund Flow Statement		Cash Flow Statement
i)	The term 'fund' refers to working capital and it shows change in position of working capital.	i)	The term 'cash' refers to cash only and it shows change in cash position of business.
ii)	This analysis is more useful in long term' planning.	ii)	This is more useful in short term planning.
iii)	This considers changes in all current assets and current liabilities.	iii)	This indicates simply cash receipt and cash payments and does not take into consideration other Current Assets.
iv)	Improvement in working capital does not mean improvement in cash position.	iv)	Cash is one constituent of working capital as improvement in cash position results in improvement in working capital.
v)	This indicates inflow of fund and outflow of fund.	v)	This indicates inflow of cash and outflow of cash.
vi)	Fund flow statement is a vast concept which includes flow of cash also.	vi)	As compared to fund flow statement, cash flow statement is a narrow concept which includes inflow and outflow of cash only.
vii)	This is a test of effective use of working capital by the management in a particulars period of time.	vii)	This a test of effective flow of cash by the management in a particular period of time.
viii)	With the help of funds statement, a financial manager can ensure that the business will have funds when required.	viii)	With the help of cash flow statement, a financial manager can ensure that the business will have liquid assets for meeting day to day expenses.
ix)	This explains in brief the changes occurred in the items in two balance sheet.	ix)	This explains the movement of cash and all those dealings which affects the cash position of the concern.
x)	It indicates the overall credit worthiness of the business.	x)	It shows how much money should be in balance in cash box at any given time.

Utility

A **Cash Flow Statement** is useful for short-term planning. A business enterprise needs sufficient cash to meet its various obligations in the near future such as payment for purchase of fixed assets, payment of debts maturing in the near future, expenses of the business, etc. The **Utility of Cash Flow Statement** is shown below in Figure 4.3.

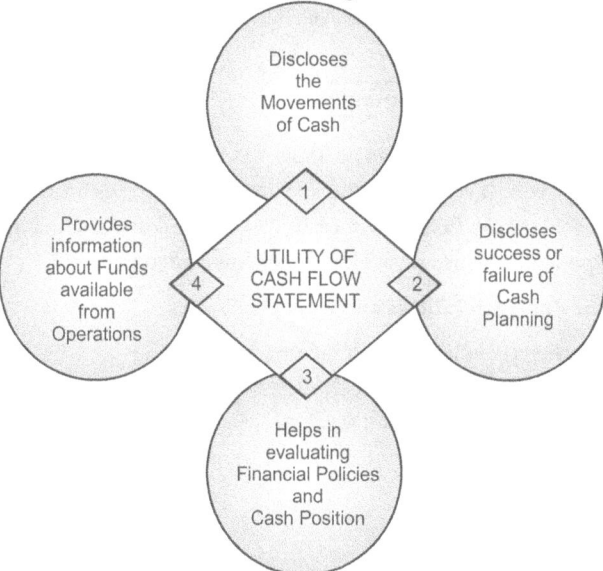

Fig. 4.3 : Utility of Cash Flow Statement

i) **Discloses the Movements of Cash :**
Cash flow statement discloses the picture of cash movement. The reason for increase in and decrease for cash can be indicated by the cash flow statement. Cash flow analysis also discloses the various reasons for low cash balance inspite of heavy operation profits or for heavy cash balance inspite of low profits.

ii) **Discloses success or failure of Cash Planning :**
With the help of comparing the projected cash flow analysis, the extent of success or failure of cash planning can be determined. The projected cash flow statement is compared with the actual cash flow statement and necessary remedial measures can be taken by the organisation.

iii) **Help in evaluating Financial Policies and Cash Position :**
Cash is the basis for all operations and hence a projected cash flow statement will enable the management to plan and co-ordinate the financial operations properly. The management can know how much cash is needed, from which source it will be derived, how much can be generated internally and how much could be obtained from outside.

iv) **Provides information about Funds available from Operations :**
Cash flow analysis provides information about funds which will be available from operations. This will help the management in determining policies regarding internal financial management, e.g., possibility of repayment of long-term debt, dividend policies, planning replacement of plant and machinery, etc. In this way, cash flow analysis helps in managing internal financial sources.

v) **Other uses of cash flow statement :**

Cash flow statement is a useful supplementary instrument. It discloses the volume as well as the speed at which the cash flows in the different segments of the business. This helps the management in knowing the amount of capital tied up in a particular segment of the business. The technique of cash flow analysis, when used in conjunction with ratio analysis, serves as a barometer in measuring the profitability and financial position of the business.

Preparation of Cash Flow Statement

A **Cash Flow Statement** is prepared to show the movements of cash between the closing dates of two Balance Sheets. It starts from the opening cash and ends with the closing balance of cash showing different sources from where cash was received and the manner in which it was utilised during the period for which Cash Flow Statement is prepared.

Transactions affecting on Cash Inflows and Cash Outflows :

The usual transactions resulting in **cash inflows** are :

i) Issue of shares;
ii) Issue of debentures,
iii) Sale of investments,
iv) Sale of assets,
v) Cash from business operations.

Cash outflows due to its application for various purpose such as :

i) Redemption of preference shares,
ii) Redemption of debentures,
iii) Sale of investments,
iv) Sale of assets,
v) Cash for business operations.

Cash outflows due to its application for various purpose such as :

i) Redemption of preference shares,
ii) Redemption of debentures,
iii) Repayment of loans,
iv) Payment of taxes,
v) Payment of dividend,
v) Cash losses due to operations.

Construction of Cash Flow Statement :

While constructing the **Cash Flow Statement**, following points are important :

i) An increase of share capital, debentures and loans clearly means that cash inflow took place due to additional issue of shares and debentures and obtaining further loans during the year.

ii) A decrease in current year figures of the liabilities will mean liquidation of liabilities and hence an application of cash.

iii) A comparison of non-current assets like Land and Buildings, Plant and Machinery, Furniture, Trade Investment, etc. will tell whether there had been increase or decrease in cash or an item resulted in cash inflow or cash outflow. (For example An increase in current year's amount of furniture clearly means cash outflow due to purchase of additional furniture. Conversely, a decrease in current years amount of furniture means sale and hence an application of cash).

iv) To calculate, how variations in non-current assets and liabilities generate or use funds (cash) the following general rules are to be kept in mind.
- Increase in Non-current Liability = Cash Inflow
- Decrease in Non-current Liability = Cash Outflow
- Increase in Non-current Asset = Cash Outflow
- Decrease in Non-current Asset = Cash Inflow

(**Note** : The net cash inflow or outflow can be arrived at only after preparing the relevant account by allowing for appropriate adjustments, if any.)

Cash from Business Operations :

The traditional Profit and Loss Account is based on certain accounting concepts and conventions such as accrual and matching principles according to which non-operating and non-cash items are also brought into it. Therefore, the net profit as shown by a traditional Profit and Loss Account cannot be equivalent to cash and as such it needs certain adjustments to arrive at net cash inflow or cash losses due to business operations. The adjustments are required in respect of the non-operating and non-cash items which do not affect the cash flows.

Adjustments for changes in current assets and current liabilities.

The changes in current assets and current liabilities affecting changes in cash position should, therefore, be taken into account in the calculation of cash from business operations.

"Notional Cash Concept" and "Actual Cash Concept".

There are two methods to deal with the current assets and current liabilities in preparation of cash from business operations. One is "**Notional Cash Concept**" and another is "**Actual Cash Concept**" Method. The variations in working capital components may either be shown in the Cash Flow Statement itself or they may be considered separately in the calculation of cash from business operations. The former course is adopted when notional concept of cash is followed and later method is applied when actual cash concept is implemented.

According to 'Notional Cash' concept, a decrease in current assets and an increase in current liability is taken as a source of cash. Similarly, an increase in current assets and decrease in current liability is considered as an application of cash. The 'Notional Cash Concept' can be understood with the help of an example. Suppose a firm has purchased raw material worth ₹ 15,000 on credit and it has not paid the amount by the end of accounting year. In this case

₹ 15,000 will appear as creditors on the liability side of the Balance Sheet of the firm, and this will be taken as a source of cash. How is this when there is no actual receipt of cash ? The '**Notional Cash Concept**' assumes that the firm will borrow ₹ 15,000 and make payment to the supplier of raw materials. Thus borrowing ₹ 15,000 means a source of cash.

In actual practice, generally, "**Actual Cash Concept**" is followed in the preparation of cash flow statement. It means actual cash received and actual cash paid are brought into the cash flow statement and the variations in the current assets and current liabilities are separately treated in the statement of cash from business operations."

Form of "Business Statement of Cash from Business Operation" :

Cash from Business Operations can be calculated by collecting and summarising the relevant informations in the following form :

Statement of Cash from Business Operations

Particulars		₹
Net Profit as per Profit and Loss Account :		
i) Add : **Decrease in Current Assets** :		
• Decrease in Debtors		
• Decrease in Stock		
• Decrease in Pre-paid Expenses		
• Decrease in Accrued Incomes	(+)	
Add : **Increase in Current Liabilities**		
• Increase in Creditors		
• Increase in Bills Payable		
• Increase in Outstanding Expenses		
• Increase in Pre-received Incomes	(+)	
ii) Less : **Increase in Current Assets** :		
• Increase in Debtors		
• Increase in Stock		
• Increase in Pre-paid Expenses		
• Increase in Accrued Incomes	(–)	
Less : **Decrease in Current Liabilities**		
• Decrease in Creditors		
• Decrease in Bills Payable		
• Decrease in Outstanding Expenses		
• Decrease in Pre-received Incomes	(–)	
3. Add : **Non-Current Expenses** :		
• Depreciation		
• Assets Discarded		
• Preliminary Expenses Written off		
• Provision for Losses, etc.	(+)	
4. Less : **Non-operating Incomes** :		
• Profit on Sale of Asset		
• Tax Refund		
• Unusual Incomes	(–)	
∴ Cash From Business Operation or Cash Lost in Business Operation		

Statement of Cash From Business Operation

Particulars		₹	₹
Net Profit as per Profit and Loss Account :			
Add : i) **Non Cash items like :**			
• Depreciation			
• Loss on Sale of Assets			
• Intangible Assets written off			
(Goodwill, Patents, Trade Marks, Copy rights etc.)			
• Deferred Revenue Expenses			
(Discount on Debentures, Brokerages, Preliminary			
Expenses etc.) written of			
• Provision for Bad and Doubtful Debts (+)		————	————
Add : ii) **Other items :**			
Decrease in Current Assets :			
• Decrease in Debtors			
• Decrease in Stock			
• Decrease in Prepaid Expenses			
• Decrease in Accrued Income			
Increase in Current Liabilities :			
• Increase in Creditors			
• Increase in Outstanding Expenses			
• Increase in Income received in Advance (+)			————
Less : i) **Non Business Incomes like :**			
• Profit of Sale of Fixed Assets			
• Rent Received			
• Dividend Received etc. (–)			
Less : ii) **Increase in Current Assets :**			
• Increase in Debtors			
• Increase in Stock			
• Increase in Prepaid Expenses			
• Increase in Accrued Incomes			
Decrease in Current Liabilities :			
• Decrease in Creditors		————	
• Decrease in Outstanding Expenses		————	
• Decrease in Income Received in Advance (–)			————
∴ Cash from Business Operation or Cash Lost in Business Operation			

If instead of "Net Profit" there is "Net Loss" the items added here will be deducted and items deducted will be added. If the total of less items is more, the resulting figures is the outflow of cash on account of operation i.e. Cash lost in operation.

4.8 PROFORMA OF CASH FLOW STATEMENT

A specimen proforma of **Cash Flow Statement** in an account form is given below :

Cash Flow Statement for the year ended 31st March ......

Inflow i.e. Sources	₹	Outflow i.e. Uses	₹
Opening Cash/Bank Balance		Cash Outflow :	
Add : Cash Inflow :		i) Purchase of Freehold Property	
i) Sale of Machinery		ii) Purchase of Plant and Machinery	
ii) Sale of Fixtures		iii) Purchase of Furniture and Fixture	
iii) Issue of Share Capital		iv) Purchase of Vehicle	
iv) Share Premium on Issue of Shares		v) Purchase of Building	
v) Increase in Creditors		vi) Purchase of Investment	
vi) Raising of Loans		vii) Repayment of Debentures	
vii) Sale of Investment		viii) Repayment of Bank Overdraft	
viii) Decrease in Sundry Debtors		ix) Repayment of Bank Loan	
ix) Sale of Vehicle		x) Payment of Dividend	
x) Raising of Bank Overdraft		xi) Payment of Tax	
xi) Loan taken from wife		xii) Increase in Prepaid Expenses (Rent)	
xii) Increase in Bank Loan		xiii) Increase in Stock (Inventory)	
xiii) Increase in Outstanding Wages		xiv) Increase in Sundry Debtors	
xiv) Decrease in Stock		xv) Increase in Accounts Receivable	
xv) Increase in Current Liabilities for goods		xvi) Decrease in Creditors	
xvi) Mortgage Loan taken		xvii) Decrease in Outstanding Expenses	
xvii) Increase in Accounts Payable		xviii) Decrease in Account Payable (Bills Payable)	
xviii) Increase in Accrued Expenses		xix) Drawings	
• **Cash from Operation** (Balancing Figure)		• Cash Lost on Operation / Operating Loss (Balancing Figure)	
		Closing Cash / Bank Balance	

Limitations of Cash Flow Statement

Following are certain Limitations of **Cash Flow Analysis**:
i) The cash balance as disclosed by the cash flow statement may not represent the real liquid position of the business since it can be easily influenced by postponing purchases and other payments.
ii) Cash flow statement cannot replace the Income Statement or the Funds Flow Statement. Each of them has a separate function to perform.
iii) Cash flow statement cannot be equated with the Income Statement. An Income Statement takes into account both cash as well as non-cash items and, therefore, net cash flow does not necessarily mean net income of the business.
iv) In cash flow statement, comparison of original forecast with actual results highlights the trends of movement of cash which may otherwise go undetected.

Now a days, in actual practice the Cash Flow Statement is prepared compulsorily as a part of annual corporate financial statements. The following specimen of a Cash Flow Statement will help to understand the practical approach to be followed in the preparation of the same.

Specimen of Cash Flow Statement

In the books of Appricon Ltd.; Andheri
Cash Flow Statement for the year ended 31st March, 2013

(₹ in Millions)

Particulars	31st March, 2013 ₹	31st March, 2012 ₹	Remarks
Cash flow from Operating Activities :			AS 3.8
			AS 3.18(d)
Profit before tax from continuing operations	5,185	4,534	
Profit before tax from discontinuing operations (+)	6	63	
Profit before tax	5,191	4,597	
Non-cash adjustment to reconcile profit before tax to net cash flows			AS 3.20 (b)
Share of (profit)/loss from investment in partnership firm	(1)	(2)	
Depreciation/amortisation on continuing operation	613	541	
Depreciation/amortisation on discontinuing operation	20	20	
Impairment/other, write off on tangible / intangible assets pertaining to continuing operation	350	-	
Impairment/other write off on tangible / intangible assets pertaining to discontinuing operation	50	-	
Loss/(Profit) on sale of Fixed Assets	2	1	
Provision for diminution in value of investments in subsidiary company	15		
Provision for diminution in value of investments (current plus other long-term)	17	9	
Employee stock compensation expense	2,369	1,907	
Unrealised foreign exchange loss	38	29	
Premium an forward exchange contract amortised	4	4	
Amortisation of ancillary cost	2	2	
Net gain on sale of current investments	(250)	(121)	
Interest expense	589	411	AS 3.20(c)
Interest income	(113)	(104)	AS 3.20(c)

Particulars	31st March, 2013 ₹	31st March, 2012 ₹	Remarks
Dividend income	(86)	(90)	AS 3.20(c)
Operating profit before working capital changes	8,810	7,204	
Movements in Working Capital :			AS 3.20(a)
Increase/(decrease) in trade payables	96	160	
Increase/(decrease) in long-term provisions	681	906	
Increase/(decrease) in short-term provisions	182	342	
Increase/(decrease) in other current liabilities	112	616	
Increase/(decrease) in other long-term liabilities	18	25	
Decrease/(increase) in trade receivables	(5,155)	(4,688)	
Decrease/(increase) in inventories	(2,426)	(2,248)	
Decrease/(increase) in long-term loans and advances	(906)	(1,072)	
Decrease/(increase) in short-term loans and advances	84	185	
Decrease/(increase) in other current assets	19	180	
Decrease/(increase) in other non-current assets	2	4	
Cash generated from/(used it) operations	1,517	1,614	
Direct taxes paid (net of refunds)	(1,334)	(1,163)	
• Net cash flow from/(used in) operating activities (A)	183	451	

Particulars	31st March, 2013 ₹	31st March, 2012 ₹	Remarks
Cash Flows from Investing Activities :			AS 3.8
Purchase of fixed assets, including intangible assets, CWIP and capital advances	(96)	(159)	AS 3.15(a)
Proceeds from sale of fixed assets	4	9	AS 3.15(b)
Proceeds of non-current investments	-	6	AS 3.15(c)
Purchase of non-current investments	(3)	-	
Purchase of current investments	(377)	(6)	AS 3.15(c)
Proceeds from sale/maturity of current investments	410	366	AS 3.15(d)
Investments in bank deposits (having original maturity of more than three months)	(832)	(537)	AS 3.15(c)
Redemption/maturity of bank deposits (having original maturity of more than three months)	767	565	AS 3.15(d)
Purchase consideration for amalgamation (note 35)	(267)	-	AS 3.38
Interest received	71	104	AS 3.30
Dividends received from subsidiary company	20	-	AS 3.30
Dividends received	86	90	AS 3.30
• Net cash flow from/(used in) investing activities (B)	(217)	438	

Particulars	31st March, 2013 ₹	31st March, 2012 ₹	Remarks
Cash flows from Financial Activities :			AS 3.8
Proceeds from issuance of share capital	1,250	-	AS 3.17(a)
Proceeds from issuance of preference share capital	-	2,500	AS 3.17(a)
Proceeds from long-term borrowings	1,025	35	AS 3.17(b)
Repayment of long-term borrowings	(311)	(186)	AS 3.17(c)
Proceeds from short-term borrowings	658	718	AS 3.17(b)
Repayment of short-term borrowings	(1,233)	(620)	AS 3.17(c)
Interest paid	(640)	(494)	AS 3.30
Dividends paid on equity shares	(1,040)	(940)	AS 3.30
Dividends paid on preference shares	(35)	-	AS 3.30
Tax on equity dividend paid	(177)	(160)	AS 3.30
Tax on preference dividend paid	(6)	-	AS 3.30
Net cash flow from/(used in) in financing activities (C)	**(509)**	**853**	
Net increase/(decrease) in cash and cash equivalents (A + B + C)	(543)	1,742	
Effect of exchange differences on cash and cash equivalents held in foreign currency	(2)	-	AS 3.25
Cash and cash equivalents at the beginning of the year	2,362	620	
Cash and cash equivalents at the end of the year	**1,817**	**2,362**	

Particulars	31st March, 2013 ₹	31st March, 2012 ₹	Remarks
Components of Cash and Cash Equivalents			AS 3.42
Cash on hand	29	1	
Cheques/drafts on hand	3	2	
With banks- on current account	1,424	2,174	
– on deposit account	350	174	
– unpaid dividend accounts*	7	6	
– unpaid matured deposits*	4	3	
– unpaid matured debentures*	–	2	
Total cash and cash equivalents (note 18)	**1,817**	**2,362**	
Summary of significant accounting policies 2.1			

* The company can utilise these balances only toward settlement of the respective unpaid dividend, unpaidmatured deposits and unpaid matured debenture liabilities.   AS 3.45

QUESTIONS FOR SELF-STUDY

I. Theory Questions :

1) Explain the following concepts :

   a) Fund, b) Flow of Fund and c) Funds Flow Statement

2) What is 'Funds Flow Statement' ? Explain the uses of Funds Flow Statement.

3) What is 'Working Capital' ? State the causes of changes in Working Capital.

4) Define the term 'Sources and Application of Funds'. Prepare the proforma of Sources and Application of Funds.

5) What is 'Adjusted Profit and Loss Account' ? Prepare the proforma of Adjusted Profit and Loss Account.

6) Define the term 'Cash Flow Statement'. Prepare the proforma of a Cash Flow Statement.

7) Differentiate between :

   a) Funds Flow Statement and Income Statement

   b) Funds Flow Statement and Cash Flow Statement

8) Write short notes on :

   a) Fund, b) Flow of Fund, c) Funds Flow Statement, d) Cash Flow Statement, e) Causes of changes in Working Capital.

✸✸✸

UNIT 5

MARGINAL COSTING

SYNOPSIS

5.1 Meaning and Definition
    5.1.1 Marginal Cost
    5.1.2 Marginal Costing
5.2 Contribution
5.3 Profit-Volume Ratio
5.4 Advantages of Marginal Costing
5.5 Limitations of Marginal Costing
• Illustrations
• Questions for Self-Study

Every manufacturing concern would like to increase its profits by increasing volume of production which will automatically involve additional cost. Such a decision would require a detailed analysis of additional costs and its behaviour as it has a direct bearing on the profitability of the concern. Any increase in the level of operation will diminish the firm's marginal profit, if it is already at its optimum level of existing operation. However, such a decision would definitely prove financially worthy if there exists any unutilised operational capacity. Thus, to reach at an accurate decision, management must know how costs will react to changes in activity. The analysis of cost behaviour reveals that the cost of a product can be divided into two major categories i.e. **Fixed Cost** and **Variable Cost**.

As it is known, **Fixed Cost** remains constant to a particular level of output whereas **Variable Cost** has tendency to change proportionally with a change in the level of output. The following example will further clarify the concept.

Axa Ltd., Anand made a sale of 20,000 units @ ₹ 1,000 per unit during the year 2013-2014 with the following details of expenditure on production.

i) Raw material required to produce one unit of finished product 2 kg @ ₹ 2 per kg.
ii) Wages ₹ 200 per unit.
iii) Rent of factory ₹ 50,000 per annum.
iv) Salary of executive ₹ 5,00,000 per annum.

In the above-mentioned example, the costs of raw-material and wages change proportionately with the change in the level of output and therefore are known as **Variable Costs**. Whereas the rent of factory and salary of executives are such costs that are not subject to change with the change in output. They remain constant at every level of output and as such are known as **Fixed Costs**. On account of this reason, it is not logical to apportion fixed costs to production. **Marginal Costing** is the technique which deals with the concept of **Variable Cost** i.e. marginal cost very carefully.

Marginal Costing which is otherwise known as **"Variable Costing"** is used as a tool for decision-making by the management. **Marginal Costing** is also known as **"Direct Costing"** and this new concept is gaining wide popularity in the field of accounting. Marginal Costing is a technique through which variable costs are taken into account for the purposes of product costing, inventory valuation and other important management decisions. The term "Marginal Costing" is commonly used in U.K. and other European Countries while the same is denoted as **"Direct Costing"** or **"Variable Costing"** in U.S.A. Marginal Costing is also known as variable or direct or differential costing. The term "Marginal Costing" seems to be inappropriate since it has an exclusive meaning in Economics. Under the above circumstances, the term 'Variable Costing' seems to be more appropriate and acceptable.

5.1 MEANING AND DEFINITION

It is absolutely necessary to understand the meaning and simplify the definitions given by various professional institutes and eminent authors in the subject concern, of various concepts frequently used in the traditional technique of Marginal Costing in the era of severe competition at the national and international level.

5.1.1 MARGINAL COST

Meaning

The term **"Marginal Cost"** is derived from the word "margin" which is a well known terminology in economics. As is used in economic parlance, the term "Marginal Cost" connotes the cost which arises from the production of additional increment of output.

Definitions

i) The **Institute of Cost and Works Accounts, London:**

Marginal Cost as "the amount at any given volume of output by which aggregate costs are changed if the volume of output is increased or decreased by one unit".

ii) **Institute of Chartered Accountants, England:**

"It is the very expense (whether of production, selling or distribution) incurred by the taking of a particular decision".

iii) **Blocker** and **Weltmore:**

"The increase or decrease in total cost which results from producing or selling additional or fewer units of a product or from a change in the method of production or distribution such as the use of improved machinery, addition or exclusion of a product or territory, or selection of an additional sales channel".

iv) The **Institute of Cost and Management Accountants, England:**

"It is the amount at any given volume of output by which aggregate costs are changed if the volume of output is increased or decreased by one unit, in practice, this is measured by the total variable cost attributable to one unit".

Thus, **Marginal Cost** is the cost incurred by a company for the additional output. It includes prime cost plus all variable overheads, but all variable overheads means actual variable together with the variable portion incorporated in semi-variable overheads.

Viewed from this angle, **Marginal Costs** in the short run will be synonymous with variable costs, i.e., prime costs and variable overheads; but in the long run the **Marginal Costs** will include fixed costs in planning production activities involving an increase in the production capacity. It is clear that the Marginal Costs are related to change in output under certain conditions.

5.1.2 MARGINAL COSTING

Meaning

Marginal Costing is an accounting technique which ascertains marginal cost by differentiating between fixed or period costs, and variable or product costs. This technique aims to charge only those costs of the cost of the product that vary directly with sales volumes. Those costs would be direct material, direct labour, and factory overhead expenses such as supplies, some indirect labour, and power. The cost of the product would not include fixed or non-variable expenses such as depreciation, factory insurance, taxes and supervisory salaries etc.

Definitions

i) **National Association of Accountants:**

"Marginal Costing method proposes that fixed factory expenses be classified as period expenses and be written off currently as is generally done with selling and administration expenses, and that only the variable costs become the basis of inventory value and profit determination".

ii) **Institute of Cost and Management Accounts, London:**

"Marginal Costing is the ascertainment of marginal costs and of the effect on profit of changes in volume or type of output by differentiating between fixed costs and variable costs. In this technique of costing, only variable costs are charged to operations, processes or products, leaving all indirect costs to be written off against profits in the period in which they arise".

iii) The **Chartered Institute of Management Accountants, England:**

Marginal Costing, "the ascertainment of marginal costs and the effect on profit of changes in volume or type of output by differentiating between fixed costs and variable costs".

iv) The **Official Terminology of the Management Accounting:**

Marginal Costing as, "a costing principle whereby variable costs are charged to cost units and the fixed costs are attributable to the relevant period is written off in full against the contribution for that period".

Thus, **Marginal Costing** is a costing technique that considers only the costs that vary directly with volume i.e. direct materials, direct labour, and variable factory overheads and ignores fixed cost in additional output decisions. Hence, the technique of Marginal Costing lies in i) differentiation between fixed and variable costs, ii) ascertainment of marginal costs, and iii) finding out effect on profit due to change in volume or type or output.

Features

The concept of Marginal Costing is evolved on the main distinction between product cost and period cost. While product cost relates to the volume of output, the period cost is mainly concerned with the period of time. Marginal Costing considers all those manufacturing costs which vary directly with the volume of output as product costs. This is in contradiction to the traditional system of costing under which all manufacturing costs - fixed as well as variable - are treated as product costs. It should also be remembered that variability with the volume of production is the basis for the classification of costs into product and period costs. Thus, marginal costing necessitates classification of costs into fixed and variable. Even the semi-variable costs have to be closely examined so as to separate fixed and variable components thereof depending upon the increase or decrease in the volume of output. Thus, marginal costs focus the effect of costs on the varying of output. **Marginal Costing** has the following four important **features**.

i) Under marginal costing, all types of **Operating Costs** i.e. factory, administrative, selling and distribution, are separated into fixed and variable components and are recorded separately.

ii) **Variable Cost** elements are handled as **product costs** i.e. they are charged to the product at the appropriate movements and follow the product through the inventory accounts, and thus are treated as expenses when the product is sold. Variable distribution costs normally are chargeable to the product at or near the moment of sale, and thus are not included in inventory values.

iii) **Fixed Costs** including fixed factory overheads, are handled as **period costs**; i.e., they are written off as expenses in the period in which they are incurred. They do not follow the inventories through the accounts but rather are treated in the way which is traditional for selling and general administrative expenses.

iv) It is a method of **recording** as well as **reporting costs**. Unlike differential cost analysis and Break-Even analysis which utilise traditional records, variable costing requires a unique method of recording cost transactions as they originally take place.

Therefore, **marginal costing** is a technique which deals with the effect on profits of changes in volume or type of output.

The classification of costs into **fixed and variable** is of special interest and importance in Marginal Costing. These two types of costs behave differently with changes in the volume of output.

i) **Fixed Costs :**

These costs remain fixed in the total amount and do not increase or decrease when the volume of production changes. But the fixed cost per unit increases when volume of production decreases and vice-versa. Fixed cost per unit decreases when the volume of production increases. The **Behaviour of Fixed Cost** is shown in a graph as follows :

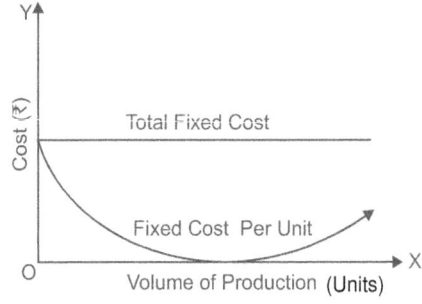

Behaviour of Fixed Cost

The line representing fixed cost per unit will not touch X axis because the fixed cost cannot be zero.

ii) **Variable Costs :**

Variable costs change in proportion to the volume of output. In other words, when volume of output increases, total variable cost also increases and vice-versa. When volume of output decreases, total variable cost also decreases. But the variable cost per unit remain fixed. The **Behaviour of Variable Cost** is shown in a graph as follows.

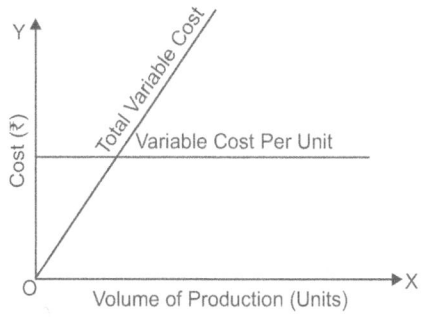

Behaviour of Variable Cost

iii) **Semi Fixed or Semi-Variable Costs :**

These costs are also separated into fixed and variable elements and added to their respective categories. Under marginal costing, fixed and variable costs are kept separate for all purpose. Only variable costs are taken into account for computing the cost of productions and thus are treated as "Product Costs". Fixed costs do not find place in the costs of products or in inventory valuation, such costs are treated as "Period Costs".

5.2 CONTRIBUTION

Meaning

In Marginal Costing, **Contribution** has greater significance. The justification for contribution lies in the fact that when two or more products are manufactured by a single unit, the apportionment of fixed costs to different products under marginal costing is simplified. **Contribution** represents the difference between sales and variable cost of sales and it is often referred to as **"Gross Margin"**. It can be considered as some sort of fund from and out of which all fixed costs are to be met. Again, the difference between contribution and fixed cost represents either profit or loss as the case may be.

The concept of **'Contribution'** is of immense use in fixing the selling prices, determining the break-even point, selecting the product mix for profit maximisation and also ascertaining the profitability of the products, departments etc.

The difference between the marginal cost of the various products manufactured and their respective selling price is the **Contribution** which each product makes towards fixed or period costs and profit.

Definition

According to *Watter W. Bigg*, "**Contribution** is the difference between sales value and the marginal cost of sales and no net profit arises until the contribution equals the fixed overheads. When this level of output is achieved, the business is said to break-even as neither profit nor loss occurs. Production in excess of that which is necessary to break-even will result in a profit equivalent to the excess units multiplied by the "contribution" per unit. Conversely, a loss is sustained if output is less than that required to break-even, amounting to the short-fall of units multiplied by the contribution."

Thus, **Contribution** is the difference between product revenue and variable cost of product. It represents the excess of sales over marginal cost (variable cost) that is the amount to meet fixed cost and profit expectation of an organisation. It can be calculated as given on the next page.

- Contribution = Sales (−) Variable cost
- Contribution per unit = Selling Price per unit (−) Variable Cost per unit
- Contribution = Fixed Cost (+) Profit
- Contribution = Sales (×) P/V Ratio
- Contribution = Fixed Cost (−) Loss

Suppose, total sales revenue is ₹ 1,50,000, variable cost is ₹ 60,000 and sale in terms of units are 1,000 then contribution will be :

$$\text{Contribution} = ₹1,50,000 (-) ₹60,000$$
$$= ₹90,000$$

or

$$\text{Contribution per unit} = ₹150 (-) ₹60$$
$$= ₹90$$

Marginal Cost Equation i.e. Relationship between Marginal Cost and Contribution :

The analysis of marginal cost statement and the contribution above reveals that,

i) Sales (−) Marginal cost = Contribution

ii) Fixed cost (+) Profit = Contribution

By combining the above two equations, we get the fundamental **marginal cost equation** i.e.

$$\text{Sales} (-) \text{Marginal Cost} = \text{Fixed Cost} (\pm) \text{Profit / Loss}$$

Or

$$S (-) V = F (+) P/L$$

The **marginal cost equation** has practical utility in the sense that if any three factors of the above equation are known, the fourth can be easily found out or computed separately.

Contribution and Profit

A product sells at ₹ 50. It has a variable cost of ₹ 30 and during the period ended 30 June 2014, 2,000 units were sold. Fixed costs for that period amounted to ₹ 25,000. The contribution and profit would be calculated, as shown in the following table.

Particulars		Per Unit ₹	2,000 Units ₹	% of Sales
Selling Price		50	1,00,000	100
Less : Variable Costs	(−)	30	60,000	60
Contribution		20	40,000	40
Less : Fixed Costs	(−)	12.50	25,000	25
∴ Profit		7.50	15,000	15

From the above table it can be observed that the contribution goes towards the recovery of the fixed overheads and profit. Marginal Costing is a technique which can be used as part of the decision making process to show the effect of possible changes in demand and or selling prices and or variable costs. For Example, it can be used to identify the most profitable projects; in make or buy decision making or in deciding whether or not to accept a special contract. Variable Costs include only those costs which can be identified with and traced to products, e.g. direct labour, direct materials, direct expenses and variable overheads. The fixed costs are those which cannot be identified with and traced to the products. They tend to vary more with time than output, and are treated as period costs. This means that the fixed costs are not included in product costs.

They are simply written off, in total, against the total contribution (s) generated from the sale, of all the firm's products, for the period in which they were incurred. (Refer to the table shown below). This treatment of fixed costs also means that because they are not included in product costs they are carried forward into the future as part of the valuation of the stocks of work in progress and finished goods.

Particulars	Products	A ₹	B ₹	C ₹	D ₹	Total ₹
Contribution		20	34	36	20	110
Less : Fixed Costs					(−)	78
∴ Profit						32

A Multi-product Environment

EXAMPLE

Compute the amount of fixed cost from the information given below :

		₹
Sales	:	2,40,000
Variable Cost	:	1,20,000
Profit	:	60,000

ANSWER

As per Marginal Cost Equation,

$$S - V = FC \pm P/L$$

∴ Sales − Variable Cost = Fixed Cost + Profit
∴ ₹ 2,40,000 − ₹ 1,20,00 = FC + ₹ 60,000
∴ ₹ 1,20,000 = FC + ₹ 60,000
∴ FC = ₹ 1,20,000 − ₹ 60,000
∴ FC = ₹ 60,000

Break- Even Analysis

Break-Even Analysis establishes the relationship between costs and profit with sales volume. It represents a specific method of presenting and studying the inter-relationship between costs, volume and profits. It also helps in the determination of that volume of sales at which costs and revenues are in equilibrium. The equilibrium point is often referred to as the 'break-even point'. The break-even point may be defined as that point of sales volume at which the total revenue is equal to the total cost. Briefly, it is a no-profit, no-loss point. It should be remembered that the break-even point is purely incidental to the Cost Volume-Profit analysis. If all costs are assumed to be variable with sales volume, the break-even point would be at zero sales. On the other hand, if all costs remain fixed, profits would vary disproportionately with sales and the break-even point would be at a point where total sales revenue and fixed cost are in equilibrium.

Break-Even Point

Break-even analysis is a costing technique that helps executives in profit planning. The narrow interpretation of break-even analysis limits it to the study of break-even point. The **Break-Even Point** is defined as the volume of activity at which total sales revenue exactly equals total costs of the output produced or sold. Since, at this level of operation sales revenue is adequate to cover all costs to manufacture and sell the product leaving no amount as profit, and therefore, this level is also known as no profit no loss level. Thus, in a situation where total costs of the output consist of only variable costs, the break-even point would be at zero of operation.

Break-even analysis need not be limited merely to seeking the break-even point. In a broader sense, break-even analysis refers to the study of relationship between cost, volume and profit at different levels of sales or production which in technical terminology is known as **Cost-Volume Profit Analysis**. Cost-Volume Profit Analysis as a planning tool analyses the inherent relationship between prices, cost structure, volume and profit. **Ahmad Belkooni** defines **Cost-Volume-Profit Analysis** as "an examination of cost and revenue behavioural patterns and their relationships with profit. The analysis separates costs into fixed and variable components and determines the levels of activity where costs and revenues are in equilibrium".

According to **Schmiedicke and Nagy**, "Cost-Volume Profit analysis is an analytical technique which uses the degrees of cost variability for measuring the effect of changes in volume or resulting profits. Such analysis assumes that the plant assets of the firm will remain the same in the short-run, therefore, the established level of fixed cost will also remain unchanged during the period being studied".

Thus, cost-volume-profit analysis is a mature model to study the inter-related relationship between cost, price and profit structure of a company. It is a formal profit planning approach based on established relationship between different factors affecting profit. The usual starting point in such an analysis is the determination of the company's break-even point. Thus, break-even analysis forms just one component of the total system of cost-volume profit analysis.

One of the important steps in cost-volume profit and break-even analysis is that of segregation of costs into fixed and variable costs. If the break-even point is to occur, it becomes essential that the business enterprise has some variable costs and some fixed costs.

Determination of Break-Even Point :

The Break-Even Point can be determined by the two following methods :
1) Algebraic Methods. (Mathematical)
   a) Contribution Margin Technique and
   b) Equation Technique.
2) Graphic Presentation
   a) Break-Even Chart and
   b) Profit Volume Graph.

The break-even point can be computed for a firm manufacturing a single product only, in terms of units of product. The BEP is reached when the total proceeds of units sold are equivalent to the total cost incurred-fixed and variable. Each unit of the product sold will cover its variable cost and leave the remainder which is known as the contribution, to cover the fixed costs. The break-even point will occur when adequate units are sold so that total contribution would become equivalent to the total fixed costs. More precisely, total contribution is equal to unit contribution multiplied by the total units sold. The profit of the unit is obtained by subtracting the fixed cost from the total contribution. The following equation can easily be remembered.

$$\text{Unit Contribution} = \text{Selling Price per unit} - \text{Variable Cost per unit}$$
$$\text{Total Contribution} = \text{Unit Contribution} \times \text{Number of units sold}$$
$$\text{Profit} = \text{Total Contribution} - \text{Fixed Costs}$$

1) Algebraic Methods (Mathematical) :
a) Contribution Margin Technique :

As has been stated earlier, contribution per unit represents the difference between selling price per unit and variable cost thereof and the profit represents the difference between the total contribution and the fixed costs. The BEP is reached when the total proceeds of units sold are equivalent to the total costs incurred - fixed and variable.

On an analysis of the above two statements, it would be clear that the Break-Even Point is reached when the profit is zero or more precisely when the total contribution is exactly equivalent to the fixed costs. The same thing can be represented in the form of equations as given below :

1) • BEP (Units) = $\dfrac{\text{Fixed Cost}}{\text{Contribution per unit}}$

2) • BEP (₹) = BEP (Units) × Selling Price per unit

3) • BEP (₹) = $\dfrac{\text{Fixed Cost}}{\text{Profit Volume Ratio}}$

4) • P/V Ratio = $\dfrac{\text{Marginal Contribution per unit}}{\text{Selling Price per unit}}$

From the above it is clear that Equation (3) is only the derivative of Equation (1). Multiplying both the numerator and the denominator with the common factor of sales, the following equation is obtained :

5) • BEP (₹) = $\dfrac{\text{Fixed Cost} \times \text{Sales}}{\text{Sales} - \text{Variable Cost}}$

Again by dividing both the numerator and the denominator of equation (5) by the common factor of sales, the following equation is obtained.

6) • BEP (₹) = $\dfrac{\text{Fixed Cost}}{1 - \dfrac{\text{Variable Cost}}{\text{Sales}}}$

Despite the existence of numerous formulae, it should be remembered that the following three formulae are always adopted for calculating the break-even point of the business rather than drawing a chart for ascertaining the same.

$$\text{BEP (₹)} = \dfrac{FC \times S}{S - VC} \text{ (or) } \dfrac{FC}{P/V \text{ Ratio}} \text{ (or) } \dfrac{FC}{1 - \dfrac{VC}{S}}$$

b) Equation Technique :

Under mathematical approach, break-even can easily by computed by engaging the technique of unit contribution which is developed on the basis of marginal cost equation.

The equation can be stated as follows :

Sales = Variable cost + Fixed Cost + Profit

At the break-even point, profit is absent, therefore, the same equation for this purpose can be re-written as follows :

Sales = Variable Cost + Fixed Cost or
Sales – Variable Cost = Fixed Cost or
Contribution = Fixed Cost

The study of the above equation reveals that sales revenue of each unit leaves a certain amount in the shape of contribution margin to meet fixed costs. Thus, in order to work out the required number of units to break-even (where the amount of contribution will be sufficient to cover total fixed cost) the total fixed cost must be divided by the unit contribution. Accordingly, the break-even point can be calculated in terms of units by using the following equation :

Break-Even Point (in terms of units) = $\dfrac{\text{Fixed Cost}}{\text{Unit Contribution Margin}} = \dfrac{FC}{SP - VC}$

where,
BEP = Break-Even Point
FC = Total Fixed Cost
SP = Selling Price per unit
VC = Variable Cost per unit

On the same basis, the break-even point in terms of rupees can be computed with the help of the equation as given under :

$$\text{BEP (in terms of rupees)} = \frac{FC}{CMR}$$

where,

FC = Total Fixed Cost
CMR = Contribution Margin Ratio

Where the selling price and variable cost per unit is not readily available, the following equation is applied to compute the break-even point.

$$\text{BEP (in terms of rupees)} = \frac{FC}{P/V \text{ Ratio}}$$

where,

FC = Total Fixed Cost
P/V Ratio = Profit Volume Ratio

EXAMPLE

Calculate the Break-Even Point from the following information :

Fixed Cost : ₹ 1,200
Variable Cost : ₹ 5,000
Sales in rupees : ₹ 7,000
Sales in units : 1,000 Units

ANSWER

$$\text{BEP (in units)} = \frac{FC}{SP - VC}$$

$$= \frac{₹ 1,200}{₹ 7 - ₹ 5}$$

$$= 600 \text{ units}$$

$$\text{BEP (in rupees)} = \frac{FC}{CMR^*}$$

$$= \frac{₹ 1,200}{₹ 0.285}$$

$$= ₹ 4,200$$

$$^*CMR = \frac{SP - VC}{SP}$$

$$= \frac{₹ 7 - ₹ 5}{₹ 7}$$

$$= ₹ 0.285$$

Working Notes :

i) Calculation of Variable Cost per unit $= \frac{₹ 5,000}{1,000 \text{ units}}$

$= ₹ 5$

ii) Calculation of Selling Price per unit $= \frac{₹ 7,000}{1,000 \text{ units}}$

$= ₹ 7$

Assumptions of Break-Even Analysis :

Break-Even Analysis data are based upon certain assumed conditions which are rarely found in practice.

Some of these basic assumptions are given below :
i) Costs can be classified into their fixed and variable components.
ii) The principle of cost variability is valid.
iii) Variable costs vary proportionately with the volume changes.
iv) Fixed costs remain constant irrespective of the level of activity.
v) Selling price does not change with the volume changes.
vi) There is no change in the general price level.
vii) There is only one product or in the case or multiple products sales mix remains constant.
viii) There is synchronisation between production and sales.
ix) Productivity per worker remains constant.
x) Revenue and costs are being compared with a common activity base, e.g., units produced or sales value of production.
xi) Plant capacity and efficiency remain unaffected.

It is clear that a change in any one of the above factors will alter the break-even point such that profits are effected by changes in factors other than volume.

Usefulness of Break-Even Analysis

Break-Even Analysis is considered to be the most useful technique of profit planning and control. It is an important device to explain the relationship between cost, volume and profit. The Usefulness of the break-Even Analysis can be summarised as follows :
i) It is a simple tool employed to graphically represent complicated accounting data.
ii) It is a more useful diagnostic tool.
iii) It provides basic information facilitating further studies on improving the profit.
iv) It is also used for analysing the risk implication of alternative actions.
v) It is useful in marketing strategies also.

The break-even analysis serves as a useful tool for considering the risk implications of alternative actions. The problem of risk evaluation can be solved by considering the effects of the alternative actions on break-even point. While taking a decision, the business unit should not only consider the profits arising from the alternatives but also the probability of reaching the break-even point.

Limitations of Break-Even Analysis

The Limitations of Break-Even Analysis can be summarised as follows :
i) The application of break-even analysis to a multi-product firm becomes very difficult.
ii) Since the break-even analysis is a short-run concept, it has a limited application in the long-range planning.
iii) The break-even tool is a static tool with very limited practical application.
iv) It is very difficult, if not impossible, to separate costs into fixed and variable components.
(v) The assumption that the total fixed cost remains constant over the entire volume range does not stand to reason.

Margin of Safety

The amount by which the current volume of sales exceeds the break-even sales volume, either in units or rupees, represents Margin of Safety. This is the difference between the total sales figures and the amount of sales at break-even point. It indicates the extent to which sales may decrease before the company suffers a loss. A margin of safety is calculated as follows :

$$M/S = S_A - S_B \text{ or } MoS = AS - BS$$

where,

M/S = Margin of safety
S_A = Actual volume of sales
S_B = Break-even volume of sales
MoS = Margin of safety
AS = Actual volume of sales
BS = Break-even volume of sales

Margin of Safety may be expressed as a percentage based either on units or rupee value. For this purpose, the following formulae are used :

$$M/S \text{ (in rupees)} = \frac{Profit}{P/V \ Ratio} \qquad M/S \text{ (in units)} = \frac{Profit}{Contribution \ per \ unit}$$

The high margin of safety is the sign of prosperity of the business. A low margin would indicate high fixed cost. Such a critical situation calls for : Increase in selling price, decrease in variable costs, replacement of existing product line by a more profitable line and increase in volume of production.

EXAMPLE

Compute Margin of Safety of Surya Ltd. Sholapur from the information given below :

Selling price	:	₹ 8 per unit
Variable cost	:	₹ 5 per unit
Fixed cost	:	₹ 45,000
Sales (current)	:	25,000 units p.a.

ANSWER

i) M/S (in rupees) = $S_A - S_B$
= ₹ 2,00,000 – ₹ 1,20,000
= ₹ 80,000

ii) M/S (in units) = 25,000 units – 15,000 units
= 10,000 units

OR

iii) M/S (in rupees) = $\frac{Profit}{P/V \ Ratio}$

= $\frac{₹ 30,000}{37.5\%} \times 100$

= ₹ 80,000

iv) $\text{M/S (in units)} = \dfrac{\text{Profit}}{\text{Contribuiton per unit}}$

$= \dfrac{₹\,30{,}000}{3}$

$= 10{,}000 \text{ units}$

Working Notes:

i) **Marginal Cost Statement: Output: 25,000 Units**

Particulars		Per Unit ₹	Total ₹
Sales		8	2,00,000
Less : Marginal cost	(−)	5	1,25,000
∴ Contribution		3	75,000
Less : Fixed cost	(−)	−	45,000
∴ Profit		−	30,000

ii) **Calculation of P/V Ratio:**

$\text{P/V Ratio} = \dfrac{\text{Contribution}}{\text{Sales}} \times 100$

$= \dfrac{₹\,75{,}000}{₹\,2{,}00{,}000} \times 100$

$= 37.50\%$

iii) **Calculation of Break-Even Point:**

$\text{BEP (Units)} = \dfrac{\text{Fixed Cost}}{\text{SP} - \text{VC}}$

$= \dfrac{₹\,45{,}000}{₹\,8 - ₹\,5}$

$= \dfrac{₹\,45{,}000}{₹\,3}$

$= 15{,}000 \text{ units}$

$\text{BEP (in rupees)} = \dfrac{\text{Fixed Cost}}{\text{Contribution Margin Ratio}}$

$= \dfrac{₹\,45{,}000}{3/8^*}$

$= \dfrac{₹\,45{,}000}{₹\,3} \times ₹\,8$

$= ₹\,1{,}20{,}000$

*Contribution Margin Ratio $= \dfrac{\text{SP} - \text{VC}}{\text{SP}}$

$= \dfrac{₹\,8 - ₹\,5}{₹\,8}$

$= \dfrac{3}{8}$

EXAMPLE

A factory manufacturing printing machines has the capacity to produce 600 machines per annum. The marginal cost of each machine is ₹ 300 and each machine is sold for ₹ 375. Fixed overheads are ₹30,000 per annum.

Calculate the Break-Even Point for output and sales.

ANSWER

$$\text{Break-Even Point (Output)} = \frac{FC}{SP - VC}$$

$$= \frac{₹\,30{,}000}{₹\,375 - ₹\,300}$$

$$= \frac{₹\,30{,}000}{₹\,75}$$

$$= 400 \text{ machines}$$

$$\text{Break-Even Point (Sales)} = \frac{FC}{CM}$$

$$= \frac{₹\,30{,}000}{₹\,0.20}$$

$$= ₹\,1{,}50{,}000$$

Working Note :

i) Calculation of Contribution Margin (CM)

$$\text{Contribution Margin} = \frac{SP - VC}{SP}$$

$$= \frac{₹\,375 - ₹\,300}{₹\,375}$$

$$= \frac{₹\,75}{₹\,375}$$

$$= ₹\,0.20$$

5.3 PROFIT VOLUME RATIO (P/V RATIO)

Meaning

Profit Volume Ratio or P/V Ratio is the ratio of contribution to sales. P/V ratio is also known as marginal income ratio or variable-profit ratio. This ratio establishes a relationship between the contribution and the sales value. This ratio is a useful guide in determining profitability of business. It is generally expressed in terms of percentage.

Definition

According to **W. W. Bigg**, "Profit-Volume Ratio, popularly known as P/V Ratio, expresses the relationship of contribution to sales value".

It is calculated with the help of the following formulae :

Formulae:

$$\text{P/V Ratio} = \frac{\text{Sales} - \text{Variable Cost}}{\text{Sales}} \times 100$$

$$\text{or} = \frac{\text{Contribution}}{\text{Sales}} \times 100$$

$$\text{or} = \frac{\text{Selling Price per unit} - \text{Variable Cost per unit}}{\text{Selling Price per unit}} \times 100$$

$$\text{or} = \frac{\text{Contribution per unit}}{\text{Selling Price per unit}} \times 100$$

Marginal Costing

$$\text{or} = \frac{\text{Fixed Cost + Profit}}{\text{Sales}} \times 100$$

$$\text{or} = \frac{\text{Change in Contribution}}{\text{Change in Sales}} \times 100$$

$$\text{or} = \frac{\text{Change in Profit}}{\text{Change in Sales}} \times 100$$

By transposition, we have,

i) Sales $= \dfrac{\text{Contribution}}{\text{P/V Ratio}}$

ii) Contribution $= \text{Sales} \times \text{P/V Ratio}$

Significance

P/V Ratio is one of the most important ratios for a business. It indicates the rate at which profit is earned. A high P/V Ratio indicates high profitability while low P/V Ratio indicates low profitability. The sectorwise profitability can be determined with the help of P/V Ratio, e.g. the profitability of the different products, processes or departments can be found out so that sales can be increased. P/V Ratio is useful in finding out the break-even point, level of output or sales for earning a desired amount of profit and determination of variable cost and profits for any volume of sales. A constant P/V Ratio, therefore, indicates steady business.

Improvement

P/V Ratio can be improved, if contribution is improved. Contribution can be improved by taking any of the following steps :
  i) Increase in sale prices.
  ii) Reducing marginal cost by efficient utilisation of men, material and machines.
  iii) Concentrating on the sale of products with relatively better P/V ratio.
  iv) Altering the sales mix. It means that the products which have low P/V Ratio will be replaced by products which have high P/V ratio.

It is interesting to note that, the P/V Ratio remains constant at various levels of output. It does not get affected with the change in the fixed cost.

Limitations

The following limitations should be borne in mind while using P/V Ratio in Break-Even Analysis :
  i) P/V Ratio heavily leans on excess of revenues over variable costs.
  ii) P/V Ratio fails to take into consideration the capital outlays required by the additional productive capacity and the additional fixed costs, that are added.
  iii) It gives only an indication of relative profitability of product/product lines and it does not help to take a final decision.
  iv) For comparing profitability through P/V Ratio, it is essential to have proper segregation of costs into fixed and variable costs. Over simplification may lead to erroneous conclusion.
  v) Higher P/V Ratio per unit of sales or per unit of production will indicate the most profitable item only when other conditions are constant.

EXAMPLE

From the following details of cost, calculate P/V Ratio
  Sales – ₹ 3,00,000, Fixed Cost – ₹ 80,000, Profit – ₹ 40,000

ANSWER

$$\textbf{P/V Ratio} = \frac{\text{Contribution}}{\text{Sales}} \times 100$$

But,

$$\text{Contribution} = \text{Fixed Cost} + \text{Profit}$$

$$\therefore \text{P/V Ratio} = \frac{\text{Fixed Cost} + \text{Profit}}{\text{Sales}} \times 100$$

$$= \frac{₹\,80,000 + ₹\,40,000}{₹\,3,00,000} \times 100$$

$$= \frac{₹\,1,20,000}{₹\,3,00,000} \times 100$$

$$= 40\%$$

EXAMPLE

Calculate P/V Ratio from the cost data given below, separately.

	₹
1) Selling Price per unit	10
Variable Cost per unit	6

2) Turnover and Profits for the two periods are as under :

Period	Turnover ₹	Profits ₹
2012-13	1,50,000	20,000
2013-14	1,70,000	25,000

ANSWER

1) P/V Ratio :

$$= \frac{\text{Contribution per unit}}{\text{Selling Price per unit}} \times 100$$

But,

$$\text{Contribution per unit} = \text{Selling Price per unit} - \text{Variable Cost per unit}$$

$$\therefore \text{P/V Ratio} = \frac{\text{Selling Price per unit} - \text{Variable Cost per unit}}{\text{Selling Price per unit}} \times 100$$

$$= \frac{₹\,10 - ₹\,6}{₹\,10} \times 100$$

$$= \frac{₹\,4}{₹\,10} \times 100$$

$$= 40\%$$

2) P/V Ratio :

$$= \frac{\text{Change in Profits}}{\text{Change in Sales}} \times 100$$

$$= \frac{₹\,25,000 - ₹\,20,000}{₹\,1,70,000 - ₹\,1,50,000} \times 100$$

$$= \frac{₹\,5,000}{₹\,20,000} \times 100$$

$$= 25\%$$

5.4 ADVANTAGES OF MARGINAL COSTING

According to **National Association of Accounts, Marginal Costing** has the following **advantages** :

i) Cost-volume-profit relationship data required for profit planning purposes are readily obtained from the regular accounting statements. Hence, management does not have to work with two separate sets of data to relate one to the other.

ii) The profit for a period is not affected by changes in absorption of fixed expenses resulting from building or reducing inventory. Other things remaining equal (e.g., selling prices, costs, sales mix) profit moves in the same direction as sales when marginal costing is in use.

iii) Manufacturing cost and income statements in the marginal cost form follow management's thinking more closely than does the absorption cost form for these statements. For this reason, management finds it easier to understand and use marginal cost reports.

iv) The impact of fixed costs on profits is emphasized, because the total amount of such cost for the period appears in the income statement.

v) Marginal income figures facilitate relative appraisal of products, territories, classes of customers and other segments of the business without having the result obscured by allocation of joint fixed costs.

vi) Marginal costing ties in with such effective plans for cost control as standard costs and flexible budgets. In fact, the flexible budget is an aspect of marginal costing and many companies thus use marginal costing methods for this purpose, without recognising them as such.

vii) Marginal cost constitutes a concept of inventory cost which corresponds closely with the current out of pocket expenditure necessary to manufacture the goods.

5.5 LIMITATIONS OF MARGINAL COSTING

According to **National Association of Accounts**, **Marginal Costing** has the following **limitations** :

i) Difficulty may be encountered in distinguishing fixed costs. In particular, certain semi-variable costs may fall in a border line area and more or less arbitrary classification may be considered necessary in order to arrive at a practical determination of fixed and variable components.

ii) Complete manufacturing cost is not determined in the process of costing of production and supplementary allocation of fixed overheads on normal or some other volume base must be made to provide product costs for long-range pricing and other long-range policy decisions.

iii) Serious taxation problems may be encountered if a change is made from full cost to marginal cost for costing inventory as definite rulings are not available for guidance.

In the light of the above mentioned advantages and limitations of marginal costing, it can be concluded that, this will prove to be an effective tool in the hands of management wherever it can be applied fruitfully. At the same time, it must be remembered that both marginal costing and absorption costing are equally important, variable costing for internal reporting and absorption costing for external users.

FORMULAE TO REMEMBER

1) **Sales or Selling Price or Market Price or Value of Turnover or Invoice Price or Inflated Price or Loaded Price :**

    = Total Cost + Profit

    = Variable Cost + Fixed Cost + Profit

    = Contribution / P/V Ratio

    = Contribution + Variable Cost

    = Marginal Cost / Marginal Cost Ratio

2) **Profit or Net Margin or Net Income :**

    = Sales − Total Cost

    = Sales − (Variable Cost + Fixed Cost)

    = Contribution − Fixed Cost

    = Margin of Safety × P/V Ratio

3) **Loss :**

    = Total Cost − Sales

    = Fixed Cost − Contribution

4) **Contribution or Gross Margin or Marginal Contribution :**

    = Sales − Variable Cost

    = Fixed Cost + Profit

    = Sales × P/V Ratio

    = Fixed Cost − Loss

    = Fixed Cost / Break-Even units

5) **Fixed Cost or Rigid Cost or Constant Cost :**

    = Total Cost − Variable Cost

    = Contribution − Profit

    = Contribution + Loss

    = Sales − (Variable Cost + Profit)

6) **Variable Cost or Marginal Cost or Differential Cost :**

    = Total Cost − Fixed Cost

    = Sales − Contribution

    = Sales − (Fixed Cost + Profit)

    = Direct Material + Direct Labour + Direct Expenses + Variable Overheads

7) **Break-Even Point i.e. BEP (in units) or (in output) :**

    $$= \frac{\text{Total Fixed Cost}}{\text{Contribution per unit}}$$

$$= \frac{\text{Break-Even Sales in ₹}}{\text{Selling Price per unit}}$$

8) **Break-Even Point i.e. BEP (Sales in Rupees):**

$$= \frac{\text{Total Fixed Cost}}{\text{Contribution per unit}} \times \text{Selling Price per unit}$$

$$= \frac{\text{Total Fixed Cost}}{\text{Total Contribution}} \times \text{Total Sales}$$

$$= \frac{\text{Total Fixed Cost}}{\text{Profit/Volume Ratio}}$$

$$= \frac{\text{Total Fixed Cost}}{1 - \left(\dfrac{\text{Variable Cost}}{\text{Sales}}\right)}$$

$$= \text{Break-Even Point (Units)} \times \text{Selling Price per unit}$$

9) **Profit/Volume Ratio or Contribution to Sales Ratio or Contribution Ratio i.e. P/V Ratio:**

$$= \frac{\text{Contribution}}{\text{Sales}} \times 100$$

$$= \frac{\text{Change in Profits}}{\text{Change in Sales}} \times 100$$

$$= \frac{\text{Change in Contribution}}{\text{Change in Sales}} \times 100$$

10) **Margin of Safety:**

$$\text{MS} = \text{Actual Sales} - \text{Break-Even Sales}$$

$$\text{MS} = \frac{\text{Profit}}{\text{P/V Ratio}}$$

$$\text{MS Ratio} = \frac{\text{Profit}}{\text{P/V Ratio}} \times 100$$

$$\text{MS Ratio} = \frac{\text{Margin of Safety}}{\text{Actual Sales}} \times 100$$

11) **Sales volume to earn required profit (in units) or Sales for desired profit (in units):**

$$= \frac{\text{Total Fixed Cost} + \text{Required Profit}}{\text{Contribution per unit}}$$

12) **Sales volume to earn required profit (in value) or Sales for desired profit (in ₹):**

$$= \frac{(\text{Total Fixed Cost} + \text{Required Profit}) \times \text{Sales}}{\text{Total Contribution}}$$

$$= \frac{\text{Total Fixed Cost} + \text{Required Profit}}{\text{P/V Ratio}}$$

ILLUSTRATIONS

ILLUSTRATION 1

Rotex India Ltd., Raipur produces 1,00,000 units and sells them @ ₹ 10 each. The variable cost per unit is ₹ 6 and Total Fixed Cost amounted to ₹ 2,00,000. Calculate Break-Even Point in units and sales by following **Formulae Method** and **Graphical Presentation Method**. Also calculate margin of safety showing angle of incidence separately.

SOLUTION

A) Formulae Method:

i) Break-Even Point (Units) = $\dfrac{\text{Total Fixed Cost}}{\text{Contribution per unit}}$

But,

Contribution per unit = Selling Price per unit − Variable Cost per unit

∴ Break-Even Point (Units) = $\dfrac{\text{Total Fixed Cost}}{\text{Selling Price per unit} - \text{Variable Cost}}$

$= \dfrac{₹\,2,00,000}{₹\,10 - ₹\,6}$

$= \dfrac{₹\,2,00,000}{₹\,4}$

= 50,000 Units

ii) Break Even Point (Sales) = Break Even Point (Units) × Selling Price per unit

= 50,000 Units × ₹ 10

= ₹ 5,00,000

iii) Margin of Safety = Actual Sales − Break Even Sales

= ₹ 10,00,000 − ₹ 5,00,000

= ₹ 5,00,000

B) Graphical Presentation Method:

Break Even Chart is a graphical representation of marginal costing. It indicates the grpahical relationship between cost, volume and profits. On the basis of cost data, the Break-Even Chart can be drawn as follows:

		₹
i)	Total Actual Sales	10,00,000
	(1,00,000 units × ₹ 10)	
ii)	Total Fixed Cost	2,00,000
iii)	Total Variable Cost	6,00,000
	(1,00,000 units × ₹ 6)	
iv)	Total Profit	2,00,000

Scale,

OX axis ... 1 cm = 10,000 units ... Output in units

OY axis ... 1 cm = ₹ 1,00,000 ... Costs and Sales Revenue

Break-Even Chart

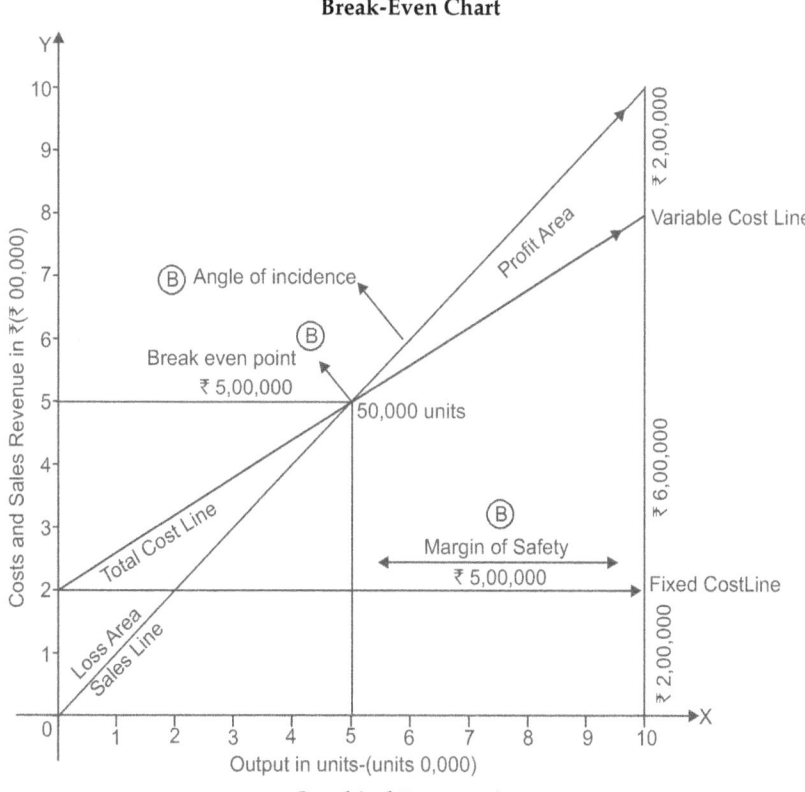

Graphical Presentation

ILLUSTRATION 2

From the following particulars calculate,

i) Contribution per unit
ii) P/V Ratio
iii) BEP (units and in rupees)
iv) What will be the selling price per unit if BEP is brought down to 25,000 units?

- Fixed Expenses ₹ 1,50,000,
- Selling Price per unit ₹ 15,
- Variable Cost per unit ₹ 10.

SOLUTION

i) Contribution per unit:

= Selling Price per unit – Variable Cost per unit
= ₹ 15 – ₹ 10
= ₹ 5

ii) **P/V Ratio:**

$$= \frac{\text{Contribution per unit}}{\text{Selling Price per unit}} \times 100$$

$$= \frac{₹5}{₹15} \times 100$$

$$= \frac{1}{3} \times 100$$

$$= 33\frac{1}{3}\%$$

iii) **BEP (in rupees):**

$$= \frac{\text{Fixed Cost}}{\text{P/V Ratio}}$$

$$= \frac{₹1,50,000}{33\frac{1}{3}\%}$$

$$= \frac{₹1,50,000}{1/3}$$

$$= ₹1,50,000 \times \frac{3}{1}$$

$$= ₹4,50,000$$

BEP (units):

$$= \frac{\text{Fixed Cost}}{\text{Contribution per unit}}$$

$$= \frac{₹1,50,000}{₹5}$$

$$= 30,000 \text{ units}$$

iv) **Selling Price per unit:**

where, BEP (units) = $\frac{\text{Fixed Cost}}{\text{Contribution per unit}}$

∴ Contribution per unit = $\frac{\text{Fixed Cost}}{\text{BEP (Units)}}$

$$= \frac{₹1,50,000}{\text{Units } 25,000}$$

= ₹6 per unit

Selling Price per unit = Variable Cost per unit + Contribution per unit

= ₹10 + ₹6

= ₹16

ILLUSTRATION 3

Find out the selling price per unit if BEP is to be brought down to 9,000 units

	₹
Marginal Cost per unit	75
Fixed Cost	2,70,000
Market Price per unit	100

SOLUTION

i) **Calculation of Contribution per unit:**

where,

BEP (units) = $\frac{\text{Fixed Cost}}{\text{Contribution per unit}}$

Management Accounting   5.23   Marginal Costing

∴ Contribution per unit = $\dfrac{\text{Fixed Cost}}{\text{BEP (Units)}}$

$= \dfrac{₹\,2,70,000}{9,000 \text{ units}}$

= ₹ 30 per unit

ii) **Calculation of Selling Price per unit :**
Where,
∴ Contribution per unit = Selling Price per unit – Variable Cost per unit
∴ Selling Price per unit = Contribution per unit + Variable Cost per unit
= ₹ 30 + ₹ 75
= ₹ 105 per unit

ILLUSTRATION 4

Find out the actual sales from the following information :

	₹
Fixed Cost	8,000
Profits	2,000
BEP (Sales)	40,000

SOLUTION

Let 'A' be the actual sales
Then,

BEP (Sales) = $\dfrac{\text{Total Fixed Cost}}{\text{Total Contribution}} \times A$

But,
Total Contribution = Fixed Cost + Profit

∴ BEP (Sales) = $\dfrac{\text{Total Fixed Cost}}{\text{Fixed Cost + Profit}} \times A$

∴ ₹ 40,000 = $\dfrac{₹\,8,000}{₹\,8,000 + ₹\,2,000} \times A$

∴ ₹ 40,000 = $\dfrac{₹\,8,000}{₹\,10,000} \times A$

∴ ₹ 40,000 = 0.8 A

∴ A = $\dfrac{₹\,40,000}{0.8}$

= ₹ 40,000 × $\dfrac{10}{8}$

= $\dfrac{₹\,4,00,000}{8}$

= ₹ 50,000

∴ Actual Sales = ₹ 50,000

ILLUSTRATION 5

Gasco Ltd., Gurgaon provides you with the following additional cost data regarding its operations for 2013-14.

- Invoice price   ₹ 20 per unit
- Works on Cost – Fixed   ₹ 61,000 p.a.
- Production Cost – Marginal   ₹ 11 per unit
- Selling Overheads – Rigid   ₹ 29,000 p.a.
- Distribution Overheads – Differential   ₹ 3 per unit

Calculate –
i) Break Even Point in amount of Sales in rupees.
ii) Number of units to be sold to earn a profit of ₹ 30,000 per year.

SOLUTION

- **Calculation of Contribution per unit :**

		Unit Cost ₹
Invoice Price		20.00
Less : Variable Cost		
i) Production Cost – Marginal	11.00	
ii) Distribution Overheads – Differential	(+) 3.00	
	(–)	14.00
∴ Contribution		06.00

- **Calculation of P/V Ratio :**

where,

$$P/V \text{ Ratio} = \frac{\text{Contribution}}{\text{Sales}} \times 100$$

$$= \frac{₹6}{₹20} \times 100$$

$$= 30\%$$

i) Break Even Point in amount of Sales in rupees :

$$= \frac{\text{Fixed Cost}}{P/V \text{ Ratio}}$$

$$= \frac{\underset{₹61,000}{\text{Works on Cost}} + \underset{₹29,000}{\text{Selling Overheads}}}{30\%}$$

$$= ₹90,000 \times \frac{100}{30}$$

$$= ₹3,00,000$$

ii) Number of units to be sold to earn a profit of ₹ 30,000 per year :

$$= \frac{\text{Fixed Cost + Desired Profit}}{\text{Contribution per unit}}$$

$$= \frac{₹90,000}{₹6}$$

$$= 15,000 \text{ units}$$

ILLUSTRATION 6

From the following cost data calculate :
i) BEP (units)
ii) BEP (units) if Selling Price is reduced by 10%.
iii) Selling Price per unit if BEP is 8,000 units.

Fixed Cost - ₹ 1,00,000, Variable Cost per unit - ₹ 10, Selling Price per unit - ₹ 20.

SOLUTION

i) BEP (units):

$$\text{BEP (units)} = \frac{\text{Fixed Cost}}{\text{Contribution per unit}}$$

But,

Contribution per unit = Selling Price per unit − Variable Cost per unit

$$\therefore \text{BEP (units)} = \frac{\text{Fixed Cost}}{\text{Selling Price per unit} - \text{Variable Cost per unit}}$$

$$= \frac{₹1,00,000}{₹20 - ₹10}$$

$$= \frac{₹1,00,000}{₹10}$$

= 10,000 units.

ii) BEP (units) if selling price is reduced by 10%:

Original Selling Price per unit − Reduction by 10% = New Selling Price per unit.

₹20 − ₹2 = ₹18

BEP (units):

$$= \frac{\text{Fixed Cost}}{\text{Contribution per unit}}$$

But,

Contribution per unit = Selling Price per unit − Variable Cost per unit

$$\therefore \text{BEP (units)} = \frac{\text{Fixed Cost}}{\text{Selling Price per unit} - \text{Variable Cost per unit}}$$

$$= \frac{₹1,00,000}{₹18 - ₹10}$$

$$= \frac{₹1,00,000}{₹8}$$

= 12,500 units

iii) Selling price per unit if BEP is 8,000 units:

Let X be the selling price per unit.

where,

$$\text{BEP (units)} = \frac{\text{Fixed Cost}}{\text{Contribution per unit}}$$

But,

Contribution per unit = Selling Price per unit − Variable Cost per unit

$$\therefore \text{BEP (units)} = \frac{\text{Fixed Cost}}{\text{Selling Price per unit} - \text{Variable Cost per unit}}$$

$$\therefore 8,000 \text{ units} = \frac{₹1,00,000}{X - ₹10}$$

∴ 8,000 units × (X − ₹10) = ₹1,00,000

∴ 8,000 X − ₹80,000 = ₹1,00,000

∴ 8,000 X = ₹1,00,000 + ₹80,000

$$\therefore X = \frac{₹1,80,000}{8,000 \text{ units}}$$

= ₹22.50

∴ Selling Price per unit = ₹22.50

ILLUSTRATION 7

From the following cost data of Onida Co. Ltd., Osmanabad calculate BEP (units) and also new BEP (units) if selling price is reduced by 10%.

	₹
Direct Materials per unit	3
Depreciation on Plant and Machinery	1,00,000
Basic Labour per unit	1.50
Salaries to Staff – Middle Level	80,000
Prime Cost Expenses per unit	0.50
Workshop Rent	20,000
Value of Turnover per unit	10

SOLUTION

i) **Calculation of Variable Cost per unit :**

	₹
Direct Materials per unit	3.00
Add : Basic Labour per unit	(+) 1.50
Add : Prime Cost Expenses per unit	(+) 0.50
∴ Total Variable Cost per unit	**5.00**

ii) **Calculation of Total Fixed Cost :**

	₹
Depreciation of Plant and Machinery	1,00,000
Add : Salaries to Staff – Middle Level	(+) 80,000
Add : Workshop Rent	(+) 20,000
∴ Total Fixed Cost	**2,00,000**

$$\text{BEP (units)} = \frac{\text{Fixed Cost}}{\text{Contribution per unit}}$$

But,

Contribution per unit = Selling Price per unit – Variable Cost per unit

$$\therefore \text{BEP (units)} = \frac{\text{Fixed Cost}}{\text{Selling Price per unit – Variable Cost per unit}}$$

$$= \frac{₹\,2,00,000}{₹\,10 - ₹\,5}$$

$$= \frac{₹\,2,00,000}{₹\,5}$$

= 40,000 units

Calculation of new BEP (units) if selling price is reduced by 10% :

Original selling price per unit – Reduction by 10% = New selling price per unit

₹ 10 – ₹ 1 = ₹ 9

$$\text{BEP (units)} = \frac{\text{Fixed Cost}}{\text{Contribution per unit}}$$

But, Contribution per unit = Selling Price per unit – Variable Cost per unit

$$\therefore \text{BEP (units)} = \frac{\text{Fixed Cost}}{\text{Selling Price per unit – Variable Cost per unit}}$$

$$= \frac{₹\,2,00,000}{₹\,9 - ₹\,5}$$

$$= \frac{₹\,2,00,000}{₹\,4}$$

= 50,000 units

ILLUSTRATION 8

Following cost details are made available by Indian Plastics Ltd., Indapur for the month April, 2014.

Prime Cost Labour per unit	₹ 3.50
Fixed Overheads	₹ 20,000
Value of Turnover per unit	₹ 20
Productive Wages – Outstanding per unit	Re. 0.50
Basic Material Cost per unit	₹ 6
Variable Overheads – 100% of Direct Labour Cost	10%

You are required to calculate –
i) Break Even Point (Sales Value)
ii) Net Profit, if Sales are 10% and 15% above the Break Even Volume.

SOLUTION

- **Calculation of Contribution per unit :**

				Unit Cost ₹
where,				
Selling Price				18.00

$$\begin{pmatrix} \text{Value of Turnover} & (-) & \text{Trade Discount @ 10\%} \\ ₹\,20 & & ₹\,2 \end{pmatrix}$$

Less : Variable Cost
i) Basic Material Cost 6.00
ii) Direct Labour Cost 4.00
   • Prime Cost Labour 3.50
   Add : Productive Outstanding Wages ... (+) 0.50
iii) Variable Overheads 4.00
   (100% of Direct Labour Cost i.e. ₹ 4) (+)_____
                                                                (–) 14.00
   ∴ **Contribution**   04.00

i) Break Even Point Units and Sales :

$$= \frac{\text{Total Fixed Cost}}{\text{Contribution per unit}}$$

$$= \frac{₹\,20{,}000}{₹\,4}$$

= 5,000 Units

		₹
Gross Sales at Break Even Point		1,00,000
(5,000 Units × ₹ 20)		
Less : Trade Discount		10,000
(10% of ₹ 1,00,000)	(–)	
∴ **Net Sales at Break Even Point**		**90,000**

ii) a) Net Profit, if Sales are 10% above break even volume :
Revised Sales are 10% above Break Even Volume i.e.
= 5,000 units + (10% of above i.e.) 500 units
= 5,500 units

- Calculation of Net Profit :
  where,

  Contribution = Fixed Cost + Profit

  ∴ Profit = Contribution – Fixed Cost
  = (5,500 units × ₹ 4) – ₹ 20,000
  = ₹ 22,000 – ₹ 20,000
  = ₹ 2,000

b) Net Profit, if Sales are 15% above break even volume :
Revised Sales are 15% above Break Even Volume i.e.
= 5,000 units + (15% above i.e.) 750 units
= 5,750 units

- Calculation of Net Profit :
  where,

  Contribution = Fixed Cost + Profit

  ∴ Profit = Contribution – Fixed Cost
  = (5,750 units × ₹ 4) – ₹ 20,000
  = ₹ 23,000 – ₹ 20,000
  = ₹ 3,000

ILLUSTRATION 9

The following is a Cost Statement of a machine manufactured by Goyal Machineries Ltd., Gondia for the year ended 31st March, 2014. During the year the company manufactured 1,000 machines and sold in the national market.

	Particulars		₹
	Basic Materials		190
Add :	Direct Wages		70
Add :	Productive Expenses	(+)	40
	Prime Cost	**(1)**	300
Add :	Fixed Manufacturing Overheads	(+)	50
	Works Cost	**(2)**	350
Add :	Constant Management Expenses	(+)	20
	Cost of Production	**(3)**	370
Add :	Rigid Selling and Distribution on Cost	(+)	30
	Cost of Sales	**(4)**	400
Add :	Profit	(5) (+)	100
	Selling Price		500

You are required to find out,
i) Break Even Point (units),
ii) The number of machines to be produced and sold to earn the same amount of profit if the price is to be increased by ₹ 50.

Management Accounting 5.29 Marginal Costing

SOLUTION

In the books of Goyal Machineries Ltd., Gondia
Profitability Statement for the year ended 31st March, 2014
(Machines Produced and Sold – 1,000)

Particulars			₹
	Sales		500
Less :	Variable Cost :		
	i) Basic Materials		190
	ii) Direct Wages		70
	iii) Productive Expenses	(–)	40
∴	Contribution		200
Less :	Fixed Cost :		
	i) Manufacturing Overheads		50
	ii) Management Expenses		20
	iii) Selling and Distribution Expenses	(–)	30
∴	**Profit**		**100**

i) Break Even Point (units) :

$= \dfrac{\text{Fixed Cost}}{\text{Contribution per unit}}$

$= \dfrac{₹1,00,000}{₹200}$

= 500 units.

ii) Number of machines to be produced and sold to earn the same amount of profit if the price is to be increased by ₹ 50 :

		₹
	New Selling Price : (₹ 500 + ₹ 50)	550
Less :	Variable Cost	(–) 300
∴	Contribution per unit	250

Sales for desired profit in units :

$= \dfrac{\text{Total Fixed Cost + Required Profit}}{\text{Contribution per unit}}$

$= \dfrac{₹1,00,000\ (₹100 \times 1,000\text{ units}) + ₹1,00,000\ (₹100 \times 1,000\text{ units})}{₹250}$

= 800 units

ILLUSTRATION 10

Bokaro India Ltd., Badalpur provides the following cost data relating to one unit of ouptut.

Productive Materials	₹ 50
Variable Works Overheads : 75% of Prime Cost Labour	
Direct Labour	₹ 80
Fixed Establishment Overheads	₹ 2,40,000 p.a.
Market Price	₹ 230

You are required to calculate,
i) the number of units to be produced and sold in a year to break even.
ii) the number of units to be manufactured and sold in a year to make a profit of ₹ 80,000.
iii) the number of units to be produced and sold to break even if the selling price is reduced by ₹ 16 each.

SOLUTION

- Calculation of Contribution per unit :
  where,

		Unit Cost ₹
Market Price		230
Less : Variable Cost		
i) Productive Materials	50	
ii) Direct Labour	80	
iii) Variable Works Overheads	(+) 60	
(75% of Prime Cost labour i.e. ₹ 80)		
	(–) 190	
∴ **Contribution**		**40**

i) Number of units to be produced and sold in a year to break even :
where, Break Even Points (units) =

$$= \frac{\text{Fixed Cost}}{\text{Contribution per unit}}$$

$$= \frac{₹ 2,40,000}{₹ 40}$$

= 6,000 units.

ii) Number of units to be manufactured and sold in a year to make a profit of ₹ 80,000.

$$= \frac{\text{Fixed Cost + Desired Profit}}{\text{Contribution per unit}}$$

$$= \frac{₹ 2,40,000 + ₹ 80,00}{₹ 40}$$

$$= \frac{₹ 3,20,000}{₹ 40}$$

= 8,000 units.

iii) Number of units to be produced and sold to break even if the selling price is reduced by ₹ 16 each.

- Calculation of Revised Selling Price :

= Old Selling Price − Reduction by
  ₹ 230   ₹ 16

= ₹ 214

- Calculation of Revised Contribution per unit :
  where,

	Unit Cost ₹
Market Price	214.00
Less : Variable Cost	(–) 190.00
∴ Contribution	24.00

  Break Even Point (units) :

  $$= \frac{\text{Fixed Cost}}{\text{Contribution per unit}}$$

  $$= \frac{₹\,2,40,000}{₹\,24}$$

  = 10,000 units

ILLUSTRATION 11

The Burma-Shell Ltd. Baramati has submitted the following data :

	₹
Selling price per unit	20
Variable cost per unit	16
Total Fixed Cost	20,000

Calculate BEP (units). Also calculate the effect on BEP (units) if

i) Selling price is increased by ₹ 1
ii) Selling price is decreased by ₹ 1
iii) Variable cost is increased by ₹ 1
iv) Variable cost is decreased by ₹ 1
v) Fixed cost is increased by ₹ 5,000
vi) Fixed cost is decreased by ₹ 5,000

SOLUTION

$$\text{BEP (units)} = \frac{\text{Fixed Cost}}{\text{Contribution per unit}}$$

But,

Contribution per unit = Selling Price per unit – Variable Cost per unit

$$\therefore \text{BEP (units)} = \frac{\text{Fixed Cost}}{\text{Selling Price per unit} - \text{Variable Cost per unit}}$$

$$= \frac{₹\,20,000}{₹\,20 - ₹\,16} = \frac{₹\,20,000}{₹\,4}$$

= 5,000 units

Calculation of effect on BEP (units) if,

i) Selling Price is increased by ₹ 1 :

Original Selling Price per unit + Increase by ₹ 1 = New Selling Price per unit

₹ 20 + ₹ 1 = ₹ 21

$$\text{BEP (units)} = \frac{\text{Fixed Cost}}{\text{Selling Price per unit} - \text{Variable Cost per unit}}$$

$$= \frac{₹\,20,000}{₹\,21 - ₹\,16}$$

$$= \frac{₹\,20,000}{₹\,5}$$

= 4,000 units

Management Accounting   Marginal Costing

ii) **Selling Price is decreased by ₹ 1 :**

Original Selling Price per unit – Decrease by ₹ 1 = New Selling Price per unit
₹ 20 – ₹ 1 = ₹ 19

$$\text{BEP (units)} = \frac{\text{Fixed Cost}}{\text{Selling Price per unit} - \text{Variable Cost per unit}}$$

$$= \frac{₹\,20,000}{₹\,19 - ₹\,16}$$

$$= \frac{₹\,20,000}{₹\,3}$$

= 6,667 units

iii) **Variable Cost is increased by ₹ 1 :**

Original Variable Cost per unit + Increase by ₹ 1 = New Variable Cost per unit
₹ 16 + ₹ 1 = ₹ 17

$$\text{BEP (units)} = \frac{\text{Fixed Cost}}{\text{Selling Price per unit} - \text{Variable Cost per unit}}$$

$$= \frac{₹\,20,000}{₹\,20 - ₹\,17}$$

$$= \frac{₹\,20,000}{₹\,3}$$

= 6,667 units

iv) **Variable Cost is decreased by Re. 1 :**

Original Variable Cost per unit – Decrease by ₹ 1 = New Variable Cost per unit
₹ 16 – ₹ 1 = ₹ 15

$$\text{BEP (units)} = \frac{\text{Fixed Cost}}{\text{Selling Price per unit} - \text{Variable Cost per unit}}$$

$$= \frac{₹\,20,000}{₹\,20 - ₹\,15}$$

$$= \frac{₹\,20,000}{₹\,5}$$

= 4,000 units

v) **Fixed Cost is increased by ₹ 5,000 :**

Original Fixed Cost + Increase by = New Fixed Cost
₹ 20,000 + ₹ 5,000 = ₹ 25,000

$$\text{BEP (units)} = \frac{\text{Fixed Cost}}{\text{Selling Price per unit} - \text{Variable Cost per unit}}$$

$$= \frac{₹\,25,000}{₹\,20 - ₹\,16}$$

$$= \frac{₹\,25,000}{₹\,4}$$

= 6,250 units

vi) **Fixed Cost is decreased by ₹ 5,000 :**

Original Fixed Cost – Decrease by = New Fixed Cost
₹ 20,000 – ₹ 5,000 = ₹ 15,000

$$\text{BEP (units)} = \frac{\text{Fixed Cost}}{\text{Selling Price per unit} - \text{Variable Cost per unit}}$$

$$= \frac{₹15,000}{₹20 - ₹16}$$

$$= \frac{₹15,000}{₹4}$$

$$= 3,750 \text{ units}$$

ILLUSTRATION 12

Fonda Ltd., Faridabad has prepared the following budget estimate for the year 2013-2014.

Sales	15,000 units
Fixed Cost	₹ 34,000
Sales Value	₹ 1,50,000
Variable Cost per unit	₹ 6

You are required to calculate,
a) P/V Ratio, BEP (Sales) and Margin of Safety
b) Also calculate the effect of the following.
  i) decrease of 10% in Selling Price
  ii) increase of 10% in Variable Cost.

SOLUTION

$$\text{Selling Price per unit} = \frac{\text{Sales Value}}{\text{Sales Units}}$$

$$= \frac{₹1,50,000}{15,000 \text{ units}}$$

$$= ₹10$$

a) i) **P/V Ratio :**

$$= \frac{\text{Contribution per unit}}{\text{Selling Price per unit}} \times 100$$

But, Contribution per unit = Selling Price per unit – Variable Cost per unit

$$\therefore \text{P/V Ratio} = \frac{\text{Selling Price per unit} - \text{Variable Cost per unit}}{\text{Selling Price per unit}} \times 100$$

$$= \frac{₹10 - ₹6}{₹10} \times 100$$

$$= \frac{₹4}{₹10} \times 100$$

$$= 40\%$$

ii) **BEP (Sales) :**

$$= \frac{\text{Fixed Cost}}{\text{P/V Ratio}}$$

$$= \frac{₹34,000}{40\%}$$

$$= ₹34,000 \times \frac{100}{40}$$

$$= ₹85,000$$

iii) **Margin of Safety:**

= Actual Sales – BEP (Sales)

= ₹1,50,000   –   ₹85,000
  (15,000 units × ₹10)

= ₹65,000

b) i) **Decrease of 10% in Selling Price:**

Original Selling Price per unit – Decrease of 10% = New Selling Price per unit

₹10   –   ₹1   =   ₹9

i) **P/V Ratio:**

$$= \frac{\text{Contribution per unit}}{\text{Selling Price per unit}} \times 100$$

But, Contribution per unit = Selling Price per unit – Variable Cost per unit

$$\therefore \quad \text{P/V Ratio} = \frac{\text{Selling Price per unit} - \text{Variable Cost per unit}}{\text{Selling Price per unit}} \times 100$$

$$= \frac{₹9 - ₹6}{₹9} \times 100$$

$$= \frac{₹3}{₹9} \times 100$$

$$= 33\tfrac{1}{3}\%$$

ii) **BEP (Sales):**

$$= \frac{\text{Fixed Cost}}{\text{P/V Ratio}}$$

$$= \frac{₹34,000}{33\tfrac{1}{3}\%}$$

$$= \frac{₹34,000}{1/3}$$

$$= ₹34,000 \times \frac{3}{1}$$

$$= ₹1,02,000$$

iii) **Margin of Safety:**

= Actual Sales – BEP (Sales)

= ₹1,35,000   –   ₹1,02,000
  (15,000 units × ₹9)

= ₹33,000

b) ii) **Increase of 10% in Variable Cost:**

Original Variable Cost per unit + Increase of 10% = New Variable Cost per unit

₹6 + ₹0.60   = ₹6.60

i) **P/V Ratio:**

$$= \frac{\text{Contribution per unit}}{\text{Selling Price per unit}} \times 100$$

But, Contribution per unit = Selling Price per unit − Variable Cost per unit

∴ P/V Ratio $= \dfrac{\text{Selling Price per unit} - \text{Variable Cost per unit}}{\text{Selling Price per unit}} \times 100$

$= \dfrac{₹\,10 - ₹\,6.60}{₹\,10} \times 100$

$= \dfrac{₹\,3.40}{₹\,10} \times 100$

$= 34\%$

ii) **BEP (Sales) :**

$= \dfrac{\text{Fixed Cost}}{\text{P/V Ratio}}$

$= \dfrac{₹\,34{,}000}{34\%}$

$= ₹\,34{,}000 \times \dfrac{100}{34}$

$= ₹\,1{,}00{,}000$

iii) **Margin of Safety :**

= Actual Sales − BEP (Sales)

= ₹ 1,50,000 − ₹ 1,00,000

= ₹ 50,000

ILLUSTRATION 13

Reliance Industries, Rameshwar provides the following information for the year 2013-2014.

	₹
Sales	2,00,000
Variable Cost	1,00,000
Fixed Cost	50,000

a) Find P/V Ratio, BEP (Sales) and Margin of Safety.
b) Also calculate the effect of the following.
  i) 10% increase in selling price
  ii) 5% decrease in variable cost
  iii) 20% decrease in selling price
  iv) 10% decrease in fixed cost

SOLUTION

a) i) **P/V Ratio :**

$= \dfrac{\text{Contribution}}{\text{Sales}} \times 100$

But, Contribution = Sales − Variable Cost

P/V Ratio $= \dfrac{\text{Sales} - \text{Variable Cost}}{\text{Sales}} \times 100$

$= \dfrac{₹\,2{,}00{,}000 - ₹\,1{,}00{,}000}{₹\,2{,}00{,}000} \times 100$

$= \dfrac{₹\,1{,}00{,}000}{₹\,2{,}00{,}000} \times 100$

$= 50\%$

ii) **BEP (Sales):**

$$= \frac{\text{Fixed Cost}}{\text{P/V Ratio}}$$

$$= \frac{₹50{,}000}{50\%}$$

$$= ₹50{,}000 \times \frac{100}{50}$$

$$= ₹1{,}00{,}000$$

iii) **Margin of Safety:**

= Actual Sales – BEP (Sales)
= ₹2,00,000 – ₹1,00,000
= ₹1,00,000

b) i) **10% increase in selling price:**

Original Selling Price + Increase by 10% = New Selling Price
₹2,00,000 + ₹20,000 = ₹2,20,000

i) **P/V Ratio:**

$$= \frac{\text{Contribution}}{\text{Sales}} \times 100$$

But, Contribution = Sales – Variable Cost

∴ P/V Ratio $= \frac{\text{Sales} - \text{Variable Cost}}{\text{Sales}} \times 100$

$$= \frac{₹2{,}20{,}000 - ₹1{,}00{,}000}{₹2{,}20{,}000} \times 100$$

$$= \frac{₹1{,}20{,}000}{₹2{,}20{,}000} \times 100$$

= 54.54%

ii) **BEP (Sales):**

$$= \frac{\text{Fixed Cost}}{\text{P/V Ratio}}$$

$$= \frac{₹50{,}000}{54.54\%}$$

$$= ₹50{,}000 \times \frac{100}{54.54}$$

= ₹91,676

iii) **Margin of Safety:**

= Actual Sales – BEP (Sales)
= ₹2,20,000 – ₹91,676
= ₹1,28,324

b) ii) **5% decrease in Variable Cost:**

Original Variable Cost – Decrease by 5% = New Variable Cost
₹1,00,000 – ₹5,000 = ₹95,000

i) **P/V Ratio:**

$$= \frac{\text{Contribution}}{\text{Sales}} \times 100$$

But, Contribution = Sales – Variable Cost

∴ P/V Ratio $= \frac{\text{Sales} - \text{Variable Cost}}{\text{Sales}} \times 100$

$$= \frac{₹\,2,00,000 - ₹\,95,000}{₹\,2,00,000} \times 100$$

$$= \frac{₹\,1,05,000}{₹\,2,00,000} \times 100$$

$$= 52.5\%$$

ii) **BEP (Sales) :**

$$= \frac{\text{Fixed Cost}}{\text{P/V Ratio}}$$

$$= \frac{₹\,50,000}{52.5\%}$$

$$= ₹\,50,000 \times \frac{100}{52.5}$$

$$= ₹\,95,238$$

iii) **Margin of Safety :**

= Actual Sales – BEP (Sales)
= ₹ 2,00,000 – ₹ 95,238
= ₹ 1,04,762

b) iii) **20% decrease in Selling Price :**
Original Selling Price – Decrease by 20% = New Selling Price
  ₹ 2,00,000   –   ₹ 40,000   =   ₹ 1,60,000

i) **P/V Ratio :**

$$= \frac{\text{Contribution}}{\text{Sales}} \times 100$$

But,

Contribution = Sales – Variable Cost

∴ $$\text{P/V Ratio} = \frac{\text{Sales – Variable Cost}}{\text{Sales}} \times 100$$

$$= \frac{₹\,1,60,000 - ₹\,1,00,000}{₹\,1,60,000} \times 100$$

$$= \frac{₹\,60,000}{₹\,1,60,000} \times 100$$

$$= 37.5\%$$

ii) **BEP (Sales) :**

$$= \frac{\text{Fixed Cost}}{\text{P/V Ratio}}$$

$$= \frac{₹\,50,000}{37.5\%}$$

$$= ₹\,50,000 \times \frac{100}{37.5\%}$$

$$= ₹\,1,33,333$$

iii) **Margin of Safety :**

= Actual Sales – BEP (Sales)
= ₹ 1,60,000 – ₹ 1,33,333
= ₹ 26,667

b) iv) **10% decrease in Fixed Cost**
Original Fixed Cost – Decrease by 10% = New Fixed Cost
  ₹ 50,000   –   ₹ 5,000   =   ₹ 45,000

i) P/V Ratio :

$$= \frac{\text{Contribution}}{\text{Sales}} \times 100$$

But, Contribution = Sales – Variable Cost

$$\therefore \text{P/V Ratio} = \frac{\text{Sales} - \text{Variable Cost}}{\text{Sales}} \times 100$$

$$= \frac{₹2,00,000 - ₹1,00,000}{₹2,00,000} \times 100 = \frac{₹1,00,000}{₹2,00,000} \times 100$$

$$= 50\%$$

ii) BEP (Sales) :

$$= \frac{\text{Fixed Cost}}{\text{P/V Ratio}}$$

$$= \frac{₹45,000}{50\%}$$

$$= ₹45,000 \times \frac{100}{50}$$

$$= ₹90,000$$

iii) Margin of Safety :

= Actual Sales – BEP (Sales)
= ₹2,00,000 – ₹90,000
= ₹1,10,000

ILLUSTRATION 14

From the following cost data you are required to calculate,
i) BEP (units and sales)
ii) Sales required to earn a profit of ₹54,000.

Selling Price per unit ₹18, Contribution per unit ₹6 and Fixed Cost ₹84,000.

SOLUTION

i) BEP (Units) :

$$= \frac{\text{Fixed Cost}}{\text{Contribution per unit}}$$

$$= \frac{₹84,000}{₹6}$$

$$= 14,000 \text{ units}$$

BEP (Sales) :

$$= \frac{\text{Fixed Cost}}{\text{Contribution per unit}} \times \text{Selling Price per unit}$$

$$= \frac{₹84,000}{₹6} \times ₹18$$

$$= 14,000 \text{ units} \times ₹18$$

$$= ₹2,52,000$$

Calculation of P/V Ratio :

$$\text{P/V Ratio} = \frac{\text{Contribution per unit}}{\text{Selling Price per unit}} \times 100$$

$$= \frac{₹6}{₹18} \times 100$$

$$= \frac{1}{3} \times 100$$
$$= 33\,{}^1/_3\%$$

ii) **Sales required to earn a profit of ₹ 54,000 :**

$$\text{P/V Ratio} = \frac{\text{Contribution}}{\text{Sales}}$$

But, Contribution = Fixed Cost + Profit

$$\therefore \quad \text{P/V Ratio} = \frac{\text{Fixed Cost + Profit}}{\text{Sales}}$$

$$\therefore \quad \text{Sales} = \frac{\text{Fixed Cost + Profit}}{\text{P/V Ratio}}$$

$$= \frac{₹\,84,000 + ₹\,54,000}{33\,{}^1/_3\%}$$

$$= \frac{₹\,1,38,000}{{}^1/_3}$$

$$= ₹\,1,38,000 \times \frac{3}{1}$$

$$= ₹\,4,14,000$$

ILLUSTRATION 15

Activa Engineering Co. Ltd., Ahmednagar provides you with the following cost details.

Non-variable Cost	₹ 2,000
Variable Cost of Sales	60%
Total Turnover	₹ 10,000
Net Margin	₹ 2,000

Calculate the following :
i) Break Even Sales
ii) Sales Volume to earn a profit of ₹ 6,000 and
iii) Margin of Safety when Sales are ₹ 25,000.

SOLUTION

As Variable Cost of Sales are 60%, the P/V Ratio will be (i.e. 100% – 60%) 40%.

i) **Break Even Sales :**

$$= \frac{\text{Fixed Cost (i.e. Non-Variable Cost)}}{\text{P/V Ratio}}$$

$$= \frac{₹\,2,000}{40\%}$$

$$= ₹\,2,000 \times \frac{100}{40}$$

$$= ₹\,5,000$$

ii) **Sales Volume to earn a profit of ₹ 6,000 :**

where, $\text{P/V Ratio} = \dfrac{\text{Contribution}}{\text{Sales}}$

But, Contribution = Fixed Cost + Profit

$$\therefore \quad \text{P/V Ratio} = \frac{\text{Fixed Cost + Profit}}{\text{Sales}}$$

$$\therefore \quad \text{Sales} = \frac{\text{Fixed Cost + Profit}}{\text{P/V Ratio}}$$

$$= \frac{₹\,2{,}000 + ₹\,6{,}000}{40\%}$$

$$= ₹\,8{,}000 \times \frac{100}{40}$$

$$= ₹\,20{,}000$$

iii) **Margin of Safety when Sales are ₹ 25,000 :**
where,
Margin of Safety = Actual Sales – Break Even Sales
= ₹ 25,000 – ₹ 5,000
= ₹ 20,000

ILLUSTRATION 16

Bajaj Auto Ltd., Bilaspur has submitted the following cost data.

	₹
Invoice Price per unit	40
Fixed Production Overheads	1,50,000
Variable Manufacturing Cost per unit	5
Selling on cost – Fixed	20,000
Prime Cost Materials per unit (Variable Cost)	18
Fixed - Distribution Expenses	10,000
Variable Selling overheads per unit	2

Calculate,
i) BEP (Sales)
ii) Number of units to be sold to earn a profit of ₹ 1,20,000.
iii) Number of units to be sold to earn an income of 25% of Sales.

SOLUTION

Calculation of Total Fixed Cost :   ₹
Fixed Production Overheads   1,50,000
Add : Selling on cost – Fixed   20,000
Add : Fixed Distribution Expenses   (+) 10,000
∴ **Total Fixed Cost**   1,80,000

Calculation of Total Variable Cost per unit   ₹
Variable Manufacturing Cost per unit   5
Add : Prime Cost materials per unit   (+) 18
Add : Variable Selling Overheads per unit   (+) 2
∴ **Variable Cost per unit**   25

Calculation of P/V Ratio :

$$= \frac{\text{Contribution per unit}}{\text{Selling Price per unit}} \times 100$$

But, Contribution per unit = Selling Price per unit – Variable Cost per unit

∴ $$\text{P/V Ratio} = \frac{\text{Selling Price per unit} - \text{Variable Cost per unit}}{\text{Selling Price per unit}} \times 100$$

$$= \frac{₹\,40 - ₹\,25}{₹\,40} \times 100$$

$$= \frac{₹\,15}{₹\,40} \times 100$$

$$= 37.50\%$$

i)   **BEP (Sales) :** $= \dfrac{\text{Fixed Cost}}{\text{Contribution per unit}} \times \text{Selling Price per unit}$

But, Contribution per unit = Selling Price per unit – Variable Cost per unit

∴   BEP (Sales) $= \dfrac{\text{Fixed Cost}}{\text{Selling Price per unit} - \text{Variable Cost per unit}} \times \text{Selling price per unit}$

$= \dfrac{₹1,80,000}{₹40 - ₹25} \times 40$

$= \dfrac{₹1,80,000}{₹15} \times ₹40$

$= ₹12,000 \text{ units} \times ₹40$

$= ₹4,80,000$

ii) **Number of units to be sold to earn a profit of ₹1,20,000 :**

where, P/V Ratio $= \dfrac{\text{Contribution}}{\text{Sales}}$

But,   Contribution = Fixed Cost + Profit

∴   P/V Ratio $= \dfrac{\text{Fixed Cost + Profit}}{\text{Sales}}$

∴   Sales $= \dfrac{\text{Fixed Cost + Profit}}{37.5\%}$

$= \dfrac{₹1,80,000 + ₹1,20,000}{37.5\%}$

$= ₹3,00,000 \times \dfrac{100}{37.5}$

$= ₹8,00,000$

But,

Number of units to be sold $= \dfrac{\text{Total Sales}}{\text{Selling Price per unit}}$

$= \dfrac{₹8,00,000}{₹40}$

$= 20,000 \text{ units}$

iii) **Number of units to be sold to earn an income of 25% on Sales :**

Let x be the number of units to be sold.

∴ $x = \dfrac{\text{Fixed Cost + Required Profit}}{\text{Contribution per unit}}$

But, Contribution per unit = Selling Price per unit – Variable Cost per unit

∴ $x = \dfrac{\text{Fixed Cost + Required Profit}}{\text{Selling Price per unit} - \text{Variable Cost per unit}}$

∴ $x = \dfrac{₹1,80,000 + 25\%(x \times 40)}{₹40 - ₹25}$

$x = \dfrac{₹1,80,000 + 10x}{15}$

∴ $15x = ₹1,80,000 + 10x$
∴ $15x - 10x = ₹1,80,000$
∴ $5x = ₹1,80,000$

∴ $x = \dfrac{₹1,80,000}{₹5}$

$= 36,000 \text{ units}$

∴   Number of units to be sold to earn an income of 25% of Sales = 36,000 units.

ILLUSTRATION 17

From the following cost data calculate,
i) Break Even Point - units
ii) Number of units to be sold to earn a profit of ₹ 40,000 per year.

	₹
Productive Material per unit	09
Selling on Cost – Rigid	19,700
Prime Cost Labour per unit	07
Administration Expenses – Fixed	24,300
Market Price per unit	32
Distribution Overheads – Constant	13,500
Marginal Production Cost per unit	02
Fixed Works Expenses	42,500
Variable Selling Cost per unit	04

SOLUTION

- **Calculation of Total Fixed Cost** ₹

Selling on Cost – Rigid	19,700
Add : Administration Expenses – Fixed	24,300
Add : Distribution Overheads – Constant	13,500
Add : Fixed Works Expenses	(+) 42,500
∴ Total	**1,00,000**

- **Calculation of Total Variable Cost per unit :** ₹

Productive Materials	09
Add : Prime Cost Labour	07
Add : Marginal Production Cost	02
Add : Variable Selling Cost	(+) 04
∴ Total	**22**

- **Calculation of Contribution per unit :**

where,

Contribution per unit = Selling Price per unit – Variable Cost per unit
= ₹ 32 – ₹ 22
= ₹ 10

i) Break Even Point (units) = $\dfrac{\text{Total Fixed Cost}}{\text{Contribution per unit}}$

= $\dfrac{₹\ 1,00,000}{₹\ 10}$

= Units 10,000

ii) Number of units to be sold to earn a profit of ₹ 40,000.

= $\dfrac{\text{Total Fixed Cost + Desired Profit}}{\text{Contribution per unit}}$

= $\dfrac{₹\ 1,00,000 + ₹\ 40,000}{₹\ 10}$

= $\dfrac{₹\ 1,40,000}{₹\ 10}$

= 14,000 units

ILLUSTRATION 18

From the following cost data, calculate :
i) P/V Ratio, ii) BEP (Sales) and iii) By how much the value of sales must be increased for the company to break even.

	₹
Variable Expenses	3,00,000
Total Sales	4,00,000
Fixed Overheads	1,80,000

SOLUTION

i) P/V Ratio :

$$= \frac{\text{Contribution}}{\text{Sales}} \times 100$$

But,

Contribution = Sales − Variable Cost

$$\therefore \text{P/V Ratio} = \frac{\text{Sales} - \text{Variable Cost}}{\text{Sales}} \times 100$$

$$= \frac{₹ 4,00,000 - ₹ 3,00,000}{₹ 4,00,000} \times 100$$

$$= \frac{₹ 1,00,000}{₹ 4,00,000} \times 100$$

$$= 25\%$$

ii) BEP (Sales) :

$$= \frac{\text{Fixed Cost}}{\text{P/V Ratio}}$$

$$= \frac{₹ 1,80,000}{25\%}$$

$$= ₹ 1,80,000 \times \frac{100}{25}$$

$$= ₹ 7,20,000$$

iii) Margin of Safety = BEP (Sales) − Actual Sales
= ₹ 7,20,000 − ₹ 4,00,000
= ₹ 3,20,000

ILLUSTRATION 19

From the following information, find out :
i) P/V Ratio ii) BEP (Sales) iii) Profit when Sales are ₹ 1,20,000.
iv) Sales required to earn a Profit of ₹ 60,000

	₹
Fixed Cost per unit	40,000
Variable Cost per unit	2
Sales	2,00,000
Selling Price per unit	10

SOLUTION

i) P/V Ratio:

$$= \frac{\text{Contribution per unit}}{\text{Selling Price per unit}} \times 100$$

But,

Contribution per unit = Selling Price per unit − Variable Cost per unit

$$\therefore \quad \text{P/V Ratio} = \frac{\text{Selling Price per unit} - \text{Variable Cost per unit}}{\text{Selling Price per unit}} \times 100$$

$$= \frac{₹10 - ₹2}{₹10} \times 100$$

$$= \frac{₹8}{₹10} \times 100$$

$$= 80\%$$

ii) BEP (Sales):

$$= \frac{\text{Fixed Cost}}{\text{P/V Ratio}}$$

$$= \frac{₹40,000}{80\%}$$

$$= ₹40,000 \times \frac{100}{80}$$

$$= ₹50,000$$

iii) Profit when Sales are ₹ 1,20,000:

where, $\quad$ P/V Ratio $= \dfrac{\text{Contribution}}{\text{Sales}}$

But, $\quad$ Contribution = Fixed Cost + Profit

$\therefore \quad$ P/V Ratio $= \dfrac{\text{Fixed Cost + Profit}}{\text{Sales}}$

$\therefore \quad$ P/V Ratio × Sales = Fixed Cost + Profit

$\therefore \quad$ Profit = (P/V Ratio × Sales) − Fixed Cost

$\therefore \quad \quad \quad = (80\% \times ₹1,20,000) - ₹40,000$

$\quad \quad \quad \quad = ₹96,000 - ₹40,000$

$\quad \quad \quad \quad = ₹56,000$

iv) Sales required to earn a profit of ₹ 60,000:

where, $\quad$ P/V Ratio $= \dfrac{\text{Contribution}}{\text{Sales}}$

But, $\quad$ Contribution = Fixed Cost + Profit

$\therefore \quad$ P/V Ratio $= \dfrac{\text{Fixed Cost + Profit}}{\text{Sales}}$

$\therefore \quad$ Sales $= \dfrac{\text{Fixed Cost + Profit}}{\text{P/V Ratio}}$

$$= \frac{₹40,000 + ₹60,000}{80\%}$$

$$= ₹1,00,000 \times \frac{100}{80}$$

$$= ₹1,25,000$$

ILLUSTRATION 20

The following information is obtained from Godrej Ltd., Gorakhpur for the year ended 31st March, 2014.

	₹
Sales (1,00,000 Units)	1,00,000
Marginal Cost	60,000
Fixed Cost	30,000

Calculate :
i) P/V Ratio,
ii) BEP (Sales-value)
iii) Sales to earn a profit of ₹ 15,000
iv) Profit when sales amounted to ₹ 1,40,000

SOLUTION

i) **P/V Ratio :**

$$= \frac{\text{Contribution}}{\text{Sales}} \times 100$$

But, Contribution = Sales – Variable Cost

$$\therefore \quad \text{P/V Ratio} = \frac{\text{Sales} - \text{Variable Cost}}{\text{Sales}} \times 100$$

$$= \frac{₹\,1,00,000 - ₹\,60,000}{₹\,1,00,000} \times 100$$

$$= \frac{₹\,40,000}{₹\,1,00,000} \times 100$$

$$= 40\%$$

ii) **BEP (Sales-value) :**

$$= \frac{\text{Fixed Cost}}{\text{P/V Ratio}}$$

$$= \frac{₹\,30,000}{40\%}$$

$$= ₹\,30,000 \times \frac{100}{40}$$

$$= ₹\,75,000$$

iii) **Sales to earn a profit of ₹ 15,000 :**

where,

$$\text{P/V Ratio} = \frac{\text{Contribution}}{\text{Sales}}$$

But, Contribution = Fixed Cost + Profit

$$\therefore \quad \text{P/V Ratio} = \frac{\text{Fixed Cost} + \text{Profit}}{\text{Sales}}$$

$$\therefore \quad \text{Sales} = \frac{\text{Fixed Cost} + \text{Profit}}{\text{P/V Ratio}}$$

$$= \frac{₹\,30,000 + ₹\,15,000}{40\%}$$

$$= ₹\,45,000 \times \frac{100}{40}$$

$$= ₹\,1,12,500$$

iv) **Profit when Sales amounted to ₹ 1,40,000 :**
where,

$$\text{P/V Ratio} = \frac{\text{Contribution}}{\text{Sales}}$$

But, Contribution = Fixed Cost + Profit

∴ $\text{P/V Ratio} = \dfrac{\text{Fixed Cost + Profit}}{\text{Sales}}$

∴ P/V Ratio × Sales = Fixed Cost + Profit

∴ Profit = (P/V Ratio × Sales) − Fixed Cost
= (40% × ₹ 1,40,000) − ₹ 30,000
= ₹ 56,000 − ₹ 30,000
= ₹ 26,000

ILLUSTRATION 21

Ashoka Ltd., Aurangabad furnishes you with the following cost data for the year 2013-2014.

Process Material per unit	₹ 3
Sales	10,000 unit
Operating Labour per unit	₹ 3
Fixed Cost	₹ 60,000
Chargeable Expenses per unit	Re. 1
Value of Sales per unit	₹ 25
Variable Overheads – 100% of Direct Labour	

You are requested to find out,
i) P/V Ratio, ii) BEP (Sales), iii) Margin of Safety.

SOLUTION

Calculation of Total Variable Cost per unit :

Particulars	₹
Variable Overheads :	
i) Process Material	3
ii) Operating Labour	3
iii) Chargeable Expenses	1
iv) Variable Overheads (100% of Direct Labour i.e. ₹ 3)	3
∴ **Variable Cost per unit**	**10**

i) **P/V Ratio :**

$$= \frac{\text{Contribution per unit}}{\text{Selling Price per unit}} \times 100$$

But, Contribution per unit = Selling Price per unit − Variable Cost per unit

∴ $\text{P/V Ratio} = \dfrac{\text{Selling Price per unit − Variable Cost per unit}}{\text{Selling Price per unit}} \times 100$

$$= \frac{₹ 25 - ₹ 10}{₹ 25} \times 100$$

$$= \frac{₹ 15}{₹ 25} \times 100$$

$$= 60\%$$

ii) **BEP (Sales):**

$$= \frac{\text{Fixed Cost}}{\text{P/V Ratio}}$$

$$= \frac{₹60,000}{60\%}$$

$$= ₹60,000 \times \frac{100}{60}$$

$$= ₹1,00,000$$

iii) **Margin of Safety:**

= Actual Sales – BEP (Sales)
= (₹25 × 10,000 units) – ₹1,00,000
= ₹2,50,000 – ₹1,00,000
= ₹1,50,000

ILLUSTRATION 22

From the following cost data relating to Force India Ltd., Faizpur you are required to calculate –
i) Sales at Break Even,
ii) Profit at budgeted sales,
iii) Profit, if actual sales be at 80% capacity.

Budgeted Sales for the year 2013-2014 (At 100% Capacity)	₹ 12,00,000
Rigid Cost in total	₹ 1,00,000
Chargeable Expenses	02% of Sales
Variable Manufacturing Overheads	10% of Sales
Administrative and Selling on Cost – Variable	08% of Sales
Direct Materials	35% of Sales
Prime Cost Labour	20% of Sales

SOLUTION

In the books of Force India Ltd., Faizpur
Profitability Statement for the year 2013-2014
(Normal Capacity – 100%)

	Particulars		₹
	Budgeted Sales		12,00,000
Less:	Variable Cost :		
	i) Chargeable Expenses (02% of Sales i.e. ₹ 12,00,000)	24,000	
	ii) Variable Manufacturing Overheads (10% of Sales i.e. ₹ 12,00,000)	1,20,000	
	iii) Administrative and Selling on Cost – Variable (08% of Sales i.e. ₹ 12,00,000)	96,000	
	iv) Direct Materials (35% of Sales i.e. ₹ 12,00,000)	4,20,000	
	v) Prime Cost Labour (20% of Sales i.e. ₹ 12,00,000)	2,40,000 (+)	
		(–)	9,00,000
	∴ Contribution		3,00,000
Less:	Fixed Cost		
	i) Rigid Cost	(–)	1,00,000
	∴ Profit at Budgeted Sales		**2,00,000**

Calculation of P/V Ratio:
where,
$$P/V \text{ Ratio} = \frac{\text{Contribution}}{\text{Sales}} \times 100$$
$$= \frac{₹3,00,000}{₹12,00,000} \times 100$$
$$= 25\%$$

i) Sales at Break Even:
where,
$$\frac{\text{Break Even Point}}{\text{Sales}} = \frac{\text{Fixed Cost}}{\text{P/V Ratio}}$$
$$= \frac{₹1,00,000}{25\%}$$
$$= ₹1,00,000 \times \frac{100}{25}$$
$$= ₹4,00,000$$

ii) Profit at Budgeted Sales:
where,
$$\text{Contribution} = \text{Fixed Cost} + \text{Profit}$$
$$\therefore \text{Profit} = \text{Contribution} - \text{Fixed Cost}$$
$$= ₹3,00,000 - ₹1,00,000$$
$$= ₹2,00,000$$

iii) Profit, if actual sales be at 80% capacity:

- Calculation of Actual Sales at 80% capacity

If 100% Capacity = ₹12,00,000 Actual Sales

∴ 80% Capacity = ?

$$= \frac{80 \times ₹12,00,000}{100}$$
$$= ₹9,60,000$$

- Calculation of profit if Actual Sales are ₹9,60,000

where,
$$P/V \text{ Ratio} = \frac{\text{Contribution}}{\text{Sales}}$$

But,
$$\text{Contribution} = \text{Fixed Cost} + \text{Profit}$$
$$\therefore P/V \text{ Ratio} = \frac{\text{Fixed Cost} + \text{Profit}}{\text{Sales}}$$
$$\therefore P/V \text{ Ratio} \times \text{Sales} = \text{Fixed Cost} + \text{Profit}$$
$$\therefore \text{Profit} = (P/V \text{ Ratio} \times \text{Sales}) - \text{Fixed Cost}$$
$$= (25\% \times ₹9,60,000) - ₹1,00,000$$
$$= ₹2,40,000 - ₹1,00,000$$
$$= ₹1,40,000$$

ILLUSTRATION 23

From the following data calculate,
i) Total Profits ii) BEP (Sales) iii) Margin of Safety
Number of units sold units – 20,000
Fixed Overheads ₹ 50,000
Selling Price per unit ₹ 10
Variable Overheads per unit ₹ 6

SOLUTION

i) Total Profits :

$$\text{Sales} = \text{Total Cost} + \text{Profit}$$

But, Total Cost = Fixed Overheads + Variable Cost

∴ Sales = Fixed Overheads + Variable Cost + Profit

∴ Profits = Sales – (Fixed Overheads + Variable Cost)
= 20,000 units × ₹ 10 – (₹ 50,000 + 20,000 units × ₹ 6)
= ₹ 2,00,000 – (₹ 50,000 + ₹ 1,20,000)
= ₹ 2,00,000 – ₹ 1,70,000
= ₹ 30,000

ii) BEP (Sales) :

$$= \frac{\text{Fixed Cost}}{\text{Contribution per unit}} \times \text{Selling Price per unit}$$

But, Contribution per unit = Selling Price per unit – Variable Cost per unit

∴ BEP (Sales) $= \frac{\text{Fixed Cost}}{\text{Selling Price per unit} - \text{Variable Cost per unit}} \times \text{Selling Price per unit}$

$= \frac{₹ 50,000}{₹ 10 - ₹ 6} \times ₹ 10$

$= \frac{₹ 50,000}{₹ 4} \times ₹ 10$

= ₹ 12,500 × ₹ 10
= ₹ 1,25,000

iii) Margin of Safety :

= Actual Sales – BEP (Sales)
= (20,000 units × ₹ 10) – ₹ 1,25,000
= ₹ 2,00,000 – ₹ 1,25,000
= ₹ 75,000

ILLUSTRATION 24

You are given the following cost data :
Total Sales ₹ 4,00,000
Total Variable Cost ₹ 2,00,000
Total Fixed Cost ₹ 1,00,000
Total Units sold Units 1,00,000

Calculate,
i) Contribution per unit ii) BEP – units and sales
iii) Margin of Safety iv) Profit
v) Units to be sold to earn a profit of ₹ 1,40,000

SOLUTION

i) Contribution per unit:

where,

$$\text{Contribution} = \text{Sales} - \text{Variable Cost}$$
$$= ₹4,00,000 - ₹2,00,000$$
$$= ₹2,00,000$$

But,

Contribution per unit:

$$= \frac{\text{Total Contribution}}{\text{Total units sold}}$$
$$= \frac{₹2,00,000}{1,00,000 \text{ units}}$$
$$= ₹2 \text{ per unit}$$

ii) BEP (units):

$$= \frac{\text{Total Fixed Cost}}{\text{Contribution per unit}}$$
$$= \frac{₹1,00,000}{₹2}$$
$$= 50,000 \text{ units}$$

Calculation of Selling price per unit:

$$\frac{\text{Total Sales}}{\text{Total units sold}} = \frac{₹4,00,000}{1,00,000 \text{ units}}$$
$$= ₹4 \text{ per unit}$$

BEP (Sales):

$$= \frac{\text{Total Fixed Cost}}{\text{Contribution per unit}} \times \text{Selling Price per unit}$$
$$= \frac{₹1,00,000}{₹2} \times ₹4$$
$$= 50,000 \text{ units} \times ₹4$$
$$= ₹2,00,000.$$

iii) Margin of Safety:

$$= \text{Actual Sales} - \text{BEP (Sales)}$$
$$= ₹4,00,000 - ₹2,00,000$$
$$= ₹2,00,000$$

iv) Profit:

where, Contribution = Fixed Cost + Profit
∴ Profit = Contribution − Fixed Cost
$$= ₹2,00,000 - ₹1,00,000$$
$$= ₹1,00,000$$

v) Units to be sold to earn a profit of ₹1,40,000:

Sales volume to earn required profit (units):

$$= \frac{\text{Total Fixed Cost} + \text{Required Profit}}{\text{Contribution per unit}}$$
$$= \frac{₹1,00,000 + ₹1,40,000}{₹2}$$
$$= \frac{₹2,40,000}{₹2}$$
$$= 1,20,000 \text{ units}$$

ILLUSTRATION 25

Kiddy Toy's Manufacturing Co., Kanpur provides the following costing data :

	% of Sales	₹
Marginal Cost	80%	8,00,000
Fixed Cost	10%	1,00,000
Profit	10%	1,00,000
Sales	100%	10,00,000

You are required to calculate :
i) P/V Ratio ii) BEP (Sales) iii) Margin of Safety iv) Margin of Safety Ratio

SOLUTION

i) P/V Ratio :

$$= \frac{\text{Contribution}}{\text{Sales}} \times 100$$

But, Contribution = Sales − Variable Cost

$$\therefore \text{P/V Ratio} = \frac{\text{Sales} - \text{Variable Cost}}{\text{Sales}} \times 100$$

$$= \frac{₹\,10,00,000 - ₹\,8,00,000}{₹\,10,00,000} \times 100$$

$$= \frac{₹\,2,00,000}{₹\,10,00,000} \times 100$$

$$= 20\%$$

ii) BEP (Sales) :

$$= \frac{\text{Fixed Cost}}{\text{P/V Ratio}}$$

$$= \frac{₹\,1,00,000}{20\%}$$

$$= ₹\,1,00,000 \times \frac{100}{20}$$

$$= ₹\,5,00,000$$

iii) Margin of Safety :

$$= \frac{\text{Profit}}{\text{P/V Ratio}}$$

$$= \frac{₹\,1,00,000}{20\%}$$

$$= ₹\,1,00,000 \times \frac{100}{20}$$

$$= ₹\,5,00,000$$

iv) Margin of Safety Ratio :

$$= \frac{\text{Actual Sales} - \text{BEP (Sales)}}{\text{Actual Sales}} \times 100$$

$$= \frac{₹\,10,00,000 - ₹\,5,00,000}{₹\,10,00,000} \times 100$$

$$= \frac{₹\,5,00,000}{₹\,10,00,000} \times 100$$

$$= 50\%$$

ILLUSTRATION 26

Following is the cost structure of a product Gemini of 2013-2014 in Cable India Ltd., Cochin.

Particulars		Unit Cost ₹
Direct Material		100
Add : Productive Wages	(+)	80
Add : Variable Overheads	(+)	20
Total Variable Overheads		200
Add : Fixed Cost	(+)	40
Total Cost		240
Add : Profit	(+)	60
Sales		300

Company produced and sold 5,000 units.
You are required to calculate,
i)   P/V Ratio
ii) BEP (Sales)
iii) Margin of Safety
iv) Profit when Sales are ₹ 30,00,000
v)   Sales when Profit are ₹ 1,00,000

SOLUTION

i) P/V Ratio :

$$= \frac{\text{Contribution per unit}}{\text{Selling Price per unit}} \times 100$$

But,

Contribution per unit = Selling Price per unit − Variable Cost per unit

$$\therefore \text{P/V Ratio} = \frac{\text{Selling Price per unit} - \text{Variable Cost per unit}}{\text{Selling Price per unit}} \times 100$$

$$= \frac{₹300 - ₹200}{₹300} \times 100$$

$$= \frac{₹100}{₹300} \times 100$$

$$= 33\,1/3\%$$

ii) BEP (Sales) :

$$= \frac{\text{Total Fixed Cost}}{\text{P/V Ratio}}$$

$$= \frac{₹40 \times 5{,}000 \text{ units}}{33\,1/3\%}$$

$$= \frac{₹2{,}00{,}000}{1/3}$$

$$= ₹2{,}00{,}000 \times \frac{3}{1}$$

$$= ₹6{,}00{,}000$$

iii) Margin of Safety :

= Actual Sales − BEP (Sales)
= (₹ 300 × 5,000 units) − ₹ 6,00,000
= ₹ 15,00,000 − ₹ 6,00,000
= ₹ 9,00,000

Management Accounting   5.53   Marginal Costing

iv) **Profit when Sales are ₹ 3,00,000 :**

where,   P/V Ratio $= \dfrac{\text{Contribution}}{\text{Sales}}$

But,   Contribution = Fixed Cost + Profit

∴   P/V Ratio $= \dfrac{\text{Fixed Cost + Profit}}{\text{Sales}}$

∴   P/V Ratio × Sales = Fixed Cost + Profit

∴   Profit = (P/V Ratio × Sales) − Fixed Cost

       = 33 $^1/_3$% × ₹ 30,00,000 − (₹ 40 × 5,000 units)

       = ₹ 10,00,000 − ₹ 2,00,000

       = ₹ 8,00,000

v) **Sales when Profit are ₹ 1,00,000 :**

where,   P/V Ratio $= \dfrac{\text{Contribution}}{\text{Sales}}$

But,

   Contribution = Fixed Cost + Profit

∴   P/V Ratio $= \dfrac{\text{Fixed Cost + Profit}}{\text{Sales}}$

∴   Sales $= \dfrac{\text{Fixed Cost + Profit}}{\text{P/V Ratio}}$

       $= \dfrac{(₹\,40 \times 5,000 \text{ units}) + ₹\,1,00,000}{33\,^1/_3\%}$

       $= \dfrac{₹\,2,00,000 + ₹\,1,00,000}{1/3}$

       $= ₹\,3,00,000 \times \dfrac{3}{1}$

       = ₹ 9,00,000

ILLUSTRATION 27

Bajaj Industries Ltd., Badalapur provides the following cost data :

	₹
Sales	1,50,000
Marginal Cost	1,20,000
Gross Profit	60,000
Fixed Overheads	20,000
Net Profit	40,000

You are required to calculate,
i)   P/V Ratio
ii)   BEP (Sales)
iii) Margin of Safety when Sales are ₹ 4,00,000
iv) Net Profit when Sales are ₹ 4,00,000
v)   Sales required to earn a profit of ₹ 80,000.

SOLUTION

i) **P/ V Ratio :**

$= \dfrac{\text{Contribution}}{\text{Sales}} \times 100$

But, Contribution = Sales − Variable Cost

$$\therefore \text{P/V Ratio} = \frac{\text{Sales} - \text{Variable Cost}}{\text{Sales}} \times 100$$

$$= \frac{₹1,50,000 - ₹1,20,000}{₹1,50,000} \times 100$$

$$= \frac{₹30,000}{₹1,50,000} \times 100$$

$$= 20\%$$

ii) **BEP (Sales):**

$$= \frac{\text{Fixed Cost}}{\text{P/V Ratio}}$$

$$= \frac{₹20,000}{20\%}$$

$$= ₹20,000 \times \frac{100}{20}$$

$$= ₹1,00,000$$

iii) **Margin of Safety when Sales are ₹4,00,000:**

Margin of Safety = Actual Sales − BEP (Sales)
 = ₹4,00,000 − ₹1,00,000
 = ₹3,00,000

iv) **Net Profit when Sales are ₹4,00,000:**

where,

$$\text{P/V Ratio} = \frac{\text{Contribution}}{\text{Sales}}$$

But,

Contribution = Fixed Cost + Profit

$$\therefore \text{P/V Ratio} = \frac{\text{Fixed Cost} + \text{Profit}}{\text{Sales}}$$

∴ P/V Ratio × Sales = Fixed Cost + Profit
∴ Profit = (P/V Ratio × Sales) − Fixed Cost
 = (20% × ₹4,00,000) − ₹20,000
 = ₹80,000 − ₹20,000
 = ₹60,000

v) **Sales required to earn a Profit of ₹80,000:**

where,

$$\text{P/V Ratio} = \frac{\text{Contribution}}{\text{Sales}}$$

But, Contribution = Fixed Cost + Profit

$$\therefore \text{P/V Ratio} = \frac{\text{Fixed Cost} + \text{Profit}}{\text{Sales}}$$

$$\therefore \text{Sales} = \frac{\text{Fixed Cost} + \text{Profit}}{\text{P/V Ratio}}$$

$$= \frac{₹20,000 + ₹80,000}{20\%}$$

$$= ₹1,00,000 \times \frac{100}{20}$$

$$= ₹5,00,000$$

ILLUSTRATION 28

Calculate,
i) P/V Ratio, if a company has fixed expenses of ₹ 90,000 with Sales at ₹ 3,00,000 and a profit of ₹ 60,000.
ii) BEP (Sales), if budgeted output is 80,000 units, fixed cost is ₹ 4,00,000, Selling price per unit is ₹ 20 and Variable cost per unit is ₹ 10.
iii) Sales, if Marginal Cost is ₹ 2,400 and P/V Ratio is 20%.
iv) Margin of Safety if profit is ₹ 20,000 and P/V Ratio is 40%.

SOLUTION

i) P/V Ratio :

$$= \frac{\text{Contribution}}{\text{Sales}} \times 100$$

But, Contribution = Fixed Cost + Profit

$$\therefore \text{P/V Ratio} = \frac{\text{Fixed Cost + Profit}}{\text{Sales}} \times 100$$

$$= \frac{₹\,90{,}000 + ₹\,60{,}000}{₹\,3{,}00{,}000} \times 100$$

$$= \frac{₹\,1{,}50{,}000}{₹\,3{,}00{,}000} \times 100$$

$$= 50\%$$

ii) BEP (Sales) :

$$= \frac{\text{Fixed Cost}}{\text{Contribution per unit}} \times \text{Selling Price per unit}$$

But,
Contribution per unit = Selling Price per unit − Variable Cost per unit

$$\therefore \text{BEP (Sales)} = \frac{\text{Fixed Cost}}{\text{Selling Price per unit} - \text{Variable Cost per unit}} \times \frac{\text{Selling Price}}{\text{per unit}}$$

$$= \frac{₹\,4{,}00{,}000}{₹\,20 - ₹\,10} \times ₹\,20$$

$$= \frac{₹\,4{,}00{,}000}{₹\,10} \times ₹\,20$$

$$= 40{,}000 \text{ units} \times ₹\,20$$

$$= ₹\,8{,}00{,}000$$

iii) Sales :

$$= \frac{\text{Marginal Cost}}{\text{Marginal Cost Ratio}}$$

But,
Marginal Cost Ratio = 100 − (P/V Ratio)

$$\therefore \text{Sales} = \frac{\text{Marginal Cost}}{100 - \text{P/V Ratio}}$$

$$= \frac{₹\,2{,}400}{100\% - 20\%}$$

$$= \frac{₹\,2{,}400}{80\%}$$

$$= ₹\,2{,}400 \times \frac{100}{80}$$

$$= ₹\,3{,}000$$

iv) Margin of Safety :

$$= \frac{\text{Profit}}{\text{P/V Ratio}}$$

$$= \frac{₹\,20{,}000}{40\%}$$

$$= ₹\,20{,}000 \times \frac{100}{40}$$

$$= ₹\,50{,}000$$

ILLUSTRATION 29

i) From the following compute the sales volume in units that will yield a profit of ₹ 25,000.

	₹
Selling Price per unit	15
Variable Cost per unit	10
Fixed Cost	25,000

ii) From the following information compute the sales in value to earn a profit of ₹ 2,40,000.

	₹
Sales	12,00,000
Variable Cost	7,50,000
Fixed Cost	3,60,000

SOLUTION

i) **Sales volume to earn the required profit in units :**

$$= \frac{\text{Fixed Cost} + \text{Required Profit}}{\text{Contribution per unit}}$$

But,

Contribution per unit = Selling Price per unit − Variable Cost per unit

∴ **Sales volume in units :**

$$= \frac{\text{Fixed Cost} + \text{Required Profit}}{\text{Selling Price per unit} - \text{Variable Cost per unit}}$$

$$= \frac{₹\,25{,}000 + ₹\,25{,}000}{₹\,15 - ₹\,10}$$

$$= \frac{₹\,50{,}000}{₹\,5}$$

$$= 10{,}000 \text{ units}$$

ii) **Sales volume to earn the required profit in value :**

$$= \frac{(\text{Fixed Cost} + \text{Required Profit}) \times \text{Sales}}{\text{Contribution}}$$

But, Contribution = Sales − Variable Cost

∴ **Sales volume in value :**

$$= \frac{(\text{Fixed Cost} + \text{Required Profit}) \times \text{Sales}}{\text{Sales} - \text{Variable Cost}}$$

$$= \frac{(₹\,3{,}60{,}000 + ₹\,2{,}40{,}000) \times ₹\,12{,}00{,}000}{₹\,12{,}00{,}000 - ₹\,7{,}50{,}000}$$

$$= \frac{₹\,6{,}00{,}000 - ₹\,12{,}00{,}000}{₹\,4{,}50{,}000}$$

$$= ₹\,16{,}00{,}000$$

Management Accounting   5.57   Marginal Costing

ILLUSTRATION 30

From the following particulars calculate :
i) Variable Cost per unit
ii) Total Profit

Sales	Units 16,000
Selling price per unit	₹ 90
Break Even Point	Units 3,000
Fixed Cost	₹ 1,80,000

SOLUTION

Calculation of Contribution per unit :

where,

$$\text{BEP (units)} = \frac{\text{Total Fixed Cost}}{\text{Contribution per unit}}$$

$$\therefore \text{Contribution per unit} = \frac{\text{Total Fixed Cost}}{\text{BEP Units}}$$

$$= \frac{₹ 1,80,000}{3,000 \text{ Units}}$$

$$= ₹ 60 \text{ per unit}$$

i) Variable cost per unit :

where,

Contribution per unit = Selling Price per unit − Variable Cost per unit

∴ Variable cost per unit = Selling Price per unit − Contribution per unit
= ₹ 90 − ₹ 60
= ₹ 30 per unit

ii) Total Profit :

where,

Total Contribution = Total Fixed Cost + Total Profit

∴ Total Profit = Total Contribution − Total Fixed Cost
= (₹ 60 × 16,000 Units) − ₹ 1,80,000
= ₹ 9,60,000 − ₹ 1,80,000
= ₹ 7,80,000

ILLUSTRATION 31

Mobilink Co., Malad has fixed overheads of ₹ 90,000 with a turnover of ₹ 3,00,000 and a profit of ₹ 60,000 during the first half year. If in the next half year they suffered a loss of ₹ 30,000, calculate :

i) P/V Ratio, BEP (Sales) and Margin of Safety for the first half year.
ii) Expected sales volume for the next half year assuming that selling price and fixed cost remain unchanged.
iii) BEP (Sales) and Margin of Safety for the whole year.

SOLUTION

(a) i) P/V Ratio :

$$= \frac{\text{Contribution}}{\text{Sales}} \times 100$$

But,

$$\text{Contribution} = \text{Fixed Cost} + \text{Profit}$$

∴ $\text{P/V Ratio} = \dfrac{\text{Fixed Cost} + \text{Profit}}{\text{Sales}} \times 100$

$= \dfrac{₹\,90{,}000 + ₹\,60{,}000}{₹\,3{,}00{,}000} \times 100$

$= \dfrac{₹\,1{,}50{,}000}{₹\,3{,}00{,}000} \times 100$

$= 50\%$

ii) **BEP (Sales)** :

$= \dfrac{\text{Fixed Cost}}{\text{P/V Ratio}}$

$= \dfrac{₹\,90{,}000}{50\%}$

$= ₹\,90{,}000 \times \dfrac{100}{50}$

$= ₹\,1{,}80{,}000$

iii) **Margin of Safety** :

$= \text{Actual Sales} - \text{BEP (Sales)}$

$= ₹\,3{,}00{,}000 - ₹\,1{,}80{,}000$

$= ₹\,1{,}20{,}000$

(b) **Expected sales volume for the next half year :**

where,

$\text{P/V Ratio} = \dfrac{\text{Contribution}}{\text{Sales}}$

But, $\text{Contribution} = \text{Fixed Cost} - \text{Loss}$

∴ $\text{P/V Ratio} = \dfrac{\text{Fixed Cost} - \text{Loss}}{\text{Sales}}$

∴ $\text{Sales} = \dfrac{\text{Fixed Cost} - \text{Loss}}{\text{P/V Ratio}}$

$= \dfrac{₹\,90{,}000 - ₹\,30{,}000}{50\%}$

$= ₹\,60{,}000 \times \dfrac{100}{50}$

$= ₹\,1{,}20{,}000$

(c) i) **BEP (Sales)** For The Whole Year :

$= \dfrac{\text{Fixed Cost for the whole year}}{\text{P/V Ratio}}$

$= \dfrac{₹\,90{,}000 + ₹\,90{,}000}{50\%}$

$= ₹\,1{,}80{,}000 \times \dfrac{100}{50}$

$= ₹\,3{,}60{,}000$

ii) **Margin of Safety :**

$$= \text{Actual Sales} - \text{BEP (Sales)}$$
$$= (₹\,3{,}00{,}000 + ₹\,1{,}20{,}000) - ₹\,3{,}60{,}000$$
$$= ₹\,4{,}20{,}000 - ₹\,3{,}60{,}000$$
$$= ₹\,60{,}000$$

ILLUSTRATION 32

Roadstar Co. Ltd., Rajapur furnished you the following information relating to half year ended 31st March, 2014.

	₹
Fixed Cost	45,000
Sales Value	1,50,000
Profit	30,000

During the second half of the year the company has projected a loss of ₹ 10,000.

Calculate,

i) Variable Cost, for the 1st half year.
ii) P/V Ratio, for the 1st half year.
iii) BEP (Sales), for the 1st half year.
iv) Margin of Safety, for the 1st half year.
v) Expected Sales Volume for the 2nd half year assuming that the P/V Ratio and Fixed Cost remains constant in the 2nd half year also.

SOLUTION

i) **Variable cost, for the 1st half year :**

where,
$$\text{Sales} = \text{Total Cost} + \text{Profit}$$

But,
$$\text{Total Cost} = \text{Fixed Costs} + \text{Variable Cost}$$
$$\therefore \text{Sales} = \text{Fixed Cost} + \text{Variable Cost} + \text{Profit}$$
$$\therefore \text{Variable Cost} = \text{Sales} - (\text{Fixed Cost} + \text{Profit})$$
$$= ₹\,1{,}50{,}000 - (₹\,45{,}000 + ₹\,30{,}000)$$
$$= ₹\,1{,}50{,}000 - ₹\,75{,}000$$
$$= ₹\,75{,}000$$

ii) **P/V Ratio, for the 1st half year :**

$$\text{P/V Ratio} = \frac{\text{Contribution}}{\text{Sales}} \times 100$$

But, Contribution = Fixed Cost + Profit

$$\therefore \text{P/V Ratio} = \frac{\text{Fixed Cost} + \text{Profit}}{\text{Sales}} \times 100$$
$$= \frac{₹\,45{,}000 + ₹\,30{,}000}{₹\,1{,}50{,}000} \times 100$$
$$= \frac{₹\,75{,}000}{₹\,1{,}50{,}000} \times 100$$
$$= 50\%$$

iii) **BEP (Sales), for the 1st half year :**

$$\text{BEP (Sales)} = \frac{\text{Fixed Cost}}{\text{P/V Ratio}}$$

$$= \frac{₹\,45{,}000}{50\%}$$

$$= ₹\,45{,}000 \times \frac{100}{50}$$

$$= ₹\,90{,}000$$

iv) **Margin of Safety, for the 1st half year:**

    Margin of Safety = Actual Sales − BEP (Sales)
                          = ₹ 1,50,000 − ₹ 90,000
                          = ₹ 60,000

v) **Expected sales volume for the 2nd half year assuming that the P/V Ratio and Fixed Cost remains constant in the 2nd half year also:**

where,   P/V Ratio $= \dfrac{\text{Contribution}}{\text{Sales}}$

But, Contribution = Fixed Cost − Loss

∴   P/V Ratio $= \dfrac{\text{Fixed Cost} - \text{Loss}}{\text{Sales}}$

∴   Sales $= \dfrac{\text{Fixed Cost} - \text{Loss}}{\text{P/V Ratio}}$

$$= \frac{₹\,45{,}000 - ₹\,10{,}000}{50\%}$$

$$= ₹\,35{,}000 \times \frac{100}{50}$$

$$= ₹\,70{,}000$$

ILLUSTRATION 33

Ravalgaon Ltd., Rahuri shows the turnover and profits for the two periods as below:

Period	Turnover ₹	Profit ₹
I	10,00,000	1,00,000
II	12,00,000	1,40,000

You are required to calculate,
i)   P/V Ratio
ii)   Sales required to earn a profit of ₹ 3,00,000.

SOLUTION

I) **P/V Ratio:**

$$= \frac{\text{Change in Profits}}{\text{Change in Sales}} \times 100$$

$$= \frac{₹\,1{,}40{,}000 - ₹\,1{,}00{,}000}{₹\,12{,}00{,}000 - ₹\,10{,}00{,}000} \times 100$$

$$= \frac{₹\,40{,}000}{₹\,2{,}00{,}000} \times 100$$

$$= 20\%$$

Calculation of Fixed Cost:

Here, P/V Ratio i.e. Contribution Margin is 20% which means Variable Cost will be 80% of Sales.

Management Accounting   5.61   Marginal Costing

∴ Sales − Variable Cost = Fixed Cost + Profit
∴   Fixed Cost = (Sales − Variable Cost) − Profit

Period I :
= (₹ 10,00,000 − 80% of ₹ 10,00,000) − ₹ 1,00,000
= (₹ 10,00,000 − ₹ 8,00,000) − ₹ 1,00,000
= ₹ 2,00,000 − ₹ 1,00,000
= ₹ 1,00,000

Period II :
= (₹ 12,00,000 − 80% of ₹ 12,00,000) − ₹ 1,40,000
= (₹ 12,00,000 − ₹ 9,60,000) − ₹ 1,40,000
= ₹ 2,40,000 − ₹ 1,40,000
= ₹ 1,00,000

ii) **Sales required to earn a profit of ₹ 3,00,000 :**

$$\text{P/V Ratio} = \frac{\text{Contribution}}{\text{Sales}}$$

But,
Contribution = Fixed Cost + Profit

$$\therefore \text{P/V Ratio} = \frac{\text{Fixed Cost + Profit}}{\text{Sales}}$$

$$\therefore \text{Sales} = \frac{\text{Fixed Cost + Profit}}{\text{P/V Ratio}}$$

$$= \frac{₹ 1,00,000 + ₹ 3,00,000}{20\%}$$

$$= ₹ 4,00,000 \times \frac{100}{20}$$

= ₹ 20,00,000

ILLUSTRATION 34

The sales and profits during the last two years of Ashoka Ltd., Ajmer were as follows :

Year	Sales ₹	Profits ₹
2012-13	15,00,000	2,00,000
2013-14	17,00,000	2,50,000

Annual fixed cost is ₹ 1,75,000. You are required to calculate,
i) P/V Ratio
ii) BEP (Sales)
iii) The profits made when Sales are ₹ 25,00,000
iv) The sales required to earn a profit of ₹ 4,00,000.

SOLUTION

i) **P/V Ratio :**

$$= \frac{\text{Change in Profits}}{\text{Change in Sales}} \times 100$$

$$= \frac{₹ 2,50,000 - ₹ 2,00,000}{₹ 17,00,000 - ₹ 15,00,000} \times 100$$

$$= \frac{₹\,50,000}{₹\,2,00,000} \times 100$$

$$= 25\%$$

ii) BEP (Sales):

$$= \frac{\text{Fixed Cost}}{\text{P/V Ratio}}$$

$$= \frac{₹\,1,75,000}{25\%}$$

$$= ₹\,1,75,000 \times \frac{100}{25}$$

$$= ₹\,7,00,000$$

iii) The profits made when sales are ₹ 25,00,000

where,

$$\text{P/V Ratio} = \frac{\text{Contribution}}{\text{Sales}}$$

But,

Contribution = Fixed Cost + Profit

∴ $\text{P/V Ratio} = \dfrac{\text{Fixed Cost + Profit}}{\text{Sales}}$

∴ P/V Ratio × Sales = Fixed Cost + Profit

∴ Profit = (P/V Ratio × Sales) − Fixed Cost

$$= (25\% \times ₹\,25,00,000) - ₹\,1,75,000$$

$$= ₹\,6,25,000 - ₹\,1,75,000$$

$$= ₹\,4,50,000$$

iv) The sales required to earn a profit of ₹ 4,00,000 :

where,

$$\text{P/V Ratio} = \frac{\text{Contribution}}{\text{Sales}}$$

But,

Contribution = Fixed Cost + Profit

∴ $\text{P/V Ratio} = \dfrac{\text{Fixed Cost + Profit}}{\text{Sales}}$

∴ $\text{Sales} = \dfrac{\text{Fixed Cost + Profit}}{\text{P/V Ratio}}$

$$= \frac{₹\,1,75,000 + ₹\,4,00,000}{25\%}$$

$$= ₹\,5,75,000 \times \frac{100}{25}$$

$$= ₹\,23,00,000$$

ILLUSTRATION 35

From the following comparative cost data of Joel India Ltd., Jabalpur for 2013 and 2014 you are required to find out : i) P/V Ratio, ii) Break Even Point, Sales Value and iii) Margin of Safety, separately.

Particulars	2013 ₹	2014 ₹
Rigid Expenses	4,000	4,000
Direct Materials	22,000	30,000
Cash Sales	10,000	15,000
Productive Wages	10,000	12,000
Credit Sales	50,000	75,000
Prime Cost Expenses	4,000	3,000
Indirect Costs – Fixed	11,000	14,000

SOLUTION

In the books of Joel India Ltd.
Profitability Statement for the period ended ......

Particulars		2013 ₹	2014 ₹
Sales : Cash + Credit		60,000	90,000
2008 : ₹ 10,000 + ₹ 50,000			
2009 : ₹ 15,000 + ₹ 75,000			
Less : Variable Cost			
i) Direct Materials		22,000	30,000
ii) Productive Wages		10,000	12,000
iii) Prime Cost Expenses	(–)	4,000	3,000
∴ Contribution		24,000	45,000
Less : Fixed Cost			
i) Rigid Expenses		4,000	4,000
ii) Indirect Costs – Fixed	(–)	11,000	14,000
∴ **Net Profit**		9,000	27,000

i) **Profit Volume Ratio :**

$$= \frac{\text{Contribution}}{\text{Sales}} \times 100$$

$$2013 = \frac{₹ 24,000}{₹ 60,000} \times 100$$

$$= 40\%$$

$$2014 = \frac{₹ 45,000}{₹ 90,000} \times 100$$

$$= 50\%$$

ii) **Break Even Point, Sales Value :**

$$= \frac{\text{Fixed Cost}}{\text{P/V Ratio}}$$

2013 $= \dfrac{₹\,15{,}000}{40\%}$

$= ₹\,37{,}500$

2014 $= \dfrac{₹\,18{,}000}{50\%}$

$= ₹\,36{,}000$

iii) **Margin of Safety :**

$$= \frac{\text{Profit}}{\text{P/V Ratio}}$$

2013 $= \dfrac{₹\,9{,}000}{40\%}$

$= ₹\,22{,}500$

20014 $= \dfrac{₹\,27{,}000}{50\%}$

$= ₹\,54{,}000$

ILLUSTRATION 36

The Sales (units) and Profit/Loss during the last two periods Cola-Cola Ltd., Gujrath were as follows :

Period	Sales Units	Profit/Loss ₹
I	7,000	10,000 (Loss)
II	9,000	10,000 (Profit)

The selling price per unit was ₹ 100. Calculate,
i) Fixed Cost
ii) BEP (Sales)
iii) The number of units to be sold to earn a profit of ₹ 40,000
iv) The amount of profits when Sales are ₹ 20,000 units.

SOLUTION

The additional Sales of ₹ 2,00,000 in Period II (2,000 units × ₹ 100) has given an additional contribution of ₹ 20,000 (i.e. change in profits ₹ 20,000), which has wiped off the loss of ₹ 10,000 of Period I and gave a profit of ₹ 10,000 for Period II.

i) **Fixed Cost :**
- **Calculation of P/V Ratio**

$$= \frac{\text{Change in Profits}}{\text{Change in Sales}} \times 100$$

$$= \frac{₹\,10{,}000\,(P) - ₹\,10{,}000\,(L)}{₹\,9{,}00{,}000 - ₹\,7{,}00{,}000} \times 100$$

$$= \frac{₹\,20{,}000}{₹\,2{,}00{,}000} \times 100$$

$$= 10\%$$

- **Calculation of Contribution of Period I**
  Contribution = Sales × P/V Ratio
  = ₹ 7,00,000 × 10%
  = ₹ 70,000
- **Calculation of Fixed Cost of Period I**
  where, Contribution = Fixed Cost − Loss
  ∴ Fixed Cost = Contribution + Loss
  = ₹ 70,000 + ₹ 10,000
  = ₹ 80,000

ii) **BEP (Sales):**
$$= \frac{\text{Fixed Cost}}{\text{P/V Ratio}}$$
$$= \frac{₹\,80,000}{10\%}$$
$$= ₹\,80,000 \times \frac{100}{10}$$
$$= ₹\,8,00,000$$

iii) **The number of units to be sold to earn a profit of ₹ 40,000:**
where, $\text{P/V Ratio} = \dfrac{\text{Contribution}}{\text{Sales}}$

But, Contribution = Fixed Cost + Profit

∴ $\text{P/V Ratio} = \dfrac{\text{Fixed Cost + Profit}}{\text{Sales}}$

∴ $\text{Sales} = \dfrac{\text{Fixed Cost + Profit}}{\text{P/V Ratio}}$
$$= \frac{₹\,80,000 + ₹\,40,000}{10\%}$$
$$= \frac{₹\,1,20,000}{10\%}$$
$$= ₹\,1,20,000 \times \frac{100}{10}$$
$$= ₹\,12,00,000$$

$\text{Sales Units} = \dfrac{\text{Total Sales}}{\text{Selling Price per unit}}$
$$= \frac{₹\,12,00,000}{₹\,100}$$
= 12,000 units

iv) **The amount of profits when Sales are 20,000 units (i.e. 20,000 units × ₹ 100 = ₹ 20,00,000)**
where,
$\text{P/V Ratio} = \dfrac{\text{Contribution}}{\text{Sales}}$

But,
Contribution = Fixed Cost + Profit

∴ $\text{P/V Ratio} = \dfrac{\text{Fixed Cost + Profit}}{\text{Sales}}$

∴ P/V Ratio × Sales = Fixed Cost + Profit

∴ Profit = (P/V Ratio × Sales) – Fixed Cost
= (10% × ₹ 20,00,000) – ₹ 80,000
∴ = ₹ 2,00,000 – ₹ 80,000
= ₹ 1,20,000

ILLUSTRATION 37

The turnover and profits of Komex Ltd., Kanpur during the two periods were as follows :

	Turnover ₹ in Lakh	Profit ₹ in Lakh
Period – I	40	4
Period – II	60	8

Assuming that the cost structure and selling prices remains the same in the two periods. Calculate :

i) P/V Ratio, ii) BEP (Sales), iii) The sales required to earn a profit of ₹ 10 lakhs, iv) Margin of Safety in Period – II, v) Profit when Sales are ₹ 50 Lakhs.

SOLUTION

i) P/V Ratio :

$$= \frac{\text{Change in Profits}}{\text{Change in Sales}} \times 100$$

$$= \frac{₹\,8,00,000 - ₹\,4,00,000}{₹\,60,00,000 - ₹\,40,00,000} \times 100$$

$$= \frac{₹\,4,00,000}{₹\,20,00,000} \times 100$$

$$= 20\%$$

ii) BEP (Sales) :

- **Calculation of Contribution –**

Contribution = P/V Ratio × Sales
= 20% × ₹ 60,00,000
= ₹ 12,00,000

- **Calculation of Fixed Cost –**

where, Contribution = Fixed Cost + Profit
∴ Fixed Cost = Contribution – Profit
= ₹ 12,00,000 – ₹ 8,00,000
= ₹ 4,00,000

- **Calculation of BEP (Sales) –**

$$= \frac{\text{Fixed Cost}}{\text{P/V Ratio}}$$

$$= \frac{₹\,4,00,000}{20\%}$$

$$= ₹\,4,00,000 \times \frac{100}{20}$$

$$= ₹\,20,00,000$$

iii) The sales required to earn a profit of ₹ 10,00,000 :

where, P/V Ratio = $\frac{\text{Contribution}}{\text{Sales}}$

But, Contribution = Fixed Cost + Profit

∴ P/V Ratio = $\dfrac{\text{Fixed Cost + Profit}}{\text{Sales}}$

∴ Sales = $\dfrac{\text{Fixed Cost + Profit}}{\text{P/V Ratio}}$

= $\dfrac{₹\,4,00,000 + ₹\,10,00,000}{20\%}$

= ₹ 14,00,000 × $\dfrac{100}{20}$

= ₹ 70,00,000

iv) **Margin of Safety in Period – II :**

Margin of Safety = Actual Sales – BEP (Sales)
= ₹ 60,00,000 – ₹ 20,00,000
= ₹ 40,00,000

v) **Profit when Sales are ₹ 50,00,000 :**

where, P/V Ratio = $\dfrac{\text{Contribution}}{\text{Sales}}$

But, Contribution = Fixed Cost + Profit

∴ P/V Ratio = $\dfrac{\text{Fixed Cost + Profit}}{\text{Sales}}$

∴ P/V Ratio × Sales = Fixed Cost + Profit

∴ Profit = (P/V Ratio × Sales) – Fixed Cost
= (20% × ₹ 50,00,000) – ₹ 4,00,000
= ₹ 10,00,000 – ₹ 4,00,000
= ₹ 6,00,000

ILLUSTRATION 38

In Ness Co. Nashik the sales and profits for the two periods are as given below :

Period	Sales ₹	Profit ₹
I	1,00,000	9,000
II	1,20,000	13,000

You are required to calculate,
i) P/V Ratio
ii) BEP (Sales)
iii) Profits when Sales are ₹ 1,50,000
iv) Sales required to earn a profit of ₹ 50,000
v) Margin of Safety in Period – II
vi) Variable Cost for both the period.

SOLUTION

i) **P/V Ratio :**

= $\dfrac{\text{Change in Profits}}{\text{Change in Sales}} \times 100$

= $\dfrac{₹\,13,000 - ₹\,9,000}{₹\,1,20,000 - ₹\,1,00,000} \times 100$

= $\dfrac{₹\,4,000}{₹\,20,000} \times 100$

= 20%

ii) **BEP (Sales):**

$$= \frac{\text{Fixed Cost}}{\text{P/V Ratio}}$$

$$= \frac{₹11,000}{20\%}$$

$$= ₹11,000 \times \frac{100}{20}$$

$$= ₹55,000$$

iii) **Profits when Sales are ₹ 1,50,000:**

where, P/V Ratio = $\frac{\text{Contribution}}{\text{Sales}}$

But, Contribution = Fixed Cost + Profit

∴ P/V Ratio = $\frac{\text{Fixed Cost + Profit}}{\text{Sales}}$

P/V Ratio × Sales = Fixed Cost + Profit

∴ Profit = (P/V Ratio × Sales) − Fixed Cost
= (20% × ₹ 1,50,000) − ₹ 11,000
= ₹ 30,000 − ₹ 11,000
= ₹ 19,000

iv) **Sales required to earn a profit of ₹ 50,000:**

where, P/V Ratio = $\frac{\text{Contribution}}{\text{Sales}}$

But, Contribution = Fixed Cost + Profit

∴ P/V Ratio = $\frac{\text{Fixed Cost + Profit}}{\text{Sales}}$

∴ Sales = $\frac{\text{Fixed Cost + Profit}}{\text{P/V Ratio}}$

$$= \frac{₹11,000 + ₹50,000}{20\%}$$

$$= ₹61,000 \times \frac{100}{20}$$

$$= ₹3,05,000$$

v) **Margin of Safety in Period II:**

Margin of Safety = Actual Sales − BEP (Sales)
= ₹ 1,20,000 − ₹ 55,000
= ₹ 65,000

vi) **Variable Cost for both the period:**

Here, P/V Ratio i.e. Contribution Margin is 20% which means Variable Cost will be 80% of Sales.

Hence,

Variable Cost = 80% of Sales

Period I: 80% of ₹ 1,00,000 = ₹ 80,000

Period II: 80% of ₹ 1,20,000 = ₹ 96,000

ILLUSTRATION 39

From the following cost-details find out –

i) Break Even Point (units).

ii) The Turnover required to earn a profit of ₹ 36,000.

iii) The available Margin of Safety, if the company is earning a profit of ₹ 36,000.

	₹
Market Price per unit	20
Variable Cost per unit – 10% of Selling Price	
Fixed Cost	1,80,000

SOLUTION

- Calculation of Contribution per unit

  $\therefore$ Contribution per unit = Selling Price per unit – Variable Cost per unit

  = ₹ 20 – ₹ 2 (10% of ₹ 20)

  = ₹ 18

- Calculation of P/V Ratio

  $\therefore$ P/V Ratio = $\dfrac{\text{Contribution per unit}}{\text{Selling Price per unit}} \times 100$

  = $\dfrac{₹ 18}{₹ 20} \times 100$

  = 90%

i) Break Even Point (Units) :

= $\dfrac{\text{Fixed Cost}}{\text{Contribution per unit}}$

= $\dfrac{₹ 1,80,000}{₹ 18}$

= 10,000 units

ii) Turnover required to earn a profit of ₹ 36,000.

P/V Ratio = $\dfrac{\text{Contribution}}{\text{Sales}}$

But, Contribution = Fixed Cost + Profit

$\therefore$ P/V Ratio = $\dfrac{\text{Fixed Cost + Profit}}{\text{Sales}}$

$\therefore$ Sales = $\dfrac{\text{Fixed Cost + Profit}}{\text{P/V Ratio}}$

= $\dfrac{₹ 1,80,000 + ₹ 36,000}{90\%}$

= $\dfrac{₹ 2,16,000}{90\%}$

= ₹ 2,40,000

iii) **The available Margin of Safety, if the company is earning a profit of ₹ 36,000.**

$$\text{Margin of Safety} = \text{Actual Sales} - \text{Break Even Sales}$$
$$= ₹ 2,40,000 - ₹ 2,00,000 \ (10,000 \text{ units} \times ₹ 20)$$
$$= ₹ 40,000$$

OR

$$\text{Margin of Safety} = \frac{\text{Net Profit}}{\text{P/V Ratio}}$$
$$= \frac{₹ 36,000}{90\%}$$
$$= ₹ 40,000$$

ILLUSTRATION 40

Anil Bajaj has invested ₹ 2,00,000 into his business and expects at least 15% return on the same. The cost analysis shows that his yearly fixed costs are ₹ 80,000 and the marginal costs are 60% of the turnover.

You are required to find out –

i) the sales volume that must be obtained to break even.

ii) the sales volume that must be obtained to get 15% return on investment.

Anil Bajaj estimates that even if he closed his business he has to incur yearly expenses of ₹ 25,000. What sales would he be better off by locking up his business ?

SOLUTION

Let us assume that Anil Bajaj has total sales of ₹ 100.

- **Calculation of Contribution :**

$$\text{Contribution per unit} = \text{Selling Price per unit} - \text{Variable Cost per unit}$$
$$= ₹ 100 - ₹ 60 \ (60\% \text{ of turnover i.e. } ₹ 100)$$
$$= ₹ 40$$

- **Calculation of P/V Ratio :**

$$\text{P/V Ratio} = \frac{\text{Contribution per unit}}{\text{Selling Price per unit}} \times 100$$
$$= \frac{₹ 40}{₹ 100} \times 100$$
$$= 40\%$$

i) **The Sales Volume to break even**

$$\text{BEP (Sales Volume)} = \frac{\text{Fixed Cost}}{\text{P/V Ratio}}$$
$$= \frac{₹ 80,000}{40\%}$$
$$= ₹ 2,00,000$$

ii) **The Sales Volume to obtain to get 15% return on investment.** ₹

15% Return on Investment of ₹ 2,00,000   30,000

Add : Fixed Cost   (+) 80,000

∴ Contribution required will be   1,10,000

$$\text{Sales Volume Required} = \frac{\text{Contribution required}}{\text{P/V Ratio}}$$

$$= \frac{₹ 1,10,000}{40\%}$$

$$= ₹ 2,75,000$$

iii) **Minimum Sales required to meet yearly Fixed Cost of ₹ 25,000.**

$$\text{Minimum Sales Required} = \frac{\text{Fixed Cost}}{\text{P/V Ratio}}$$

$$= \frac{₹ 25,000}{40\%}$$

$$= ₹ 62,500.$$

ILLUSTRATION 41

From the following cost data, calculate the Break-Even Point expressed in terms of units and also the new BEP, if the inflated price decreases by 10% and increases by 30%.

Depreciation on Plant and Machinery	₹ 87,900
Raw Materials	₹ 3 per unit
Salaries to Administrative Staff	₹ 91,800
Direct Labour	₹ 1.60 per unit
Rent of Sales Depot	₹ 20,300
Productive Expenses	Re. 0.40 per unit
Selling Price	₹ 10 per unit

SOLUTION

- **Calculation of Total Fixed Cost**   ₹

  Depreciation on Plant and Machinery   87,900

  Add : Salaries to Administrative Staff   91,800

  Add : Rent of Sales Depot   (+) 20,300

      ∴ Total   2,00,000

- **Calculation of Total Variable Cost per unit**   ₹

  Raw Materials   3.00

  Add : Direct Labour   1.60

  Add : Productive Expenses   (+) 0.40

      ∴ Total   5.00

i) Break-Even Point (Units):

$$= \frac{\text{Fixed Cost}}{\text{Contribution per unit}}$$

But,

Contribution per unit = Selling Price per unit − Variable Cost per unit

= ₹ 10 − ₹ 5

= ₹ 5

∴ Break-Even Point (units) = $\frac{₹ 2,00,000}{₹ 5}$

= 40,000 units

ii) BEP (units), if Inflated Price i.e. Selling Price decreases by 10%:

| Original Selling Price per unit ₹ 10 | (−) | Decrease by 10% Re. 1 | = | New Selling Price per unit ₹ 9 |

Break-Even Point (units) = $\frac{\text{Fixed Cost}}{\text{Contribution per unit}}$

But,

Contribution per unit = Selling Price per unit − Variable Cost per unit

= ₹ 9 − ₹ 5

= ₹ 4

∴ Break-Even Point (units) = $\frac{₹ 2,00,000}{₹ 4}$

= 50,000 units

iii) BEP (units) if Inflated Price i.e. Selling Price increases by 30%:

| Original Selling Price per unit ₹ 10 | (+) | Increase by 30% ₹ 3 | = | New Selling Price per unit ₹ 13 |

Break-Even Point (units) = $\frac{\text{Fixed Cost}}{\text{Contribution per unit}}$

But,

Contribution per unit = Selling Price per unit − Variable Cost per unit

= ₹ 13 − ₹ 5

= ₹ 8

Break-Even Point (units) = $\frac{₹ 2,00,000}{₹ 8}$

= ₹ 25,000 units

Management Accounting 5.73 Marginal Costing

ILLUSTRATION 42

The budget forecast of Adwani Ltd., Akola is as follows :

Particulars	Constant ₹	Marginal ₹	Total ₹
Estimated Turnover @ ₹ 25 per unit			50,00,000
Less : Budgeted Costs			
i) Raw Materials		12,00,000	
ii) Prime Cost Labour		6,00,000	
iii) Productive Expenses		1,00,000	
iv) Manufacturing Overheads	10,20,000	3,40,000	
v) Management Overheads	6,80,000	2,70,000	
vi) Selling and Distribution Overheads (+)	1,00,000	90,000	
Total	18,00,000	26,00,000	(−) 44,00,000
∴ Forecasted Profit			6,00,000

Determine the Break-Even Point in units and in value in the following situations separately if,
a) a 10% increase is effected in fixed costs.
b) a 10% decrease is effected in variable costs.
c) a 10% increase is effected in sales price which will result in reduction in units sold by 5%.
d) a 10% increase in fixed costs and 5% decrease in variable cost is effected.

SOLUTION

- **Calculation of Budgeted Sales units :**

$$= \frac{\text{Total Sales}}{\text{Selling Price per unit}}$$

$$= \frac{₹\,50,00,000}{₹\,25}$$

= 2,00,000 units

Statement showing Computation of BEP(units) and BEP (value) under different situations

	Particulars	Situations			
		(a) 10% increase in Fixed Costs	(b) 10% increase in Variable Costs	(c) 10% increase in Sales Price and 5% reduction in Sales Volume	(d) 10% increase in Fixed Costs and 5% decrease in Variable Costs
1)	Selling Price per unit	25.00	25.00	27.50 (10% increase)	25.00
2)	Variable Cost per unit (₹ 26,00,000/2,00,000 units)	13.00	14.30 (10% increase)	13.00	12.35 (5% decrease)
3)	Contribution per unit (3 = 1 − 2)	12.00	10.70	14.50	12.65
4)	Fixed Costs	19,80,000 (10% increase)	18,00,000	18,00,000	19,80,000 (10% increase)
5)	Break-Even Point (units) (4 ÷ 3)	1,65,000	1,68,224	1,24,138	1,56,522
6)	Break-Even Point (value) (5 × 1)	41,25,000	42,05,600	34,13,795	39,13,050

ILLUSTRATION 43

Caterpillar Co. Ltd., Cochin manufacturers a small machine the cost structure of which is as under :

Direct Materials	₹ 50
Prime Cost Labour	₹ 80

Variable Production Overheads : 60% of Labour Cost

Variable Administration Overheads : 15% of Labour Cost

Yearly Fixed Overheads of the company amounted to ₹ 2,40,000 and the invoice price of the machine is ₹ 230 each.

You are required to find out the number of machines to be manufactured and sold

a) in a year in order to break even.

b) to make a profit of ₹ 1,00,000 per year.

c) to break even if the selling price is reduced by ₹ 15 each.

SOLUTION

- **Calculation of Total Variable Cost per unit**

	₹
Direct Material	50
Add : Prime Cost Labour	80
Add : Variable Production Overheads	48
(60% of Labour Cost i.e. ₹ 80)	
Add : Variable Administration Overheads	12
(15% of Labour Cost i.e. ₹ 80) (+)	
∴ Total	190

- **Calculation of Contribution per unit :**

Contribution per unit = Selling Price per unit − Variable Cost per unit

= ₹ 230 − ₹ 190

= ₹ 40

a) Number of machines to be manufactured and sold in a year in order to break even.

$$\text{BEP (units)} = \frac{\text{Total Fixed Cost}}{\text{Contribution per unit}}$$

$$= \frac{₹\ 2,40,000}{₹\ 40}$$

= 6,000 machines.

b) Number of machines to be manufactured and sold to make a profit of ₹ 1,00,000 per year.

$$= \frac{\text{Total Fixed Cost + Desired Profit}}{\text{Contribution per unit}}$$

$$= \frac{₹ 2,40,000 + ₹ 1,00,000}{₹ 40}$$

$$= \frac{₹ 3,40,000}{₹ 40}$$

= 8,500 machines.

c) Number of machines to be manufactured and sold to break even if the selling price is reduced by ₹ 15 each.

- **Calculation of New Selling Price :**

$$\underset{₹ 230}{\text{Old Selling Price}} \; (-) \; \underset{₹ 15}{\text{Reduction by}} = \underset{₹ 215}{\text{New Selling Price}}$$

- **Calculation of Revised Contribution :**

Contribution per unit = Selling Price per unit − Variable Cost per unit

= ₹ 215 − ₹ 190

= ₹ 25

$$\text{BEP (Units)} = \frac{\text{Total Fixed Cost}}{\text{Contribution per unit}}$$

$$= \frac{₹ 2,40,000}{₹ 25}$$

= 9,600 machines.

ILLUSTRATION 44

The results of Kingfisher Ltd., Kalyan for the two periods revealed the following :

Year	Value of Sales ₹	Cost of Sales ₹
2013	40,00,000	44,00,000
2014	60,00,000	56,00,000

Calculate, a) P/V Ratio, b) Fixed Cost, c) Break-Even Sales, d) Sales required to earn a profit of ₹ 10,00,000, e) Sales required to earn a profit of 20% on sales.

SOLUTION

Calculation of profit or loss for the two periods :

Year	Value of Sales ₹	Cost of Sales ₹	Profit/Loss ₹
2013	40,00,000	44,00,000	4,00,000 (Loss)
2014	60,00,000	56,00,000	4,00,000 (Profit)

Thus, additional sales of ₹ 20,00,000 in the year 2014 has given an additional contribution of ₹ 8,00,000 (i.e. change in profits ₹ 8,00,000), which has wiped off the loss of ₹ 4,00,000 of the year 2010 and resulted in a profit of ₹ 4,00,000 for the year 2014.

a) $$\text{P/V Ratio} = \frac{\text{Change in Profits}}{\text{Change in Sales}} \times 100$$

$$= \frac{₹\,4,00,000\,(P) - ₹\,4,00,000\,(L)}{₹\,60,00,000 - ₹\,40,00,000} \times 100$$

$$= \frac{₹\,8,00,000}{₹\,20,00,000} \times 100$$

$$= 40\%$$

- **Calculation of Contribution :**

   Contribution = Sales × P/V Ratio

   2013 = ₹ 40,00,000 × 40%

   = ₹ 16,00,000

   2014 = ₹ 60,00,000 × 40%

   = ₹ 24,00,000

b) **Fixed Cost :**

   Contribution = Fixed Cost ± Profit/Loss

   2013 : Contribution = Fixed Cost − Loss

   ∴ Fixed Cost = Contribution + Loss

   = ₹ 16,00,000 + ₹ 4,00,000

   = ₹ 2,00,000

   2014 : Contribution = Fixed Cost + Profit

   ∴ Fixed Cost = Contribution − Profit

   = ₹ 24,00,000 − ₹ 4,00,000

   = ₹ 20,00,000

Thus, Fixed Cost remains constant at ₹ 20,00,000 for both the years.

c) **Break Even Sales :**

$$\text{Break Even Sales} = \frac{\text{Fixed Cost}}{\text{P/V Ratio}}$$

$$= \frac{₹\,20,00,000}{40\%}$$

$$= ₹\,50,00,000$$

d) **Sales required to earn a profit of ₹ 10,00,000 :**

$$\text{P/V Ratio} = \frac{\text{Contribution}}{\text{Sales}}$$

But, Contribution = Fixed Cost + Profit

∴ $$\text{P/V Ratio} = \frac{\text{Fixed Cost + Profit}}{\text{Sales}}$$

∴ $$\text{Sales} = \frac{\text{Fixed Cost + Profit}}{\text{P/V Ratio}}$$

Management Accounting 5.77 Marginal Costing

$$= \frac{₹20,00,000 + ₹10,00,000}{40\%}$$

$$= \frac{₹30,00,000}{40\%}$$

$$= ₹75,00,000$$

e) **Sales required to earn a profit of 20% on Sales :**

$$P/V \text{ Ratio} = \frac{\text{Contribution}}{\text{Sales}}$$

But, Contribution = Fixed Cost + Profit

∴ $$P/V \text{ Ratio} = \frac{\text{Fixed Cost + Profit}}{\text{Sales}}$$

∴ $$\text{Sales} = \frac{\text{Fixed Cost + Profit}}{P/V \text{ Ratio}}$$

$$\text{Sales} = \frac{₹20,00,000 + 20\% \text{ of Sales}}{40\%}$$

$$\text{Sales} = \frac{₹20,00,000 + 0.2 \text{ Sales}}{0.4}$$

∴ 0.4 Sales = ₹20,00,000 + 0.2 Sales

∴ 0.4 Sales − 0.2 Sales = ₹20,00,000

∴ 0.2 Sales = ₹20,00,000

∴ $$\text{Sales} = \frac{₹20,00,000}{0.2}$$

$$= ₹20,00,000 \times \frac{10}{2}$$

$$= ₹1,00,00,000$$

ILLUSTRATION 45

Doxy Ltd., Delhi manufactures and sells four types of products under the brand names A, B, C and D. The sales mix in total value comprises 33.33%, 41.67%, 16.67% and 8.33% of A, B, C and D respectively. The total estimated monthly turnover at 100% is ₹ 60,000. The operating costs for the same are as follows :

i) Rigid costs : ₹ 14,700 per month.

ii) Marginal Costs : (Percentage on market price)

- Products   :   A   B   C   D
- Percentage :   60   68   80   40

You are required to calculate the Break-Even Point (Sales Value) for the products on overall basis.

SOLUTION

Statement showing Profit on Overall Basis

Particulars	Products Amount	A ₹	B ₹	C ₹	D ₹	Total ₹
Sales		20,000	25,000	10,000	5,000	60,000
A – 33.33% of ₹ 60,000						
B – 41.67% of ₹ 60,000						
C – ₹ 16.67% of ₹ 60,000						
D – 8.33% of ₹ 60,000						
Less : Variable Costs		12,000	17,000	8,000	2,000	39,000
A – 60% of ₹ 20,000						
B – 68% of ₹ 25,000						
C – 80% of ₹ 10,000						
D – 40% of ₹ 5,000	(–)					
∴ Contribution		8,000	8,000	2,000	3,000	21,000
Less : Fixed Costs	(–)				(–)	14,700
∴ **Profit**						**6,300**

- **Calculation of P/V Ratio :**

  $= \dfrac{\text{Contribution}}{\text{Sales}} \times 100$

  $= \dfrac{₹ 21,000}{₹ 60,000} \times 100$

  $= 35\%$

- **Calculation of Break-Even Point (Sales Value) :**

  $= \dfrac{\text{Fixed Cost}}{\text{P/V Ratio}}$

  $= \dfrac{₹ 14,700}{35\%}$

  $= ₹ 42,000$

ILLUSTRATION 46

Godrej Steel Ltd., Gangapur makes an average profit of ₹ 1.25 per steel glass on a selling price of ₹ 16 per glass by producing 60,000 glasses or 60% of the potential capacity, its cost of sales per glass is,

	₹
Direct Materials	5.00
Direct Labour	1.65
Manufacturing Overheads (50% Variable)	5.00
Administration Overheads (75% Fixed)	0.40

During the current year, it intends to produce the same number, but anticipates that his fixed costs will increase by 10% whereas rates of direct labour and direct materials will increase by 3% and 6% respectively. There is no scope for increasing the selling price due to keen competition under this situation. It obtains from Air India an offer for a further 20% of the capacity. What minimum price per glass would be quoted to Air India to ensure that it earns an overall profit of ₹ 2,47,200 ?

SOLUTION

Statement showing Contribution under Present and Revised Situation

Present Situation		Revised Situation	
Particulars	₹	Particulars	₹
Selling Price	16.00	Selling Price	16.00
Less : Variable Cost		**Less :** Variable Cost	
i) Direct Materials 5.00		i) Direct Materials 5.30	
		₹ 5 + (6% of ₹ 5	
		i.e. Re. 0.30)	
ii) Direct Labour 1.65		ii) Direct Labour 1.70	
		₹ 1.65 + (3% of	
		₹ 1.65 i.e. Re. 0.05)	
iii) Manufacturing Overheads		iii) Manufacturing Overheads	
(V – 50% of ₹ 5) 2.50		(V – 50% of ₹ 5) 2.50	
iv) Administration Overheads		iv) Administration Overheads	
(V – 25% of Re. 0.40) 0.10	9.25	(V – 25% of Re. 0.40) 0.10	9.60
(–)		(–)	
∴ **Contribution per unit**	**6.75**	∴ **Contribution per unit**	**6.40**

- Calculation of Fixed Cost under present situation ₹
  - i) Manufacturing Overheads   1,50,000
    F) 50% of ₹ 5 = ₹ 2.50 × 60,000 units
  - ii) Administration Overheads   18,000
    F) 75% of Re. 0.40 = Re. 0.30 × 60,000 units   (+) _____
          ∴ Total   1,68,000

- Calculation of Profit under present situation :
  (C = F + P ∴ P = C – F)

  Profit = Total Contribution – Total Fixed Cost
  = (60,000 units × ₹ 6.75) – ₹ 1,68,000
  = ₹ 4,05,000 – ₹ 1,68,000
  = ₹ 2,37,000

- **Calculation of Fixed Cost under revised situation :**

  Total Fixed Cost ₹ 1,68,000 (+) Increase by 10% ₹ 16,800 = Revised Fixed Cost ₹ 1,84,800

- **Calculation of Contribution required to earn an overall profit of ₹ 2,47,200.**

  Contribution Required = Revised Fixed Cost ₹ 1,84,800 (+) Desired Profits ₹ 2,47,200

  = ₹ 4,32,000

- **Calculation of Contribution required per unit**

  $= \dfrac{\text{Contribution required}}{\text{Units to be produced}}$

  $= \dfrac{₹ 4,32,000}{60\% \text{ of Potential Capacity i.e. 60,000 units} \;(+)\; \text{Further 20\% of Capacity i.e. 20,000 units}}$

  $= \dfrac{₹ 4,32,000}{80,000 \text{ units}}$

  = ₹ 5.40 per unit

Hence,

Minimum Price per glass to be quoted

= Contribution required per unit (+) Variable Cost under revised situation per unit

= ₹ 5.40 + ₹ 9.60

= ₹ 15

ILLUSTRATION 47

Ajantha Chemicals Ltd., Amalner produces two products viz. Cee and Dee. The company has the following three alternative choices of product mix.

(a) 200 units of Cee and 400 units of Dee.

(b) 300 units of Cee and 300 units of Dee.

(c) 400 units of Cee and 200 units of Dee.

The cost data made available is as follows :

Particulars	Product Cee ₹	Product Dee ₹
Market Price per unit	400	300
Total Fixed Cost	16,000	16,000
Marginal Cost per unit	320	240

State which alternative sales mix you would recommend to the management as the best profitable mix.

SOLUTION

- **Calculation of Contribution per unit of product.**

    where,

    Contribution = Selling Price per unit − Variable Cost per unit

    ∴   Product Cee = ₹ 400 − ₹ 320

                           = ₹ 80

    ∴   Product Dee = ₹ 300 − ₹ 240

                           = ₹ 60

In the Books of Ajantha Chemicals Ltd., Amalner

Statement showing Comparative Profitability of Alternative Sales Mix for the period ended ...

Particulars		Alternative Sales Mix Proposals		
where, C = F + P ∴ P = (C − F)		(a) Cee + Dee 200 + 400 ₹	(b) Cee + Dee 300 + 300 ₹	(c) Cee + Dee 400 + 200 ₹
Contribution		40,000	42,000	44,000
(a) Cee : 200 units × ₹ 80 =	₹ 16,000			
Dee : 400 units × ₹ 60 =	₹ <u>24,000</u>			
(b) Cee : 300 units × ₹ 80 =	₹ 24,000			
Dee : 300 units × ₹ 60 =	₹ <u>18,000</u>			
(c) Cee : 400 units × ₹ 80 =	₹ 32,000			
Dee : 200 units × ₹ 60 =	₹ <u>12,000</u>			
Less : Fixed Cost		16,000	16,000	16,000
	(−)			
∴ Profit		24,000	26,000	28,000

Recommendation :

Out of the three different alternative choices of product mix given in the budget for the next period, alternative sales mix proposals (c) i.e. producing 400 units of Cee and 200 units of Dee is more desirable to adopt since it,

    i)   generates maximum contribution of ₹ 44,000 and

    ii)   yields highest profit of ₹ 28,000,

as compared to other proposals, hence proposal (c) should be recommended very strongly to the management, as it is the most profitable one.

ILLUSTRATION 48

Disha Manufacturing Co., Dombivali produces two different kinds of products AC and BC, the limiting factor is the availability of labour. From the following cost details for 2010 show which product is more profitable.

Particulars		Product AC per unit ₹	Product BC per unit ₹
Direct Materials		5.00	5.00
Add : Productive Labour		3.00	1.50
• AC : 6 Hours @ Re. 0.50			
• BC : 3 Hours @ Re. 0.50			
Add : Overheads			
• Fixed (50% of Direct Labour)		1.50	0.75
• Variable	(+)	1.50	1.50
∴ Total Cost		11.00	8.75
Add : Profit	(+)	3.00	2.25
∴ Selling Price		14.00	11.00
Total Monthly Production	Units	500	600

Maximum Monthly Capacity   Hrs. 4,800
Maximum Capacity of Product BC   Units 1,000

SOLUTION

In the books of Disha Manufacturing Co., Dombivali

Statement showing Contribution per unit

Particulars		Product AC ₹	Product BC ₹
Selling Price		14.00	11.00
Less : Variable Cost			
i) Direct Materials		5.00	5.00
ii) Productive Labour		3.00	1.50
iii) Variable Overheads	(−)	1.50	1.50
∴ Contribution per unit		4.50	3.00

Since availability of labour is a limiting factor, contribution per labour hour is very necessary to find out the more profitable product.

$$\text{Contribution per hour} = \frac{\text{Contribution per unit}}{\text{Time required to produce one unit}}$$

Product AC = ₹4.50 / 6 Hours = ₹0.75

Product BC = ₹3.00 / 3 Hours = ₹1.00

Management Accounting 5.83 Marginal Costing

Comment :

As contribution per labour hour of Product BC (i.e. ₹ 1 per labour hour) is more than Product AC (i.e. ₹ 0.75 per labour hour), Product BC is more profitable. As the maximum capacity of Product BC is 1,000 units, it will require 3,000 labour hours (i.e. 1,000 units × 3 hours per unit) which means remaining 1,800 labour hours (i.e. Maximum capacity 4,800 Hours – Time require to produce product BC 3,000 Hours) can be utilise the to produce product AC conveniently.

ILLUSTRATION 49

The cost accounts of Jindal Ltd., Jaipur are expected to reveal a profit of ₹ 14,00,000 after charging costs of ₹ 10,00,00 for the year ended 31st March, 2014. The selling price of the product is ₹ 50 per unit and the marginal cost per unit is ₹ 20. Market investigations suggest the following responses to the price changes.

Alternatives	Selling Price decreases by %	Quantity sold increased by %
A	5	10
B	7	20
C	10	25

Evaluate these alternatives and state which of the alternatives, on profitability consideration, should be adopted for the forthcoming year.

SOLUTION

- **Calculation of Present Quantity sold**

i) **Total Contribution**

$$\text{Contribution} = \text{Fixed Cost} + \text{Profit}$$
$$= ₹ 10,00,000 + ₹ 14,00,000$$
$$= ₹ 24,00,000.$$

ii) **Unit Contribution :**

$$\text{Contribution per unit} = \text{Selling price per unit} - \text{Variable Cost per unit}$$
$$= ₹ 50 - ₹ 20$$
$$= ₹ 30$$

iii) **Quantity Sold**

$$= \frac{\text{Total Contribution}}{\text{Contribution per unit}}$$
$$= \frac{₹ 24,00,000}{₹ 30}$$
$$= 80,000 \text{ units}$$

In the books of Jindal Ltd., Jaipur
Profitability Statement for the period ended ...

Particulars		Alternatives		
		A	B	C
Selling Price	₹	47.50	46.50	45.00
A) ₹ 50 – (i.e. 5% of ₹ 50) ₹ 2.50				
B) ₹ 50 – (i.e. 7% of ₹ 50) ₹ 3.50				
C) ₹ 50 – (i.e. 10% of ₹ 50) ₹ 5.00				
Less : Variable Cost (@ ₹ 20 per unit) ₹		20.00	20.00	20.00
	(–)			
∴ **Contribution per unit**	₹	27.50	26.50	25.00
Quantities Sold	Units	88,000	96,000	1,00,000
A) 80,000 units + (i.e. 10% of 80,000) 8,000 units				
B) 80,000 units + (i.e. 20% of 80,000) 16,000 units				
C) 80,000 units + (i.e. 25% of 80,000) 20,000 units				
∴ **Total Contribution**	₹	24,20,000	25,44,000	25,00,000
= Quantities Sold × Contribution per unit				
A) 88,000 units × ₹ 27.50				
B) 96,000 units × ₹ 26.50				
C) 1,00,000 units × ₹ 25.00				
Less : Fixed Cost	₹ (–)	10,00,000	10,00,000	10,00,000
∴ **Profit**		14,20,000	15,44,000	15,00,000

Comment :

On profitability consideration, alternative B should be adopted for the forthcoming year, as total contribution and the profit is the highest one as compared to alternative A and C.

ILLUSTRATION 50

Atlas Machine Ltd., Aurangabad produces small machines with a invoice price at ₹ 400 per machine. The cost data to manufacture the same are as follows :

	₹
Prime Cost Materials	140
Direct Labour Cost	30
Productive Expenses	10
Variable Works Overheads	35
Marginal Office Overheads	05
Yearly Fixed Overheads	5,00,000

Variable Selling Overheads – 30% on market price.

The company was producing 10,000 units as current production. However, they had the capacity to produce 1,000 units more without any additional rigid overheads. A suggestion to increase production by 1,000 units but at a selling price of ₹ 320 per unit and half the variable selling overheads for this transaction is under consideration. As a management accountant of the company do you recommend this change ?

Prepare a statement of profitability to be submitted to the board of directors with specific recommendations based on the statement.

SOLUTION

In the books of Atlas Machines Ltd., Aurangabad

Profitability Statement for the period ended ......

Particulars		Present Production	Additional Production	Total Production
Sales Volume	Units	10,000	1,000	11,000
Selling Price per unit	₹	400	320	–
		₹	₹	₹
Sales		40,00,000	3,20,000	43,20,000
Less : Variable Cost				
i) Prime Cost Materials @ ₹ 140		14,00,000	1,40,000	15,40,000
ii) Direct Labour Cost @ ₹ 30		3,00,000	30,000	3,30,000
iii) Productive Expenses @ ₹ 10		1,00,000	10,000	1,10,000
iv) Variable Works Overheads @ ₹ 35		3,50,000	35,000	3,85,000
v) Marginal Office Overheads @ ₹ 5		50,000	5,000	55,000
vi) Variable Selling Overheads				
• Present Production : 30% of ₹ 40,00,000		12,00,000	48,000	12,48,000
• Additional Production : 15% of ₹ 3,20,000	(+)			
∴ **Total Variable Cost**	(–)	34,00,000	2,68,000	36,68,000
∴ Contribution		6,00,000	52,000	6,52,000
Less : Fixed Cost	(–)	5,00,000	–	5,00,000
∴ **Profits**		1,00,000	52,000	1,52,000

Comments :

The proposal to increase the production by 1,000 units will have the corresponding effect of increasing the profits by ₹ 52,000, since there is no increase in fixed overheads. Hence, as a management accountant of the company it should be strongly recommended to the board of directors that the proposal may be accepted, provided this does not create any depressing trend in prices, in the existing market.

QUESTIONS FOR SELF-STUDY

I. Theory Questions :

1) Define the concept of 'Marginal Cost' and 'Marginal Costing'. State the important characteristics of Marginal Costing.
2) What is 'Marginal Costing' ? Explain the objectives of Marginal Costing.
3) State the advantages and limitations of Marginal Costing.
4) Explain Marginal Costing as a technique of costing.
5) Explain the following concepts :
   a) Fixed Cost, b) Variable Cost, c) Marginal Cost, d) Contribution, e) Profit Volume Ratio.

6) Explain the technique of Marginal Costing and state its importance in decision-making.
7) How are variable costs and fixed costs treated in Marginal Costing ?
8) Define the term 'Marginal Costing'. Explain the practical uses of Marginal Costing.
9) State the utility of Marginal Costing in price fixation during trade depression and for export promotion.
10) In what circumstances would you recommend the management to make use of Marginal Costing ?
11) What is 'Contribution' ? How does it differ from 'Profit' ?
12) What do you understand by P/V Ratio ? Discuss the importance of P/V Ratio. How can P/V Ratio can be improved ?
13) What is Break-Even Analysis ? State the assumptions of Break-Even Analysis.
14) State the advantages and limitations of Break-Even Analysis.
15) What is Break-Even Point ? Explain the importance of Break-Even Point.
16) Explain the concept of 'Break-Even Point'. What factors influence Break-Even Point ?
17) "Limitations of Break-Even Charts arise from the assumptions involved in preparing such charts". Discuss.
18) What is Break-Even Chart ? State the important purposes of constructing Break-Even Chart.
19) Discuss the importance of the following in relation to Marginal Costing :
   i) Break-Even Point, ii) Contribution, iii) P/V Ratio.
20) Write short notes on :
   a) Marginal Cost, b) Fixed Cost, c) Marginal Costing, d) Variable Cost, e) Contribution, f) Profit Volume Ratio, g) Break-Even Analysis, h) Break-Even Point, i) Objectives of Marginal Costing, j) Limitations of Marginal Costing, k) Advantages of Marginal Costing, l) Importance of Profit Volume Ratio, m) Limitations of Break-Even Analysis, n) Importance of Break-Even Point.
21) Differentiate between :
   a) Fixed Cost and Variable Cost, (b) Contribution and Profit.

II. Practical Problems :

1) The following are the budgeted cost data of Atlas Co. Ltd., Ahmedabad.

	₹
Total Turnover	6,00,000
Marginal Costs	3,00,000
Fixed Costs	1,50,000

Find out the Break-Even Point at i) the budgeted data and ii) 20% increase in variable cost.

2) The turnover and profits during the two periods were as follows :

Period	Sales ₹	Profit ₹
One	40,00,000	4,00,000
Two	60,00,000	8,00,000

Assuming that the cost structure and selling price remains the same in the two periods. Calculate – i) Profit-Volume Ratio, ii) Break-Even Point (Sales Value), iii) The sales required to earn a profit of ₹ 10,00,000, iv) Margin of Safety in period two, v) Profit when Sales are ₹ 50,00,000.

3) From the following cost data calculate – i) Fixed Cost, ii) Break-Even Point, iii) The number of units to be sold to earn a profit of ₹ 40,000.

The selling price is ₹ 100 per unit.

Period	Sales (Units)	Profit/Loss ₹
One	7,000	Loss – 10,000
Two	9,000	Profit - 10,000

4) From the following find out, i) P/V Ratio, ii) Break-Even Point, iii) Net Profit if the sales were ₹ 2,50,000, iv) Sales to earn a profit of ₹ 70,000.

Particulars		₹
Value of Turnover		2,00,000
Less :Variable Cost	(–)	1,20,000
∴ Contribution		80,000
Less :Fixed Cost	(–)	20,000
∴ Profit		60,000

5) Morgan Ltd., Mahim has prepared the following budget estimates for the year 2008-09.

               Sales – 20,000 units
          Sales Value – ₹ 2,00,000
   Variable Cost per unit – ₹ 5
           Fixed Cost – ₹ 20,000.

You are required to calculate –

a)   P/V Ratio, Break-Even Point and Margin of Safety in each of the following cases.
    i)   Decrease of 10% in selling price.
    ii)   Increase of 10% in variable cost.

6) Calculate the Break-Even point in the following cases :

          Sales (estimated) – ₹ 5,00,000
               Fixed Costs – ₹ 2,00,000
   Variable Cost per unit – ₹ 10
   Selling Price per unit – ₹ 50

7) Amol Industries, Ajmer supply you with the following information :

               Sales – ₹ 2,00,000
           Fixed Cost – ₹ 1,00,000
         Variable Cost – ₹ 1,30,000

Find out the increase in sales required to break-even.

8) Chaby Ltd., Chalisgaon furnishes you with the following information. Calculate the break-even point and show the same by drawing a graph.

           Sales (value) – ₹ 1,50,000
           Sales (units) – 15,000
             Fixed Cost – ₹ 50,000
         Variable Costs –
        Direct Material – ₹ 40,000
         Direct Labour – ₹ 45,000
   Variable overheads – ₹ 35,000

9) From the following particulars draw a break-even chart and find out the break-even point.

   Variable cost per unit – ₹ 15
   Fixed Cost – ₹ 54,000
   Selling price per unit – ₹ 20

10) From the following particulars find out i) P/V Ratio, ii) BEP (Sales) and iii) Margin of Safety.

	₹	% of Sales
Variable Cost	– 10,000	80%
Fixed Cost	– 5,000	5%
Profit	– 15,000	15%
	30,000	100%

11) The sales and profit during two years are given below :

	Sales	Profit
2013	– ₹ 20 lakhs	₹ 2 lakhs
2014	– ₹ 30 lakhs	₹ 4 lakhs

Calculate (a) P/V Ratio, (b) Sales required to earn a profit of ₹ 5 lakhs.

12) Ashim Ltd., Ambegaon gives you the following information :

Sales	–	₹ 50,000
Variable Cost	–	₹ 25,000
Fixed Cost	–	₹ 10,000

Calculate P/V Ratio, BEP and Margin of Safety. Also calculate the effect of 20% increase in sales price and 20% decrease in sales price.

13) The following are the figures obtained from the cost records of Neel Industries, Nagpur :

		₹	₹
Sales – 5,000 units @ ₹ 4 per unit			20,000
Direct Material –		4,000	
Direct Labour –		5,000	
Variable Overheads –	(+)	3,000	
		12,000	
Fixed Overheads –	(+)	4,000	(+) 16,000
∴ Net profit			4,000

The company has decided to reduce the selling price by 10%.
What extra units should be sold to obtain the same amount of profit ?

14) The P/V Ratio and Margin of Safety of Bardhan Industries, Badalapur are 50% and 40% respectively. The Company has a sales volume of ₹ 8,00,000.
Calculate the net profit.

UNIT 6

BUDGET AND BUDGETARY CONTROL

SYNOPSIS

6.1 Budget and Budgetary Control
    6.1.1 Meaning
    6.1.2 Definitions
    6.1.3 Nature
    6.1.4 Objectives
    6.1.5 Limitations
6.2 Steps in Budgetary Control
6.3 Types or Classification of Budgets
    6.3.1 According to Time
        6.3.1.1 Short-Term Budget
        6.3.1.2 Long-Term Budget
    6.3.2 According to Flexibility
        6.3.2.1 Fixed Budget
        6.3.2.2 Flexible Budget
• Illustrations
• Questions for Self-Study

6.1 BUDGET AND BUDGETARY CONTROL

Managerial Control becomes essential in case of public limited companies and Government undertakings which are run by hired managerial personnel with little interest in the results of such enterprises. The proprietors have, therefore, to think of a device which may encourage the management to work with greater care and caution to serve the interests of all by optimising the use of investments in the form of man, money, machines, methods, manpower and materials. **Budgeting** is one such device which helps the management to understand the business programmes in their right perspective and take steps to achieve the business objectives.

Budgeting means planning for future. It involves the preparation of departmental budgets, budgetary control and related issues. The **Budgetary Control** is concerned with the management of business activities with the help of budgets. In this way, budgets serve as a control device.

6.1.1 MEANING

A **Budget** is a plan which relates to a definite period of time and which is expressed in quantitative terms. It is thus a predetermined statement which incorporates the policy of the management during a given period and serves as a standard for comparing the actual results. Thus, a **Budget** is a tool in the hands of the management which serves as a guide to all the employees in achieving their goals, objectives and targets.

A **Budget** helps in planning and co-ordination with all the employees and departments, but the most important factor is that it is used for control purposes at all levels of management.

There is a difference between **Budget** and **Budgetary Control**. A **Budget** is a quantitative statement prepared in advance and keeping it as the base, the actuals are compared. **Budgetary Control** on the other hand means use of the budgets. Thus, **Budgetary Control** involves use of the budgeting techniques to help the management for carrying out the various functions viz. Planning, Organising, Co-ordinating and Controlling the activities of a business.

The **Budgetary Control** technique includes :

i) Establishment of Budgets for each department.

ii) Variance Analysis is done for taking suitable action.

iii) To see that the mistake of the past are not repeated in future.

iv) Comparing the budgets with the actual which is known as **Variance.**

6.1.2 DEFINITIONS

The term **Budget** has been defined by the professional institutes and eminent authors as follows :

i) **The Chartered Institute of Management Accountants (CIMA), London :**

"a financial and/or quantitative statement, prepared and approved prior to a defined period of time, of the policy to be pursued during the period for the purpose of attaining a given objective. It may include income, expenditure and employment of capital".

ii) **Kohler :**

"a financial plan serving as a pattern for and a control over future operations".

iii) **Brown and Howard :**

"it is a pre-determined statement of management policy during a given period which provides a standard for comparison with the results actually achieved".

iv) **George Terry :**

"Budget is an estimate of future needs, arranged according to an orderly basis, covering some or all of the activities of an enterprise for a definite period of time".

Thus, from the above definitions the important **Features of Budget** are outlined as follows :

i) it is a statement expressed in numbers.

ii) it is a financial and/or quantitative statement.

iii) it is prepared for a future specified period of time.

iv) it is prepared and approved prior to the budget period.

v) it is based on the policies to be pursued.

vi) it is prepared for the purpose of attaining a given objective.

vii) it may relate to incomes, expenses, capital receipts and expenditure.

viii) it may be prepared for a short, medium or long period.

ix) it may relate to whole of the organisation or for various divisions of the organisation.

x) it is an instrument of financial control.

The term **Budgetary Control** has been defined by the professional institutes and eminent authors as follows :

i) **The Chartered Institute of Management Accountants (CIMA), London :**

"the establishment of budgets relating to the responsibilities of executives to the requirements of a policy, and the continuous comparison of actual with the budgeted results, either to secure by individual action the objective of that policy or to provide a basis for its revision".

ii) **W. W. Bigg :**

"the term Budgetary control is applied to a system of management and accounting control by which all operations and output are forecast as far ahead as possible and actual results when known, are compared with the budget estimates".

iii) **J. A. Scot :**

"it is the system of management control and accounting in which all operations are forecasted and planned so far as possible ahead, and the actual results compared with the forecasted and planned ones".

iv) **Robert Anthony :**

"it is process by which the managers assure that efficiently in the accomplishment of the goals of the organisation".

v) **George Terry :**

"Budgetary Control is a process of comparing actual results with the corresponding budget data in order to approve accomplishment or to remedy differences by either adjusting the budget estimates or correcting the causes of the differences. A budget is a means and budgetary control is the end result".

Thus, from the above definitions the important **Features of Budgetary Control** are outlined as follows :

i) establishment of budgets for each department or function of the organisation.

ii) co-ordination of various budgets as a total plan for the entire organisation.

iii) recording and reporting of actual results.

iv) comparing the actual result continuously with the budgeted performance.

v) finding out the variances.

vi) analysing the reasons for such variables.

vii) fixing the responsiblities for every controllable variances.

viii) taking corrective action wherever possible.

ix) to see that the mistakes of the past are not repeated in the future.

x) revising the budgets in the light of changes in plans and policies.

Thus, Budgetary control is an important tool very frequently used by the management for the purpose of planning, co-ordination and control.

Rowland and Harr, the professional authority on the subject of 'Budgeting for Management Control' has made a clearcut variation between the original concepts of **Budget**, **Budgeting** and **Bugetary Control** as follows.

- **'Budgets'** are the individual objectives of a particular department in the organisation.
- **'Budgeting'** is the ultimate process of building up the specific budget.
- **'Budgetary Control'** includes all this and additionally, it is the science of planning the budgets themselves and the utilisation of the same to effect an overall management tool for the effective business planning and efficient control.

Hence, **Budgets** are the future estimates. **Budgeting** is based on incrementalism. Budgetary Control is a broader term than budgeting. **Budgtary Control** is a most useful technique of implementing the objectives of the company with minimum possible cost and maximum possible efficiency.

6.1.3 NATURE

Budgeting as an instrument of short planning and control is invaluable to management. A budget is a quantified plan for future action. It is a document of formal financial planning and control as it lists the future objectives and the means of attaining them in quantitative terms. Usually, a year is the basic time frame, though it could be for a quarter or a month. There are many kinds of budgets, but according to functions they are classified into operating budgets, financial budgets, capital budgets and R and D budgets.

The budgeting process to be successful should be in the first place a participative bottomup, not top down budget. Budget should be flexible in that set of budgets should be prepared at a few possible level of activity. A flexible budget is a volume-adjusted budget rather than a static budget at one in single volume of activity.

From control point of view, actual results should be compared with the budgeted results for the achieved level of activity. Behavioural considerations are not less important in developing the budget than quantitative estimates. The benefits of budgeting flow from the fact that forecasting is its important dimension. It aims to anticipate change and enables the firm to meet that change in an advantageous way.

However, one must realise the limitations of budgeting. It is after all a tool, a guide or a blue print for action, the benefits therefrom will depend upon how best it is used. A budget itself does not measure, control or improve it does not control or improve costs any more than a thermometer the weather. Rather, it is a tool which managers use to evaluate performance. Budgeting Control offers only definite and tangible benefits related to the basic functions of management.

6.1.4 OBJECTIVES

Generally Budgetary Control is concerned with three aspects viz. planning, co-ordination and control. All these factors depend on each other and hence we cannot isolate them. Hence the basic objectives of Budgetary Control can be summarised as follows :

i) **Planning :**

A Budget is nothing but a plan. Without planning any modern business cannot function, planning is related to production sales, stocks, requirement of labour, etc. The advantage of planning is to anticipate the problems before hand. Planning through budgetary control is necessary at all levels of management. There is the process of thinking which enables to provide new ideas to the management.

ii) **Co-ordination :**

It means co-operation by the different people in the organisation to achieve the common goal. To have co-ordination, there should be proper communication. Communication can be through the budgets. Planning helps co-ordination and hence if the planning is good, there is effective co-ordination. A detailed Budgetary control system is one where the plans are made and are circulated to all the levels of management.

iii) **Control :**

It ensures that the goals of the management as stated in the Budgetary control system have been achieved. For this purpose fixing of standards is necessary. Thus, through the budgets the standards are fixed which enables the management to control the activities so that the goals are achieved. Thus, through budgetary control, it is possible to compare the standards with the actuals and the analysis of the variances can made and corrective action taken wherever necessary. It encourages research and development as budgetary control schedules are usually based on past experiences.

Advantages of Budgetary Control

Following are certain important **advantages of Budgetary Control System**.
  i) It locates the inefficient areas and persons in the business.
  ii) It helps to increase the efficiency, reduce wastages and control costs.
  iii) It helps to co-ordinate the activities of the various employees, departments and thus helps to achieve the goal of the management.
  iv) With the help of budgeting, the responsibilities of the managers can be fixed for planning, so that they can think ahead, anticipate and be prepared to meet the challenges ahead.
  v) Maximisation of profits is possible through budgeting.
  vi) It helps to introduce the standard costing technique.
  vii) It helps to ensure cash flow and hence bank credit can be obtained.

viii) It creates cost consciousness in the minds of all the employees in the organisation.

ix) Authority can be delegated and responsibilities fixed.

x) It rewards the efficient workers and the managers can show their efficiency by achieving the goals fixed by the management through the budgets.

xi) It ensures that the capital of the firm is utilised in a proper way and that there is no misutilisation of funds.

xii) Vital decisions can be taken by the management based on the budgets.

xiii) Actual results can be compared with the budgets so that corrective action can be taken in time.

xiv) It is like a barometer which enables us to study the changes in the business conditions.

6.1.5 LIMITATIONS

Though there are many advantages of Budgetary Control System, it suffers from many defects also. Hence, the persons using the budgets should be very careful and should be fully aware of the limitations. Following are certain important **limitations of Budgetary Control System**.

i) **Budgetary Control does not replace Management :**

It cannot replace the management because in businesses all vital decisions have to be taken by the management.

ii) **Too much reliance on Budgets is harmful :**

Budgetary control is only a technique and tool in the hands of the management. To execute the budget, all the employees must take active part and co-operate with each other so that the budgetary goal can be achieved. But the budgets should not be taken as the only means through which the business should run. Though sometimes, through budgetary control it is possible to have utmost success in business, it should not be depended upon totally.

iii) **Less Flexibility :**

A Budgetary control system should be more flexible and should be changed according to the changing circumstances. The alternative systems should be added, deleted, improved, replaced or compared with the present system of budgetary control.

iv) **Budgets are based on Estimated Figures :**

Budgets are prepared in anticipation of various factors. These factors are estimated by knowing the past and forecasting for the future. Hence, forecasting is done which may or may not happen in actual life. Thus, it is not an exact prediction of figures, but based on estimates.

v) **Costly System :**

The installation of the system and its execution is expensive affair. This is because specialised persons have to be appointed and extra costs have to be incurred for carrying out the operations. Hence, small scale units cannot go in for budgetary control system.

vi) **Budgetary Control deals with Quantitative Data only :**

In budgetary control system, only the figures are considered and hence the quantitative data i.e. the facts are not considered. e.g. if a worker is inefficient, we should analyse the various reasons for his inefficiency as he may be inefficient because of the conditions or environment or the work is not suitable to his health. Here budgets are of no use because, budgets will only measure his efficiency in terms of quantity produced and will not considered other factors.

Scope of Budget and Budgetary Control

Normally, a budget statement is expressed in both the terms-currency and quantitative units. Currency refers to the cost or value and quantity refers to the activity level or volume of function. Certain budgets can be expressed only in currency as the function cannot be quantified. A budget is a statement of estimated performance for a specific period of time. The natural means of performance evaluation is the comparison between the ideas and the actual. Here, the ideas are the budgeted or standard specifications which are set before the budget period begins. So the actual performance is compared with the standard performance and such comparison gives an idea about the degree of success as a result of the actual performance. The scope of budgetary control is very wide and broad based and it includes within its fold, a variety of aspects of business operations. The scope of budgetary control extend to cover the operation of a department of the whole organisation. e.g. budgets are prepared for production department, selling and distribution department, purchase department, research and development department etc. and also for the whole company. Therefore, budgetary control is more extensive in its scope. Budgetary control can be applied over to a part of the business. Budgetary control system can be operated without standard costing.

6.2 STEPS IN BUDGETARY CONTROL

Budgetary Control system involves the following steps :

i) Preparation of various types of budgets
ii) Measurement of actual performance at the end of the budget period.
iii) Comparison of actual performance with the budgetary performance to find out whether the company has achieved the target set in the budget.
iv) Analysis of the reasons for not achieving the target, so that remedial measures may be taken.

Budgetary Control is largely a matter of management action which is taken on the basis of information on variances. It could be described as **'forwarding costing'**, establishment of budgets and then their application with a view to monitoring and controlling the activities of a concern.

In recent years, there have been some notable changes in the concept and techniques of budgets. These are zero base budgeting and performance budgeting. These approaches are particularly useful in government and non-profit organisations where benefits cannot be traced to the costs.

Requirement of a good Budgeting System

The following are the requirements of a good budgeting system.

i) **Sound Organisation :**
A good organisation is absolutely necessary to carry out the plans and policies of the management. It means that the organisational structure should be such that each one knows what the management expects from him and also his responsibilities.

ii) **Cost Factor :**
The cost benefit analysis should be made before the budget is introduced. It means that the cost of operation of the budget should be less than the benefits derived out of it.

iii) **Interpersonal Relationship :**
The management should develop interpersonal relationships, which means that the management should be able to know the personal difficulties of the executives and managers

in implementing the budgets. This will ensure that the budget is not imposed on anyone without studying his ability to undertake the responsibility.

iv) Systematic Accounting Systems :

It is necessary so that the management can hold the concerned person responsible in the organisation in terms of monetary consideration.

v) High Profits :

The main aim or goal of the management should be to earn maximum profits and this factor should be kept in mind while preparing the budget.

vi) Goals should be Achievable :

The management should fix the goals in such a way that they should be attainable, otherwise there will be confusion in the organisation.

vii) Constant Review :

Constant review of the performance should be made to evaluate the actual results as compared with the budgets, so that corrective action can be taken at the right time.

viii) Fixing of Responsibilities and Preparation of Budget :

It should be noted that the person who will execute the budget should be made responsible for the preparation of it.

ix) Budget Committee :

A budget committee is necessary to carry out the policies effectively, so that the committee consisting of the directors and the executives of various departments are responsible for its implementation.

x) Involvement of Top Management :

Unless the top management co-operates in implementing the budget in true spirit, the budgetary control system cannot be successfully implemented. It means that the top management should carry out the plans and policies as laid down in the budget strictly.

Procedure to be followed in Budget Preparation :

When control through budgets is desired, the budgetary control organisation has to be busy with the following preliminaries.

i) Establishment of Budget Centres :

A budget centre is a section of the organisation of an undertaking defined for each of which a budget will be set with the help of the head of department concerned, e.g. labour budget, production cost budget etc. by the accountant in conjunction with production managers and other executives.

ii) Preparation of an Organisation Chart :

An organisation chart when properly drafted will show the functional responsibilities of each member of management and ensure that he knows his position in the organisation and his relationship to other members. The organisation chart may have to be adjusted to ensure that, each centre is controlled by an appropriate member of the staff.

Figure 6.1 shows the specimen of **Organisational Chart** for implementation of budgetary control system.

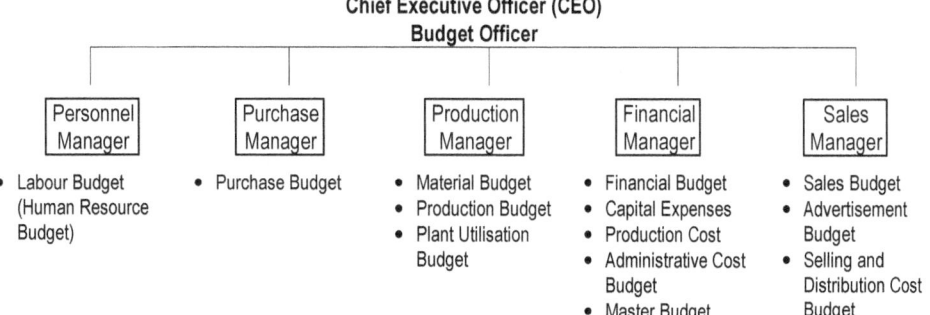

Fig. 6.1 : Organisational Chart

iii) **Preparation of Adequate Accounting Records :**

It is essential that the accounting system should be able to record and analyse the transactions involved. An "accounts code" should be maintained which may be linked with the budget centres for establishment of budgets and finally control through budgets.

iv) **Formation of Budget Committee :**

In small sized organisations a budget officer may establish budget and co-ordinate all the work involved, but in large organisations a budget committee consisting of chief executive, budget officer and heads of departments or budget centres, is established. The main functions of a budget committee are as follows :

- to accept and scrutinise all budgets.
- to decide over all policy to be followed.
- to suggest revision of functional budgets, where necessary.
- to approve finally revised budgets.
- to receive and deal with budget and comparison statements.
- to recommend action to be taken under the different situations.

v) **Preparation of Budget Manual :**

A budget manual is a document setting out the responsibilities of the persons engaged in the routine of and the forms and records required for, budgetary control. A budget manual helps in standardising methods and procedures and the risk of overlapping of functions is eliminated.

vi) **Fixation of Budget Period :**

A budget period is the period of time for which a budget is prepared and employed. Except in case of Capital Expenditure Budget, the budget period is generally the accounting year sub-divided into four quarters or twelve months.

vii) **Determination of Governing Factors :**

A governing factor or key factor or principal budget factor is that factor the extent of whose influence must be assessed first in order to ensure that, functional budgets are reasonably capable of fulfilment. The key factor serves as a starting point for preparation of budget.

Generally, sales become the key factor, but other factors of production, such as men, material, machine, capital etc. may also be factors.

The top management appoints an officer to supervise and guide the Budget Committee in the discharge of its functions. This officer is designated as Budget Officer, Budget Director, Budget Co-ordinator or Budgetary Controller in different organisations. He is generally a controller or chief accountant well versed with accounting and budgeting matters. The budgetary controller is attached to the chief executive to whom he is accountable in matters of budgeting. The **Budgetary Control** is expected to perform the following **functions** :

i) To call meetings of the departmental heads and educate them in the mechanism of budgeting.
ii) To prepare budget programme and budget schedules.
iii) To develop necessary forms for the preparation of budgets and other reports.
iv) To review and maintain budget manual.
v) To co-ordinate the efforts of departmental heads who are involved in budget preparation.
vi) To act as the secretary or co-ordinator of Budget committee and guide its functioning.
vii) To prepare summary budgets for the consideration of the Budget Committee.
viii) To get the budgets approved by the Board of Management before they are passed on to the departmental heads for execution.
ix) To consider the proposals of the departments in the Budget Committee.
x) To conduct special studies needed for the preparation and finalisation of budgets. It should be noted that the functions of the Budget Committee and that of Budgetary Controller are not different. In fact, the functions of Budget Committee form part of the duties of Budgetary Controller who performs most of his functions through the Budget Committee. However, the Budgetary Controller is responsible and accountable to management for the smooth functioning of the Budgetary control system. He seeks the instructions of the Board which formulates budget policies and set business objectives.

6.3 TYPES OR CLASSIFICATION OF BUDGETS

The budgets are of different types which are classified according to the various bases as shown in Figure 6.2 as under :

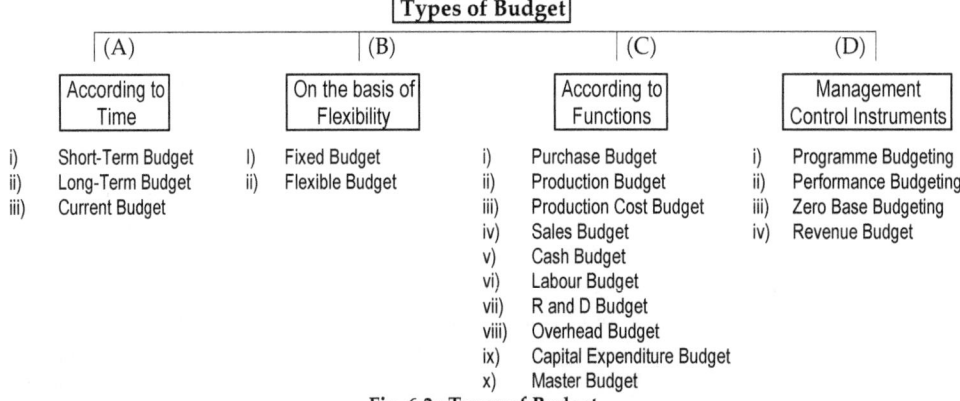

Fig. 6.2 : Types of Budget

Budgeting in an undertaking may be done for a particular segment or it may cover all the activities depending upon the need and resources of the enterprise. The large scale business enterprises prepare different types of budgets covering almost all activities where control is desired. In order to understand the nature of budgets, it is desirable to know their classification which is usually done on time, flexibility, functions and management control instrument basis.

6.3.1 ACCORDING TO TIME

Based on time factor budgets can be classified into three types such as Short-Term Budget, Long-Term, Budget and Current Budget etc.

6.3.1.1 Short-Term Budget

These budgets are prepared mainly for the purposes of exercising effective control. Usually these budgets cover a period of one to two years.

6.3.1.2 Long-Term Budget

These budgets are concerned with long term planning activities such as plant expansion and development programme, huge amount of capital expenditure, research and development programme, new product promotional activities, latest technological improvements scheme. Usually, these budgets cover a period of three to five years or even more than that.

6.3.2 ACCORDING TO FLEXIBILITY

On the basis of flexibility budgets can be classified into two types such as fixed budgets and flexible budgets. A **Fixed Budget** is one which rigidly specifies the targets for a particular level of activity. The targets are not revised during the budget period irrespective of the fact that the actual level of activity attained is much different from the budgeted figure. Consequently, the variances are violent and it becomes difficult to isolate the reasons for variances due to change in the level of activity. **Fixed Budgets** can serve the purpose only if the budgets can be prepared with high degree of accuracy and budget period is short, because the forecast for short period can be made with reasonable degree of accuracy. On the other hand, a **Flexible Budget** is one which permits the change in accordance with the changes in the level of activity. According to **Flexible Budgeting**, budgets for different levels of activity are prepared and the management enjoys the benefit of adopting any one of them according to changes in the attainment of the level of activity. Thus, the **Flexible Budget** has a series of fixed budgets for different levels of activity. It is always preferable to prepare flexible budget particularly when the economic conditions frequently change and it is difficult to forecast with any fair degree of accuracy.

6.3.2.1 Fixed Budget

Meaning

Fixed Budgets are prepared for only one level of activity under the same conditions. It is unchangeable budget which is drawn on the assumption that the level of activity will remain the same. Hence, the changes in the expenses due to changes in the conditions are not provided for in this budget. Thus, a fixed budget becomes useful when the actual level of activity is equal to the budgeted level of activity. However, in real life, the level of activity and business conditions due to the internal constraints as well as external factors like changes in the demand, price, shortage of materials, cut in the electricity, etc. go on changing. Thus, a fixed budget is not that successful because it does not consider the variable, semi-variable and fixed costs as separate items and also does not consider change in costs due to change in the level of activity.

Definition

ICMA, London defines **Fixed Budget** as, "a budget which is designed to remain unchanged irrespective of the volume of output or turnover achieved".

The **reasons** why fixed budgets are **not considered to be useful** are given below :

i) In fixed budgets the managers become helpless as they cannot do anything beyond the budget.

ii) In case of Fixed Budgets, if the actual level differs widely as compared to the fixed budget, we find large variances.

iii) In the real life, we find that the cost of material, labour and overheads go on changing. Hence, fixed budgets are not useful because these changes do not have any effect on the budgeted figures.

iv) Since, it is fixed in nature, it is not suitable for long-term planning.

6.3.2.2 Flexible Budget

Meaning

A Flexible Budget is one which is designed to change according to the level actually achieved. The budgeted figures can be changed according to the changing conditions. Hence, a Flexible Budget is just the opposite of a fixed budget. Thus, it is more elastic, practical and useful in the real life. These budgets are prepared for the purpose of cost control.

Definition

ICMA, London Terminology defines a **Flexible Budget** as, *"one which by recognising the difference between fixed, semi-fixed and variable costs, is designed to change in relation to the level of activity attained"*.

Suitability

Generally, flexible budgets are prepared under the following suitable situations :

i) Where the business depends upon some scarce material.

ii) Where the exact demand cannot be estimated e.g. in new business.

iii) Where the business depends upon nature e.g. rainfall.

iv) In some business where the sales cannot be predicted.

v) Where sufficient labour force is necessary for running the business smoothly.

Distinction between Fixed Budget and Flexible Budget

Following are the major points of differences between Fixed Budget and Flexible Budget.

Fixed Budget	Flexible Budget
i) It is prepared for a particular level of activity.	i) It is designed to change in accordance with the level of activity actually attained.
ii) It is prepared only for one level of activity.	ii) It is prepared for any level of activity.
iii) It is static and does not change with the changes in the level of activity attained.	iii) It is variable and can change on the basis of activity level to be achieved.
iv) Here costs are not classified according to behaviour.	iv) Here, costs are classified according to the behaviour i.e. fixed, variable and semi-variable.
v) Formation of budget equation is not necessary.	v) Budget equation is formed for each and every cost.
vi) It is difficult to ascertain the cost under changing circumstances.	vi) It is possible to ascertain cost at different levels of activity.
vii) Fixation of price do not give a correct picture.	vii) It facilitates fixation of selling price.
viii) It has very limited use in controlling costs.	viii) It is more useful technique for cost control.
ix) Tendering quotations do not give correct picture.	ix) It helps a lot in tendering quotations.
x) It is not useful for performance evaluation.	x) It is useful for performance evaluation.

Methods of Preparing Flexible Budgets

A Flexible Budget can be prepared in the following manner :

At first a number of fixed budgets are prepared for each manufacturing budget centre. Within the limits of these budgets, the flexible budgets are prepared. In Flexible budgets clear differences are drawn between fixed, semi-fixed and variable costs.

There are three **methods of preparing Flexible Budgets** which are as follows :

i) **Tabular Method :**
In this method, a table is prepared wherein different capacities are shown in horizontal columns and the budget, the budgeted figures are shown against different capacities in the vertical columns. The expenses are recorded as variable, semi-variable and fixed. Various capacity levels showing different volumes of production are shown in the flexible budgets.

ii) **Charting Method :**
In this method, the expenses are analysed according to their nature or behaviour i.e. variable, semi-variable and fixed. The budgeted expenses are prepared and these are plotted on a graph paper against different levels of activity. The budgeted expenses relating to the level of activity actually attained can be read from this chart.

iii) **Ratio Method :**
If the activities of a company are standardised and the expenses are of uniform nature, most of the expenses can be worked out as percentage level of activity. The method is that the common cost are estimated. For the normal production, i.e. the normal level of activity. From this we can work out various ratios which show the relationships of each expenses with each increase in the level of activity. Then the budgeted cost for any level of activity can be ascertained by using these ratios.

Uses

The uses of Flexible Budget can be summarised as follows:
i) It is more realistic and has great practical utility in the business.
ii) The efficiency of the managers can be measured.
iii) It helps to control the costs.
iv) It is more realistic than a fixed budget because a fixed budget deals with only one level of activity or condition.
v) The figures in a flexible budget can be changed according to the change in the volume of activity.

Proforma of Flexible Budget

The proforma of a Flexible Budget as per Tabular Method is given as follows:

In the books of a Company

Flexible Budget

Normal Activity : Units
Capacity : %

Production	Units	–		–		–	
Capacity	%	–		–		–	
Particulars		Unit Cost ₹	Total Cost ₹	Unit Cost ₹	Total Cost ₹	Unit Cost ₹	Total Cost ₹
A) Fixed Expenses: • Salaries • Depreciation • Insurance • Rent B) Variable Expenses: • Direct Material • Direct Labour • Direct Expenses • Indirect Material/Labour/Expenses • Variable Overheads C) Semi-Variable Expenses: • Electricity • Repairs and Maintenance • Administrative Expenses • Selling Expenses • Distribution Expenses (+)							
∴ Total Cost							
Add: Profit (+) or Less: Loss (−)							
∴ Sales							

ILLUSTRATIONS

ILLUSTRATION 1

The statement given below gives the Flexible Budget at 60% capacity of Finolex Cable Ltd., Faizpur. Prepare a tabulated statement giving the budget figures at 75% and 90% capacity where no indication has been given and make your own classification of expenses between fixed, variable and semi-variable expenses.

Particulars	60% capacity ₹
Prime Cost Materials	1,60,000
Depreciation	60,000
Productive Wages	40,000
Rent	12,000
Indirect Materials	48,000
Insurance of Machinery	12,000
Indirect Labour	40,000
Electric Power (40% Fixed)	8,000
Repairs and Maintenance (60% Fixed)	20,000

SOLUTION

In the books of Finolex Cable Ltd., Faizpur
Flexible Budget

Normal Activity : Units
Capacity : 60%

Production Capacity			Units %		60	75	90
Particulars					Total Cost ₹	Total Cost ₹	Total Cost ₹
A)	Fixed Expenses :						
	i)	Depreciation			60,000	60,000	60,000
	ii)	Rent			12,000	12,000	12,000
	iii)	Insurance of Machinery			12,000	12,000	12,000
B)	Variable Expenses :						
	i)	Prime Cost Materials			1,60,000	2,00,000	2,40,000
	ii)	Productive Wages			40,000	50,000	60,000
	iii)	Indirect Materials			48,000	60,000	72,000
	iv)	Indirect Labour			40,000	50,000	60,000
C)	Semi-Variable Expenses						
	i)	Electric Power		8,000			
		• Fixed – 40%	3,200		3,200	3,200	3,200
		• Variable – 60%	(+) 4,800		4,800	6,000	7,200
	ii)	Repairs and Maintenance		20,000			
		• Fixed – 60%	12,000		12,000	12,000	12,000
		• Variable – 40%	(+) 8,000	(+)	8,000	10,000	12,000
		∴ Total			4,00,000	4,75,200	5,50,400

ILLUSTRATION 2

The expenses budgeted for production at 100% capacity of Infosys Ltd., Islampur are given below.

Particulars	At 100% capacity ₹
Direct Materials	6,00,000
Variable Works Overheads	2,00,000
Basic Wages	2,00,000
Fixed Production Overheads	80,000
Productive Expenses – Marginal	40,000
Administrative Expenses – Rigid	40,000
Selling Overheads (10% Fixed)	1,20,000
Distribution on Cost (80% Variable)	60,000

Prepare a Flexible Budget for the production at 60% and 80% capacity showing separately the, i) Prime Cost, ii) Works Cost, iii) Cost of Production, and iv) Cost of Turnover.

In the Books of Infosys Ltd., Islampur
Flexible Budget

Normal Activity : Units —
Capacity : 100%

Production Capacity	Units %			60	80	100
Particulars				Total Cost ₹	Total Cost ₹	Total Cost ₹
Direct Materials				3,60,000	4,80,000	6,00,000
Add: Basic Wages				1,20,000	1,60,000	2,00,000
Add: Productive Expenses – Marginal			(+)	24,000	32,000	40,000
Prime Cost			i)	**5,04,000**	**6,72,000**	**8,40,000**
Add: Factory Overheads						
i) Variable Works Overheads				1,20,000	1,60,000	2,00,000
ii) Fixed Production Overheads			(+)	80,000	80,000	80,000
Works Cost			ii)	**7,04,000**	**9,12,000**	**11,20,000**
Add: Administrative Expenses – Rigid			(+)	40,000	40,000	40,000
Cost of Production			iii)	**7,44,000**	**9,52,000**	**11,60,000**
Add: Selling and Distribution Overheads						
i) Selling Overheads –		1,20,000				
• Fixed – 10%	12,000			12,000	12,000	12,000
• Variable – 90%	(+) 1,08,000			64,800	86,400	1,08,000
ii) Distribution on Cost –		60,000				
• Fixed – 20%	12,000			12,000	12,000	12,000
• Variable – 80%	(+) 48,000		(+)	28,800	38,400	48,000
Cost of Turnover			iv)	**8,61,600**	**11,00,800**	**13,40,000**

ILLUSTRATION 3

From the following information relating to Castrol Ltd., Cochin prepare a Flexible Budget at 60% and 80% capacity.

Particulars		70% capacity ₹
A) Variable Overheads :		
• Indirect Material		5,000
• Indirect Labour		15,000
B) Semi-variable Overheads :		
• Electricity		50,000
Variable – 60%		
Fixed – 40%		
• Repairs and Maintenance		5,000
Variable – 65%		
Fixed – 35%		
C) Fixed Overhead :		
• Salaries to Staff		10,000
• Depreciation on Machines		14,000
• Insurance on Machines		(+) 6,000
∴ Total		1,05,000

The company estimated the direct labour hours to be worked at 70% capacity as 70,000 hours. Also calculate the overhead recovery rate at 60%, 70% and 80% capacities.

SOLUTION

In the Books of Castrol Ltd., Cochin
Flexible Budget

Normal Activity : Units
Capacity : 70%

Production Capacity	Units %			60	70	80
Particulars				Total Cost ₹	Total Cost ₹	Total Cost ₹
A) Variable Overheads :						
i) Indirect Material				4,286	5,000	5,714
ii) Indirect Labour				12,857	15,000	17,143
B) Semi-variable Overheads :						
i) Electricity			50,000			
• Variable - 60%	30,000			25,714	30,000	34,286
• Fixed - 40%	20,000			20,000	20,000	20,000
ii) Repairs and Maintenance			5,000			
• Variable - 65%	3,250			2,786	3,250	3,714
• Fixed - 35%	1,750			1,750	1,750	1,750
C) Fixed Overheads :						
i) Salaries to Staff				10,000	10,000	10,000
ii) Depreciation on Machines				14,000	14,000	14,000
iii) Insurance on Machines			(+)	6,000	6,000	6,000
∴ Total				97,393	1,05,000	1,12,607
Calculation of Overhead Recovery Rate on the basis of Direct Labour Hours : $= \dfrac{\text{Total Overheads}}{\text{Direct Labour Hours}}$				$= \dfrac{₹\,97{,}393}{60{,}000\text{ Hrs.}}$ = ₹ 1.62	$= \dfrac{₹\,1{,}05{,}000}{70{,}000\text{ Hrs.}}$ = ₹ 1.50	$= \dfrac{₹\,1{,}12{,}607}{80{,}000\text{ Hrs.}}$ = ₹ 1.41

ILLUSTRATION 4

Dupont Chemicals Ltd., Delhi has submitted the actual cost data working on two capacity levels as follows :

Particulars	Capacity – Cost Amount –	60% Total ₹	70% Total ₹
Distribution on Cost		30,000	40,000
Prime Cost Labour		3,00,000	3,50,000
Factory Overheads		2,00,000	2,20,000
Chargeable Expenses		1,20,000	1,40,000
Raw Materials		3,60,000	4,20,000
Selling Expenses		60,000	70,000
Office on Cost (Rigid)		1,00,000	1,00,000

Prepare a Flexible Budget at 80%, 90% and 100% capacity showing clearly the i) Direct Cost, ii) Works Cost, iii) Cost of Production, and iv) Total Cost.

The costs have a rising tendency according to the change in capacity levels.

SOLUTION

Working Notes :

As per the cost data arising tendency according to the change in capacity levels is being observed which can be summarised as follows :

i) Raw Materials Cost increases by ₹ 60,000 per 10% increase in capacity.
ii) Prime Cost Labour increases by ₹ 50,000 per 10% increase in capacity.
iii) Factory Overheads increase by ₹ 20,000 per 10% increase in capacity.
iv) Office on Cost are rigid hence remain fixed at various capacity levels.
v) Selling Expenses and Distribution on Cost increases by ₹ 10,000 per 10% increase in capacity.

In the books of Dupont Chemicals Ltd., Delhi
Flexible Budget

Normal Activity : Units
Capacity : 60% and 70%

Production Units Capacity %			– 60	– 70	– 80	– 90	– 100
Particulars			Total Cost ₹	Total Cost ₹	Total Cost ₹	Total Cost ₹	Total Cost ₹
Raw Materials			3,60,000	4,20,000	4,80,000	5,40,000	6,00,000
Add : Prime Cost Labour			3,00,000	3,50,000	4,00,000	4,50,000	5,00,000
Add : Chargeable Expenses		(+)	1,20,000	1,40,000	1,60,000	1,80,000	2,00,000
∴ **Direct Cost**		i)	7,80,000	9,10,000	10,40,000	11,70,000	13,00,000
Add : Factory Overheads		(+)	2,00,000	2,20,000	2,40,000	2,60,000	2,80,000
Works Cost		ii)	9,80,000	11,30,000	12,80,000	14,30,000	15,80,000
Add : Office-on-Cost		(+)	1,00,000	1,00,000	1,00,000	1,00,000	1,00,000
Cost of Production		iii)	10,80,000	12,30,000	13,80,000	15,30,000	16,80,000
Add : Selling Expenses			60,000	70,000	80,000	90,000	1,00,000
Add : Distribution on Cost		(+)	30,000	40,000	50,000	60,000	70,000
Total Cost		iv)	11,70,000	13,40,000	15,10,000	16,80,000	18,50,000

ILLUSTRATION 5

From the following cost data made available by Ambuja Metals Co. Ltd., Ahmednagar for a quarterly period, forecast the results by preparing a Flexible Budget at 70%, 80% and 90% capacity level where the estimated turnover amounted to ₹ 1,26,000, ₹ 1,34,000 and ₹ 1,42,000 respectively. It is assumed that –

i) Marginal expenses varies due to change in production capacity level,
ii) Rigid expenses remain constant at various production capacity level and
iii) Semi-fixed expenses are constant between 55% and 75% capacity, increases by 10% between 75% and 85% capacity and increases by 20% between 85% and 90% capacity.

The expenses and sales at 60% capacity level are as under :

Particulars	₹
A) Fixed Expenses :	
i) Workshop Salary	9,300
ii) Office Rent	6,100
iii) Machinery Depreciation	8,600
B) Variable Expenses :	
i) Basic Materials	24,000
ii) Direct Labour	9,000
iii) Productive Expenses	3,000
C) Semi-Variable Expenses :	
i) Repairs and Maintenance	10,000
ii) Telephone Charges	6,000
iii) Indirect Labour	(+) 4,000
∴ Total Cost of Sales	80,000
Value of Sales	1,10,000

Also find out the percentage of profit to sales and submit a report to the management indicating your critical comments on the position at various production capacity level.

SOLUTION

In the books of Ambuja Metals Co. Ltd., Ahmednagar

Flexible Budget

Normal Activity : Units
Capacity : 60%

Production Capacity	Units	–	–	–	–
	%	60	70	80	90
Particulars		Total Cost ₹	Total Cost ₹	Total Cost ₹	Total Cost ₹
A) Fixed Expenses :			9,300	9,300	9,300
i) Workshop Salary		9,300	6,100	6,100	6,100
ii) Office Rent		6,100	8,600	8,600	8,600
iii) Machinery Depreciation		8,600			
B) Variable Expenses					
i) Basic Materials		24,000	28,000	32,000	36,000
ii) Direct Labour		9,000	10,500	12,000	13,500
iii) Productive Expenses		3,000	3,500	4,000	4,500

Production	Units	–	–	–	–
Capacity	%	60	70	80	90
Particulars		Total Cost ₹	Total Cost ₹	Total Cost ₹	Total Cost ₹
C) Semi-Variable Expenses :					
i) Repairs and Maintenance		10,000	10,000 (constant)	11,000 (increases by 10%)	12,000 (increases by 20%)
ii) Telephone Charges		6,000	6,000 (constant)	6,600 (increases by 10%)	7,200 (increases by 20%)
iii) Indirect Labour	(+)	4,000	4,000 (constant)	4,400 (increases by 10%)	4,800 (increases by 20%)
∴ Total Cost of Sales	i)	80,000	86,000	94,000	1,02,000
Add : Profits	ii) (+)	30,000	40,000	40,000	40,000
Total Turnover		1,10,000	1,26,000	1,34,000	1,42,000
Percentage of Profit to Sale (%)	iii)	27.27	31.75	29.85	28.17

Reporting to the Management :

A critical analysis of the forecasted results as shown above in the flexible budgets reveals that at 70% production capacity level the percentage of profit to sales (i.e. 31.75%) is more as compared to other production levels. Hence, it is suggested to the management that,

i) the company should increase their production capacity level from 60% to 70%.

ii) additional efforts are necessary to reduce the cost substantially by introducing effective techniques to control variable cost.

iii) the company should concentrate on increasing the turnover sizably.

ILLUSTRATION 6

In Burma Plastics Co., Badalpur, the cost of an article at a capacity level of 5,000 units is given under 'A' below for a variation of 25% in capacity above or below this level, the individual variation as indicated 'B' below.

Particulars	A ₹	B Variation
Raw Materials	25,000	100% varying
Direct Labour	15,000	100% varying
Stores Overhead	1,000	100% varying
Productive Expenses	10,000	100% varying
Repairs and Maintenance	2,000	75% varying
Power	1,250	50% varying
Inspection	500	20% varying
Office Overheads	5,000	25% varying
Selling on Cost	3,000	25% varying

Prepare a flexible budget at production levels of 4,000 units and 6,000 units.

SOLUTION

In the books of Burma Plastic Co., Badalpur
Flexible Budget

Normal Activity : Units 5,000
Capacity : –

	Production		Units			4,000		5,000		6,000	
	Capacity		%			60		80		–	
	Particulars				Nature of Cost	Unit Cost ₹	Total Cost ₹	Unit Cost ₹	Total Cost ₹	Unit Cost ₹	Total Cost ₹
A)	Variable Expenses :										
	i)	Raw Materials			Variable	5.00	20,000	5.00	25,000	5.00	30,000
	ii)	Direct Labour			Variable	3.00	12,000	3.00	15,000	3.00	18,000
	iii)	Stores Overhead			Variable	0.20	800	0.20	1,000	0.20	1,200
	iv)	Productive Expenses			Variable	2.00	8,000	2.00	10,000	2.00	12,000
B)	Semi-Variable Expenses :				Semi-variable						
	i)	Repairs and Maintenance		2,000							
		• Fixed : 25%	500			0.13	500	0.10	500	0.08	500
		• Variable : 75%	1,500			0.30	1,200	0.30	1,500	0.30	1,800
	ii)	Power		1,250	Semi-variable						
		• Fixed : 20%	250			0.06	250	0.05	250	0.04	250
		• Variable : 80%	1,000			0.20	800	0.20	1,000	0.20	1,200
	iii)	Inspection		500	Semi-variable						
		• Fixed : 80%	400			0.10	400	0.08	400	0.07	400
		• Variable : 20%	100			0.02	80	0.02	100	0.02	120
	iv)	Office Overheads,		5,000	Semi-variable						
		• Fixed : 75%	3,750			0.94	3,750	0.75	3,750	0.63	3,750
		• Variable : 25%	1,250			0.25	1,000	0.25	1,250	0.25	1,500
	v)	Selling on Cost		3,000	Semi-variable						
		• Fixed : 75%	2,250			0.56	2,250	0.45	2,250	0.38	2,250
		• Variable : 25%	750		(+)	0.15	600	0.15	750	0.15	900
		∴ Total				12.91	51,630	12.55	62,750	12.32	73,870

ILLUSTRATION 7

Thomas Cook Ltd., Talegaon provides the following cost data for a 60% working capacity, from which you are required to prepare a Flexible Budget for the production at 80% and 100% capacity level.

Current Production	Units 600
Selling Price (Fixed) per unit	₹ 300
Process Material Cost per unit	₹ 100
Productive Wages per unit	₹ 40
Prime Cost Expenses	₹ 10
Total Works Overheads (40% Fixed)	₹ 40,000

Total Office, Selling and Distribution Overheads (50% Variable) ₹ 30,000.

SOLUTION

In the books of Thomas Cook Ltd., Talegaon
Flexible Budget

Normal Activity : Units 600
Capacity : 60%

Production	Units		600		800		1,000	
Capacity	%		–		–		100	
Particulars			Unit Cost ₹	Total Cost ₹	Unit Cost ₹	Total Cost ₹	Unit Cost ₹	Total Cost ₹
Process Material Cost			100.00	60,000	100.00	80,000	10.00	1,00,000
Add : Productive Wages			40.00	24,000	40.00	32,000	40.00	40,000
Add : Prime Cost Expenses		(+)	10.00	6,000	10.00	8,000	10.00	10,000
∴ Prime Cost		i)	150.00	90,000	150.00	1,20,000	150.00	1,50,000
Add : Works Overheads	40,000							
• Fixed : 40%	16,000		26.67	16,000	20.00	16,000	16.00	16,000
• Variable : 60%	24,000	(+)	40.00	24,000	40.00	32,000	40.00	40,000
∴ Works Cost		ii)	216.67	1,30,000	210.00	1,68,000	206.00	2,06,000
Add: Office, Selling and Distribution Overheads	30,000							
• Fixed : 50%	15,000		25.00	15,000	18.75	15,000	15.00	15,000
• Variable : 50%	15,000	(+)	25.00	15,000	25.00	20,000	25.00	25,000
∴ Total Cost		iii)	266.67	1,60,000	253.75	2,03,000	246.00	2,46,000
Add : Profit		iv) (+)	33.33	20,000	46.25	37,000	54,000	54,000
Selling Price			300.00	1,80,000	300.00	2,40,000	300.00	3,00,000

ILLUSTRATION 8

Activa Co. Ltd., Anand produces computer hardware. The estimated unit cost is as under:

Particulars	Unit Cost ₹
Direct Material	15
Direct Wages	10
Direct Expenses	4
Variable Overheads	(+) 6
∴ Total	35

The Fixed Overheads are estimated at ₹ 1,00,000. The semi-Vaiable Overheads are ₹ 50,000 at 100% capacity i.e. 10,000 units. The semi-variable expenses vary in stages of ₹ 4,000 for each change in output of 1,000 units. Selling Price per unit is ₹ 70. You are required to prepare a Flexible Budget at 50%, 70%, 90% and 100% capacities and determine the profit at each level.

SOLUTION

In the Books of Activa Co. Ltd., Anand
Flexible Budget

Normal Activity : 10,000 units
Capacity : 100%

Production Capacity	Units %		5,000 50		7,000 70		9,000 90		10,000 100	
Particulars			Unit Cost ₹	Total Cost ₹	Unit Cost ₹	Total Cost ₹	Unit Cost ₹	Total Cost ₹	Unit Cost ₹	Total Cost ₹
Direct Material			15.00	75,000	15.00	1,05,000	15.00	1,35,000	15.00	1,50,000
Add : Direct Wages			10.00	50,000	10.00	70,000	10.00	90,000	10.00	1,00,000
Add : Direct Expenses		(+)	4.00	20,000	4.00	28,000	4.00	36,000	4.00	40,000
Prime Cost		i)	29.00	1,45,000	29.00	2,03,000	29.00	2,61,000	29.00	2,90,000
Add : Variable Overheads			6.00	30,000	6.00	42,000	6.00	54,000	6.00	60,000
Add : Fixed Overheads			20.00	1,00,000	14.29	1,00,000	11.11	1,00,000	10.00	1,00,000
Add : Semi-Variable Overheads		(+)	6.00	30,000	5.43	38,000	5.11	46,000	5.00	50,000
Total Cost		ii)	61.00	3,05,000	54.72	3,83,000	51.22	4,61,000	50.00	5,00,000
Add : Profit		iii) (+)	9.00	45,000	15.28	1,07,000	18.78	1,69,000	20.00	2,00,000
Selling Price		iv)	70.00	3,50,000	70.00	4,90,000	70.00	6,30,000	70.00	7,00,000

ILLUSTRATION 9

The expenses for the production at 5,000 units at 50% capacity in Baroda Chemicals Ltd., Bhavnagar given as follows :

Particulars	Unit Cost ₹
Materials	50
Labour	20
Variable Overheads	15
Fixed Overheads (₹ 50,000)	10
Administrative Expenses (5% Variable)	10
Selling Expenses (20% Fixed)	6
Distribution Expenses (10% Fixed)	(+) 5
Total Cost of Sales	116

You are required to prepare a Flexible Budget for 70% and 90% production capacity, assuming that 90% capacity cost of materials will increase by 10% where as labour cost will decrease by 5%.

SOLUTION

In the Books of Baroda Chemicals Ltd., Bhavnagar
Flexible Budget

Normal Activity : 5,000 units
Capacity : 50%

Production Capacity		Units %	5,000 50		7,000 70		9,000 90	
Particulars			Unit Cost ₹	Total Cost ₹	Unit Cost ₹	Total Cost ₹	Unit Cost ₹	Total Cost ₹
A)	**Fixed Expenses :**							
	i) Fixed Overheads		10.00	50,000	7.14	50,000	5.56	50,000
B)	**Variable Expenses :**							
	i) Materials		50.00	2,50,000	50.00	3,50,000	55.00 (50 + 10% i.e. ₹ 5)	4,95,000
	ii) Labour		20.00	1,00,000	20.00	1,40,000	19.00 (20 – 5% i.e. ₹ 1)	1,71,000
	iii) Variable Overheads		15.00	75,000	15.00	1,05,000	15.00	1,35,000
C)	**Semi-Variable Expenses :**							
	i) Administrative Expenses 10.							
	a) Fixed 95% 9.50		9.50	47,500	6.79	47,500	5.28	6,000
	b) Variable 5% (+) 0.50		0.50	2,500	0.50	3,500	0.50	4,500
	ii) Selling Expenses 6.							
	a) Fixed 20% 1.20		1.20	6,000	0.86	6,000	0.67	6,000
	b) Variable 90% (+) 4.80		4.80	24,000	4.80	33,600	4.80	43,200
	iii) Distribution Expenses 5.							
	a) Fixed 10% 0.50		0.50	2,500	0.36	2,500	0.28	2,500
	b) Variable 90% (+) 4.50 (+)		4.50	22,500	4.50	31,500	4.50	40,500
∴	**Total Cost of Sales**		116.00	5,80,000	109.95	7,69,600	110.59	9,95,200

ILLUSTRATION 10

Dabur Chemicals Ltd., Delhi has given you the following information at 50% capacity of the production of 5,000 units during the month of March, 2014.

Particulars	Unit Cost ₹
Materials	50
Labour	30
Variable Overheads	20
Fixed Overheads (₹ 50,000)	10
Administrative Overheads	10
Selling Expenses (25% Fixed)	8
Distribution Expenses (20% Fixed)	5
Total Cost	**133**

You are required to prepare Flexible Budgets at 60%, 70% and 80% capacity presuming that at 80% capacity material cost will be less by 5% and variable selling expenses will increase by 10%.

SOLUTION

In the Books of Dabur Chemicals Ltd., Delhi
Flexible Budget

Normal Activity : 5,000 units
Capacity : 50%

Production Units			5,000		6,000		7,000		8,000	
Capacity %			50		60		70		80	
Particulars			Unit Cost ₹	Total Cost ₹	Unit Cost ₹	Total Cost ₹	Unit Cost ₹	Total Cost ₹	Unit Cost ₹	Total Cost ₹
A) Fixed Expenses										
i) Fixed Overheads			10.00	50,000	8.33	50,000	7.14	50,000	6.25	50,000
B) Variable Expenses										
i) Materials			50.00	2,50,000	50.00	3,00,000	50.00	3,50,000	47.50 (₹50 – 5% i.e. ₹2.50)	3,80,000
ii) Labour			30.00	1,50,000	30.00	1,80,000	30.00	2,10,000	30.00	2,40,000
iii) Variable Overheads			20.00	1,00,000	20.00	1,20,000	20.00	1,40,000	20.00	1,60,000
C) Semi-Variable Expenses :										
i) Administration Overheads		10.								
a) Fixed 90%	9.		9.00	45,000	7.50	45,000	6.43	45,000	5.62	45,000
b) Variable 10%	(+) 1.		1.00	5,000	1.00	6,000	1.00	7,000	1.00	8,000
ii) Selling Expenses		8.								
a) Fixed 25%	2.		2.00	10,000	1.67	10,000	1.43	10,000	1.25	10,000
b) Variable 75%	(+) 6.		6.00	30,000	6.00	36,000	6.00	42,000	6.60 (₹6 + 10% i.e. .60)	52,800
iii) Distribution Expenses		5.								
a) Fixed 20%	1.		1.00	5,000	0.83	5,000	0.71	5,000	0.62	5,000
b) Variable 80%	(+) 4.	(+)	4.00	20,000	4.00	24,000	4.00	28,000	4.00	32,000
Total Cost			133.00	6,65,000	129.33	7,76,000	126.71	8,87,000	122.84	9,82,000

ILLUSTRATION 11

Crysta Ltd., Cochin is currently working at 50% capacity and produces 1,000 units at a cost of ₹ 180 per unit as per the details shown below.

Particulars	Unit Cost ₹
Direct Material	100
Direct Labour	30
Factory Overhead (40% Fixed)	30
Administrative Overhead (50% Fixed)	20

The current selling price is ₹ 200 per unit. At 60% capacity working, raw material cost increases by 2% and selling price falls by 20%. At 80% capacity working, material cost increases by 5% and selling price falls by 5%. Estimate profits of the company at 60% and 80% capacity by preparing Flexible Budgets and offer your critical comments.

Management Accounting 6.26 Budget and Budgetary Control

SOLUTION

In the Books of Crysta Ltd., Cochin
Flexible Budget

Normal Activity : 1,000 units
Capacity : 50%

Production Capacity		Units %		1,000 50		1,200 60		1,600 80	
Particulars				Unit Cost ₹	Total Cost ₹	Unit Cost ₹	Total Cost ₹	Unit Cost ₹	Total Cost ₹
Direct Material				100.00	1,00,000	102.00 (100 + 2% i.e. ₹ 2)	1,22,400	105.00 (100 + 5% i.e. ₹ 5)	1,68,000
Add : Direct Labour				30.00	30,000	30.00	36,000	30.00	48,000
			(+)						
Prime Cost			i)	130.00	1,30,000	132.00	1,58,400	135.00	2,16,000
Add : Factory Overheads		30							
Fixed	40%	12		12.00	12,000	10.00	12,000	7.50	12,000
Variable	60%	18		18.00	18,000	18.00	21,600	18.00	28,800
Add : Administrative Overhead		20							
Fixed	50%	10		10.00	10,000	8.33	10,000	6.25	10,000
Variable	50%	10		10.00	10,000	10.00	12,000	10.00	16,000
			(+)						
∴ **Total Cost**			ii)	180.00	1,80,000	178.33	2,14,000	176.75	2,82,800
Add : Profits			iii)	20.00	20,000	17.67	21,200	13.25	21,200
			(+)						
Selling Price			iv)	200.00	2,00,000	196.00 (200 − 2% i.e. ₹ 4)	2,35,200	190.00 (200 − 5% i.e. ₹ 10)	3,04,000

Comments :

After making critical anlaysis, it is suggested that production capacity should not be increased as profits remain constant at 60% and 80% capacity level.

ILLUSTRATION 12

Sudarshan Co., Satara is engaged in manufacturing Full Scape Note Books is working currently at 40% capacity and produces 10,000 note books per month. The cost and price details for one note book is as under :

Particulars	Unit Cost and Price ₹
On Cost (40% Variable)	5
Productive Expenses	1
Direct Labour Cost	2
Basic Materials Cost	10
Market Price	20

You are required to prepare a Flexible Budget showing separately the profit at 50% and 90% capacities and the break-even-points at the production capacity levels assuming that –
  i) at 50% capacity the invoice price falls by 3% and
  ii) at 90% capacity the selling price falls by 5%
accompanied by a similar fall in the price of Direct Material.

SOLUTION

In the books of Sudarshan Co., Satara
Flexible Budget

Normal Activity : Units 10,000
Capacity % : 40

Production Capacity	Units %	10,000 40		12,500 50		22,500 90	
Particulars		Per Unit ₹	Total ₹	Per Unit ₹	Total ₹	Per Unit ₹	Total ₹
Sales		20.00	2,00,000	19.40 (fall by 3%)	2,42,500	19.00 (fall by 5%)	4,27,500
Less : Variable Cost							
i) Basic Material Cost		10.00	1,00,000	10.00	1,25,000	9.50 (fall by 5%)	2,13,750
ii) Direct Labour Cost		2.00	20,000	2.00	25,000	2.00	45,000
iii) Productive Expenses		1.00	10,000	1.00	12,500	1.00	22,500
iv) On Cost (40% of ₹ 5.00)	(–)	2.00	20,000	2.00	25,000	2.00	45,000
∴ Contribution where, (C = S – V)		5.00	50,000	4.40	55,000	4.50	1,01,250
Less : Fixed Cost							
i) On Cost (60% of ₹ 5.00)	(–)	3.00	30,000	2.40	30,000	1.33	30,000
∴ Profit where, (P = C – F)		2.00	20,000	2.00	25,000	3.17	71,250
∴ Break Even Point (Units) where, BEP (Units) = Total Fixed Cost / Contribution per unit		= ₹30,000 / ₹5.00 = 6,000 units		= ₹30,000 / ₹4.40 = 6,818 units		= ₹30,000 / ₹4.50 = 6,667 units	

QUESTIONS FOR SELF-STUDY

I. **Theory Questions :**
  1) Define the term 'Budget', 'Budgeting' and 'Budgetary Control'.
  2) What is 'Budget' ? State the nature of Budget and Budgetary Control.
  3) Define the term 'Budgetary Control'. What are the objectives of Budgetary Control ?
  4) What is 'Budgetary Control' ? Explain the objectives and limitations of Budgetary Control.
  5) What do you understand by 'Budgetary Control' ? Explain the necessary steps involved in a Budgetary Control System.
  6) What is 'Budget' ? State the types of budgets according to time.
  7) Define the term 'Budget'. State the types of budgets according to flexibility.

8) Short Notes :
a) Nature of Budget and Budgetary Control, b) Objectives of Budgetary Control, c) Limitations of Budgetary Control, d) Steps in Budgetary Control, e) Short-term Budget, f) Long-term Budget, g) Fixed Budget, h) Flexible Budget.
9) Differentiate between :
a) Budget and Budgetary Control, b) Long-term and Short-term Budget, c) Fixed and Flexible Budget.

II. Practical Problems :

1) The following budget estimates are available from Monica Industries Ltd. Manipur working at 50% capacity.

	₹
Variable Costs	50,000
Semi-variable Costs	25,000
Fixed Costs	10,000

You are required to prepare a budget for 80% capacity assuming that semi-variable expenses increases by 10% for every 20% increases in capacity.

2) In a factory, a cost centre works at 60% capacity and the following overhead expenses are incurred.

Particulars	₹
Salary of Supervisor	2,000
Salary of Assistant Supervisor	1,000
Wages of workers	5,000
Repairs of machines	8,000
Spoiled Work	2,500
Spoiled Work	2,500
Oils and Lubricants	2,000
Depreciation of Machine	10,000
Total	**33,000**

Prepare a Flexible Budget for 75%, 100% and 125% capacities.

3) Kwality Industries Ltd., Kalbadevi produces a consumer product. The estimated costs per unit are given below :

Particulars	₹
Raw Material	500
Direct Labour	300
Factory Overhead	400 (30% fixed)
Administrative Overheads	200 (60% fixed)
Cost per unit	1,400

The selling price per unit is ₹ 1,800. At 50% capacity it produces 5,000 units. Find out the profits when it works at 60% and 80% capacity.

Notes :
i) The cost per unit of ₹ 1,400 is at 50% capacity.
ii) At 60% capacity raw material cost increases by 3% and selling price falls by 3%.
iii) At 80% capacity raw material cost increases by 4% and selling price falls by 5%.
Draw a proforma of a Flexible Budget using imaginary figures for 50%, 60% and 70% capacity levels.

***

AT A GLANCE
GLOSSARY

1. **Management Accounting :**

   It is the presentation of accounting information in such a way so as to assist management in the creation of policy and in the day-to-day operation of an undertaking.

2. **Stewardship Accounting :**

   It is associated with the need of business owners to keep records of their day-to-day transactions to manage their properties.

3. **Financial Accounting :**

   It is the art of recording, classifying and summarising in a significant manner and in terms of money transactions and events which are in part atleast of a financial character and interpreting the results thereof.

4. **Cost Accounting :**

   It is the application of costing and cost accounting principles, methods and techniques to the science, art and practice of cost control and ascertainment of profitability, which includes the presentation of information derived therefrom for the purpose of managerial decision-making.

5. **Financial Statement Analysis :**

   It is a process of evaluating the relationship between component parts of a financial statement to obtain a better understanding of a firm's position and performance.

6. **Ratio :**

   It is a mathematical yardstick that measures the relationship between two figures which are related to each other and mutually inter-dependent.

7. **Ratio Analysis :**

   It is a method by which the relationship of items or groups of items in the financial statements are computed, determined and presented.

8. **Financial Statement :**

   It is a statement prepared for evaluating past performance and predicting future performance.

9. **Funds :**

   It includes all cash resources used in the business or all financial resources which flow through working capital and fixed capital accounts or all working capital i.e. current assets minus current liabilities.

10. **Funds Flow Statement :**

    It is a statement prepared to show the sources from where the funds have been generated and where they have been applied.

11. **Trading on Equity :**

    A company is said to be trading on equity when it uses equity financing and loan financing for financing its business activities.

12. **Flow of Fund :**

    It represents the movements to and fro working capital area.

13. **Cash Flow Statement :**

    It is a statement that provides valuable information about cash flows associated with the operations of the company, which is more useful in short-term planning.

14. **Working Capital :**

    It is represented by the excess of current assets over current liabilities and identifies the relatively liquid position of the total enterprise capital which constitutes a margin of buffer for maturing obligations within the ordinary operating cycle of the business.

15. **Gross Working Capital :**

    It refers to the sum total of all current assets employed in the business process.

16. **Net Working Capital :**

    It refers to the funds which have been procured to support that portion of current assets which is in excess of current liabilities.

17. **Negative Working Capital :**

    It refers to the current liabilities and provisions which exceeds the current assets.

18. **Tangible Working Capital :**

    It refers to the working capital which excludes the non-moving and obsolete items from inventories.

19. **Permanent Working Capital :**

    It refers to the quantum of current assets which are required on a continuing basis for an entire year.

20. **Temporary Working Capital :**

    It refers to the working capital which is influenced by seasonal fluctuations of the business concerned.

21. **Positive Working Capital :**

    It refers to the current assets which exceeds the current liabilities.

22. **Current Assets :**

    It refers to those assets of short duration which are used for day-to-day activities of the firm, e.g. cash and bank, stock-in-trade, sundry debtors etc.

23. Current Liabilities :

It refers to that part of obligations which the firm has to clear with the outsiders in a short period, generally within a year, e.g. bank overdraft, sundry creditors etc.

24. Working Capital Cycle :

It refers to the time period required to complete the whole operating cycle of events starting with cash and ending up with cash plus.

25. Working Capital Management :

It is the management of maintaining sufficient working capital and to make availability of necessary funds as and when required.

26. Marginal Cost :

It is the amount of any given volume of output by which aggregate costs are changed if the volume of output is increased or decreased by one unit.

27. Marginal Costing :

It is the ascertainment of marginal costs and of the effect on profit of changes in volume or type of output by differentiating between fixed and variable costs.

28. Fixed Cost :

It is a cost which accrues in relation to the passage of time and which, within certain output and turnover limits, tends to be unaffected by fluctuations in the level of the activity, e.g. rent, rates, insurance etc.

29. Variable Cost :

It is a cost which in the aggregate, tends to vary in the direct proportion to the changes in the volume of the production or the turnover, e.g. direct material, direct labour, direct expenses etc.

30. Semi-variable Cost :

It is the cost which has an element of fixity and also of variability, e.g. telephone charges, electricity charges, repairs and maintenance etc.

31. Contribution :

It is the excess of selling price over the variable costs.

32. Profit-Volume Ratio :

It is a ratio that expresses the relationship of contribution to sales value as percentage.

33. Break-Even Point :

It is the point at which total sales revenue equals the total costs.

34. Break-Even Analysis :

It is the analysis used to determine the probable profit or loss at any level of operations.

35. **Margin of Safety :**

    It is the difference between actual sales and break-even sales.

36. **Angle of Incidences :**

    It is the angle formed through intersection of total cost line and sales line.

37. **Budget :**

    A financial and/or quantitative statement prepared and approved prior to a defined period of time, of the policy to be pursued during that period for the purpose of attaining a given objective. It may include income, expenditure and employment of capital.

38. **Budgetary Control :**

    The establishment of budgets relating to the responsibilities of executives to the requirements of a policy, and the continuous comparison of actual with budgeted results, either to secure by individual action the objective of that policy or to provide a basis for its revision.

39. **Budgeting :**

    It is the ultimate process of building up the specific budget.

40. **Budget Centre :**

    It is a section of the organisation of an undertaking defined for the purposes of budgetary control.

41. **Budget Manual :**

    It is a document which sets out the responsibilities of the person engaged in, the routine of, and the forms and records required for budgetary control.

42. **Budget Period :**

    It is a period for which a budget is prepared and employed.

43. **Fixed Budget :**

    It is a budget which is designed to remain unchanged irrespective of the volume of output or turnover achieved.

44. **Flexible Budget :**

    It is a budget which, by reasoning the difference in behaviour between fixed and variable costs in relation to fluctuations in output, turnover or other variable factors such as number of employees, is designed to change appropriately with such fluctuations.

45. **Short-term Budget :**

    It is a budget prepared for a period of one to two years.

46. **Long-term Budget :**

    It is a budget prepared for a period of three to five years.

***

OBJECTIVE QUESTIONS

(i) True or False Statements

- **State whether the following statements are True or False :**
    1. Management Accounting is concerned with the adjustment in the value of assets, and of profit in the light of changes in the price level.
    2. Financial Accounting is a discipline, which is employed in industry and commerce to record, classify and summarise the mercantile transactions that occur in an organisation.
    3. Inflation Accounting helps the management in planning and controlling the costs relating to both, production and distribution activities.
    4. The changes in the economic conditions of the country have direct impact on the business position of an organisation.
    5. The main objective of financial accounting is to identify the profitable areas of business.
    6. Human Resource Accounting serves as a vital source of information for effective and efficient planning.
    7. Management Accounting furnishes useful accounting data and statistical information for the decision-making process.
    8. Stewardship Accounting provides means to motivate the employees of the company organisation.
    9. The principle of objectivity is followed in its real spirit in management accounting.
    10. Management Accounting is not based on double-entry system.
    11. It is compulsory for a joint stock company to install a system of Management Accounting.
    12. Management Accounting is nothing more than use of cost and financial information for administrative purposes.
    13. Corporate Accounting assists in the corporate planning process.
    14. Social Responsibility Accounting plays a vital role in planning, organising, decision-making and controlling functions performed by management.
    15. Limitations of Financial Accounting results into introduction of Management Accounting.
    16. Financial Accounting and Cost Accounting cannot replace each other.
    17. Financial Statement analysis helps in determining credit risk.
    18. Financial Statements are historical in nature.
    19. Ratio Analysis is one of the popular tools of financial statement analysis.
    20. The transactions which decrease working capital are sources of funds.
    21. The basic object of cash flow statement is to find out increase or decrease in the working capital during a particular period.
    22. Ratio Analysis provides necessary basis for inter-firm as well as intra-firm comparison.
    23. Ratio Analysis does not help in investment decisions.

24. Solvency Ratios measure the ability of a firm to meet its short-term obligations.
25. Leverage ratios indicate the degree of debt-financing in a firm.
26. Activity Ratios are also known as efficiency and performance ratios.
27. Liquidity Ratios are intended to reflect the overall efficiency of the organisation.
28. Ratio Analysis is considered as an invaluable tool of analysis.
29. A current ratio serves as an index of short-term solvency.
30. Over-investment in stock leads to low liquid ratio inspite of a favourable current ratio.
31. Liquid Ratio shows the firms ability to meet its immediate obligations very promptly.
32. Quick liabilities are those current liabilities which are fluctuating and fall due for payment at any time during the year.
33. Proprietary Ratio is a test of the financial and credit strength of the business.
34. Debt-Equity Ratio indicates the relationship between short-term and long-term borrowings.
35. Higher debt-equity ratio indicates too much dependence on short-term debts.
36. Turnover Ratio brings out the relationship between gross profit and net sales.
37. Liquid Ratio is a yardstick that measures the efficiency of all the operational activities of the business.
38. When more capital is required, the operating ratio should be very high.
39. Financial Statements are indicators of the performance of a business firm.
40. Trend Analysis facilitates the ratio analysis.
41. Ratio Analysis is an important tool for predicting the sickness of a business unit.
42. Funds Flow Statement acts as a tool for allocation of financial resources.
43. A Funds Flow Statement cannot replace the traditional financial statements.
44. Increase in the value of current assets decreases the working capital.
45. Decrease in the value of current liabilities increases the fixed capital.
46. A Funds Flow Statement deals with financial resources required for running the business activities.
47. Improvement in working capital means improvement in cash position.
48. A Cash Flow Statement is very much useful for short-term planning.
49. A Cash Flow Statement is a useful supplementary instrument.
50. It is obligatory to prepare a Funds Flow Statement.
51. The primary objective of Funds Flow Statement is to identify the sources and applications of funds.
52. Preparation of a Cash Flow Statement is more practical and relevant.
53. A Cash Flow Statement indicates the financial strength and weakness of the business.

54. Cash generated from business operations can be determined from income statement.
55. Working Capital from business operations can be determined from profit and loss appropriation account.
56. Cash Flows are inflows and outflows of cash and cash-equivalents.
57. 'Going Concern' concept is the base of gross working capital.
58. The Gross Working Capital represents total current assets minus total current liabilities.
59. As the volume of sales increases, the investment of working capital substantially increases.
60. Time Factor plays a major role in managing the current assets.
61. Usually in a manufacturing concern the operating cycle is very long as the firm has to offer credit facility for improving sales.
62. A liberal credit policy followed by a firm will result in decreasing the need for working capital.
63. Marginal Cost includes direct cost plus all rigid costs.
64. An increase in production will result in a decrease in per unit marginal cost.
65. Contribution is the difference between the turnover price and the marginal cost.
66. Margin of Safety can be improved by lowering the volume of sales.
67. The size of margin of safety is an extremely valuable guide to know the strength of a business.
68. P/V Ratio can be improved, if contribution is improved.
69. The effect of price reduction is always to raise the break-even point.
70. The angle of incidence is affected by changes in fixed cost.
71. The contribution per unit remains unchanged regardless of the level of activity.
72. Marginal Cost = Cost of Turnover (−) Constant Cost.
73. Marginal Costing technique emphasises on behavioural classification of cost.
74. Fixed Costs are directly associated with the volume of production.
75. Variable Costs are not time based.
76. P/V Ratio can be improved by reducing marginal cost.
77. Under Marginal Costing only variable costs are charged to products.
78. Prices of products are based on fixed cost of products plus contribution margin.
79. The decision regarding make or buy is guided by fixed cost of internal production.
80. With increase in fixed cost break-even point will go up.
81. An increase in per unit selling price reduces the break-even point.
82. If contribution is less than the fixed cost, the shortfall is a loss.
83. A larger angle of incidence denotes a higher P/V Ratio.

84. The industries which have high fixed cost burden but low variable cost have smaller angle of incidence.
85. Break-Even chart offers a static analysis.
86. In practical life certain semi-variable costs are difficult to separate into fixed and variable overheads.
87. Budgeting is nothing but profit planning.
88. Budgets are half used if they serve only as planning devices.
89. Flexible Budgeting is more suitable for seasonal industries.
90. Budgetary Control and Standard Costing go together.
91. A budget is both a plan as well as a control tool.
92. Forecasting leads to budgeting and budgeting leads to budgetary control.
93. A Flexible Budget is one which is prepared for changing level of activity.
94. Budgets are not always for a specified future period of time.
95. Forecasting is a process of predicting or estimating a future happening.
96. Budgets should be periodically reviewed, revised and updated in the light of changes.
97. Fixed Budgets are more useful where fixed costs are of step character and differ at different levels of output.
98. Limitations of budgetary control arise mainly due to poor implementation of the budgetary process.
99. Budgets are a communication device also.
100. Budgets should adopt a participative approach.

ANSWERS

True :

2, 4, 7, 10, 16, 17, 18, 19, 22, 25, 26, 28, 29, 30, 31, 32, 33, 36, 39, 41, 42, 43, 46, 48, 49, 51, 52, 56, 57, 59, 61, 65, 66, 67, 68, 69, 71, 72, 73, 75, 76, 77, 80, 81, 82, 83, 85, 86, 87, 88, 89, 90, 91, 92, 93, 95, 96, 97, 98, 99, 100.

False :

1. inflation accounting, 3. cost accounting, 5. cost accounting, 6. management accounting, 8. management Accounting, 9. is not followed. 11. not compulsory, 12. management purpose, 13. management accounting, 14. management accounting, 15. introduction of cost accounting, 20. application of funds, 21. fund flow statement, 23. helps investment decisions, 24. liquidity ratios, 27. profitability ratios, 34. between owned capital and borrowed capital ratio, 38. very low, 40. ratio analysis facilitates the trend analysis, 44. increases the working capital, 45. increases the working capital, 47. does not mean improvement in cash position, 50. it is not obligatory, 53. funds flow statement, 54. from cash flow statement, 55. profit and loss account, 58. net working capital, 60. minor, 62. increasing the need, 63. all variable costs, 64. per unit variable cost remains constant, 70. not affected, 74. are not associated, 78. based on variable cost of products plus contribution margin, 79. guided by variable cost of internal production, 84. larger angle of incidence, 94. are always.

***

(ii) Fill in the Blanks

1. ...... Accounting is concerned with measurement of the cost and value of people for the organisation.
2. The important objective of ...... accounting is to organise the accumulated financial data into meaningful information.
3. ...... accounting is the adoption and analysis of accounting information and its diagnosis and explanation in such a way so as to assist the decision-makers.
4. Management Accounting is also known as Management ...... Accounting.
5. The important objective of Management Accounting is to submit comprehensive reports with quantitative and ...... information.
6. Planning is that function of ...... which requires an efficient system of decision-making.
7. The publication of companies annual report is an important task of a ...... accountant.
8. Financial ...... ensures effective utilisation of available financial resources in the long period.
9. ...... costs are pre-determined targets against which actual results are evaluated.
10. Financial Accounting data is primarily meant for ...... users.
11. ...... Accounting is often called as a tool for management.
12. ...... Accounting is an extension of ...... Accounting.
13. Management Accounting is a mid-way between Financial Accounting and ...... Accounting.
14. ...... Accounting is the blending together of financial accounting, cost accounting and financial management.
15. Management Accounting begins where ...... accounting ends.
16. Cost Accountant should report to the ...... management.
17. Financial Statement Analysis is a ...... tool in predicting the bankruptcy and failure probability of business enterprises.
18. Financial Statements do not show ...... changes which undoubtedly affect greatly the performance of an undertaking.
19. Common-size Comparative Statements provide a better ...... perspective of an undertaking.
20. The transactions which increase working capital are ...... of funds.
21. ...... statement is also termed as statement of sources and applications of funds.
22. A Cash Flow Statement records the transactions which have a direct impact on ....
23. A ...... Flow Statement fails to convey the quantum of inflow and outflow of cash.
24. ...... is an arithmetical relationship between two figures.
25. Ratio Analysis acts as an ...... of efficiency of an enterprise.
26. ...... Analysis is an instrument for diagnosis of financial health of an enterprise.
27. Ratio Analysis ensures effective cost ....
28. Quick Ratio is to be used to analyse the ...... of a firm.
29. Ratios are expressed as a percentage relations when the simple ratios are multiplied by ....

30. ...... Ratios measure the relationship between proprietors funds and borrowed funds.
31. Two to one ratio expresses the relationship between ...... and ....
32. As current ratio indicates the working capital position of the business, it is also known as ...... ratio.
33. It is advisable to consider bank overdraft as a ...... liability.
34. ...... means the practice of bolstering and improving the current ratio through manipulation to make it appear more colourful.
35. ...... Ratio is also known as one to one ratio.
36. The purpose of liquid ratio is to measure the immediate ...... of the business.
37. Too much reliance on ...... ratio without detailed investigation should be avoided.
38. ...... Ratio is employed to indicate the long-term solvency of the business.
39. ...... Ratio brings out the relationship between two types of capital of a limited company.
40. The important advantage of high gearing is ...... on equity.
41. ...... the operating ratio, better is the operational efficiency of the business.
42. ...... study the past and relate the findings to the present.
43. Ratios are increasingly used in ...... analysis.
44. A ...... statement is also termed as 'where got and where gone' statement.
45. A Funds Flow Statement is a test of effective use of ...... by the management during a particular period.
46. A Funds Flow Statement can be used as a ...... device to make the financial planning more effective.
47. ...... Statement is a vast concept which includes flow of cash also.
48. According to ...... Cash Concept, a decrease in current assets and an increase in current liability is taken as a source of cash.
49. A Funds Flow Statement is a statement of changes in ...... and ...... of an organisation.
50. Preparation of Funds Flow Statement is more ...... in nature.
51. Cash Flow Statement based on AS-3 indicates change in ....
52. Decrease in creditors ...... cash.
53. Increase in prepaid expenses ...... cash.
54. ...... assets are those which change their character swiftly.
55. ...... capital is the difference between inflow and outflow of funds.
56. The ...... cash inflow is the excess of current assets over current liabilities and provisions.
57. ...... Capital may be regarded as the life blood of a business.
58. A Gross Working Capital is also termed as ...... Capital, as current assets are rotating in their nature.
59. Working Capital is treated as a financial ...... which keeps the business operations going.
60. Working Capital is rightly an adjunct of ...... capital investment.
61. Public Deposits maturing within one year represent ......
62. Advance payment of tax is an example of ...... asset.
63. The minimum amount of investment in all current assets which is required at all times to carry on minimum level of business activities is termed as ...... working capital.

64. Tandon Committee referred fixed working capital as …… Current Assets.
65. The extra working capital required to support the changing production and sales activities is known as …… Working Capital.
66. The …… Working Capital is controlling technical insolvency.
67. …… Capital helps in controlling technical insolvency.
68. The objective of …… is to finance accounts receivables and inventories.
69. The …… manager has to devote considerable time to manage current assets more effectively.
70. The inventory requirement of public utility concerns are usually …….
71. The overall profitability …… if a firm maintains a large holding of current assets.
72. During …… demand periods, the need for working capital also comes down.
73. In the organisation, if the sales are mostly on …… basis, the operating cycle is also very short.
74. In a competitive market because of liberal credit policy …… amount of working capital will be required.
75. If a liberal dividend policy is followed by the company, …… working capital will be required.
76. Higher the margin of safety …… are the trading operations.
77. At break-even point total contribution is exactly sufficient to recover …… cost.
78. Computation of break-even point is very useful at …… stage.
79. The industries which have low fixed cost but high per unit variable cost have …… angle of incidence.
80. Marginal Costing is not a …… of costing such as job costing.
81. Marginal Cost does not include …… cost.
82. At the break-even point, the Margin of Safety is …….
83. Break-even point is …… by changes in Fixed Costs.
84. Sales minus Marginal Costs = Rigid Cost plus …….
85. Contribution minus …… Costs = Profit.
86. The Margin of Safety is the difference between …… Sales and Break-Even Sales.
87. At Break-Even Point …… is equals to fixed costs.
88. A higher P/V ratio reflects …… profitability.
89. If nothing is produced, the loss will be equal to …… cost.
90. The Break-even point, …… when selling price is decreased.
91. At Break-even point, total cost is equal to ……
92. Marginal Costing is a very significant technique widely used for managerial …… making.
93. …… is a very important indicator of profit earning capacity of the business.
94. Marginal Costing is a technique which segregates total cost into …… and …….
95. Technique of Marginal Costing is a valuable aid to the …….
96. Under Marginal Costing stock of work-in-progress is valued at …… cost only.
97. Marginal Costing is a …… run technique of costing.
98. …… is the act of building budgets.
99. The …… is an impersonal policeman that maintains ordered effort and brings about efficiency in results.
100. Budgetary Control is …… to the system of standard costing.
101. …… budgets cannot be used for cost-ascertainment and price fixation.

102. ...... budgets are more useful where the overall business situation is highly dynamic and fast changing.
103. A fixed budget is prepared for only ...... level of activity.
104. ...... budgets are more useful for performance evaluation.
105. Budgets are ...... for action.
106. Budgetary control process involves checking and evaluation of ...... performance.
107. The document which describes the budgeting organisation, procedures etc. is known as budget ....
108. The budget is an aid to ....
109. Flexible budget is also known as ...... budget.
110. Cost ...... is the primary objective of budgetary control.
111. ...... are generally made for a longer period than budgets.
112. Budgets are a ...... device also.
113. Scope of ...... control is much wider than that of standard costing.
114. Budgetary Control system facilitates effective ...... of authority.
115. Budgetary Control technique is an ...... tool.
116. Budget is a ...... plan for a period of time.
117. A ...... budget is a most dynamic tool of controlling overhead costs.
118. A ...... is an estimate of future needs.
119. A ...... budget is a concise statement of how costs are related to fluctuations in output.
120. A sound system of budgetary control should provide a ...... against which actual results can be compared.

ANSWERS

1. human resource, 2 financial, 3. management, 4. oriented, 5. qualitative, 6. management, 7. management, 8. planning, 9. standard, 10. external, 11. management, 12, financial, 13. cost, 14. management, 15. cost, 16. top, 17, significant, 18. qualitative, 19. historical, 20. sources, 21. fund flow, 22. cash, 23. fund, 24. ratio, 25. index, 26. ratio, 27. control, 28. liquidity, 29. 100, 30. leverage, 31. current assets and current liabilities, 32. working capital, 33. current, 34. window dressing, 35. liquid, 36. solvency, 37. liquid, 38. proprietary, 39. capital gearing, 40. trading, 41. lower, 42. ratios, 43. trend, 44. funds flow, 45. working capital, 46. control, 47. fund flow, 48. notional, 49. assets-liabilities, 50. academic, 51. cash and cash equivalents, 52. decreases, 53. decreases, 54. current, 55. working, 56. net, 57. working, 58. circulating, 59. lubricant, 60. fixed, 61. current liability, 62. current, 63. permanent, 64. core, 65. variable/temporary, 66. negative, 67. working, 68. working capital, 69. finance, 70. less, 71. reduces, 72. low, 73. cash, 74. larger, 75. more, 76. safer, 77. fixed, 78. project, 79. smaller, 80. method, 81. fixed, 82. nil, 83. affected, 84. profit, 85. fixed, 86. actual, 87. contribution, 88. higher, 89. fixed, 90. increases, 91. revenue, 92. decision, 93. P/V Ratio, 94. fixed-variable, 95. management, 96. variable, 97. short, 98. budgeting, 99. budget, 100. complementary, 101. fixed, 102. flexible, 103. one, 104. flexible, 105. blue prints, 106. actual, 107 manual, 108. management, 109. variable, 110. control, 111. forecasts, 112. communication, 113. budgetary, 114. delegation, 115. expensive, 116. cost, 117. flexible, 118. budget, 119. flexible, 120. yardstick.

***

FORMULAE

3. ANALYSIS AND INTERPRETATION OF RATIOS

	Ratios	Formulae
1)	Current Ratio	$\dfrac{\text{Current Assets}}{\text{Current Liabilities}}$
2)	Net Working Capital Ratio	$\dfrac{\text{Net Working Capital}}{\text{Net Assets}}$
3)	Quick Ratio	$\dfrac{\text{Quick Assets}}{\text{Liquid Liabilities}}$
4)	Cash Position Ratio	$\dfrac{\text{Cash (+) Marketable Securities}}{\text{Liquid Liabilities}}$
5)	Proprietary Ratio	$\dfrac{\text{Shareholders' Fund}}{\text{Total Asset (or) Total Resources}}$
6)	Solvency Ratio	$\dfrac{\text{Outside Liabilities}}{\text{Total Assets}}$
7)	Fixed Assets to Proprietors Fund Ratio	$\dfrac{\text{Fixed Assets}}{\text{Proprietors' Fund}}$
8)	Current Assets to Proprietors' Fund Ratio	$\dfrac{\text{Current Assets}}{\text{Proprietors' Funds}}$
9)	Capital Gearing Ratio	$\dfrac{\text{Fixed Interest Bearing Funds}}{\text{Equity Share Capital}}$
10)	Debt-Equity Ratio	$\dfrac{\text{External Equities}}{\text{Internal Equities}}$ or $\dfrac{\text{Outsiders Fund}}{\text{Shareholders Fund}}$
11)	Fixed Assets to Current Assets	$\dfrac{\text{Fixed Assets}}{\text{Current Assets}}$
12)	Reserves to Equity Capital Ratio	$\dfrac{\text{Revenue Reserve}}{\text{Equity Capital}}$
13)	Gross Profit Ratio	$\dfrac{\text{Gross Profit}}{\text{Net Sales}} \times 100$
14)	Operating Ratio	$\dfrac{\text{Cost of Goods Sold (+) Operating Exp.}}{\text{Net Sales}} \times 100$
15)	Material Consumed Ratio	$\dfrac{\text{Material Consumed}}{\text{Net Sales}} \times 100$
16)	Conversion Cost Ratio	$\dfrac{\text{Manufacturing Exp. (--) Material Cost}}{\text{Net Sales}} \times 100$
17)	Particular Expense Ratio	$\dfrac{\text{Particular Expense}}{\text{Net Sales}} \times 100$
18)	Net Profit Ratio	$\dfrac{\text{Net Profit}}{\text{Net Sales}} \times 100$
19)	Return on Assets	$\dfrac{\text{Net Profit}}{\text{Total Assets}} \times 100$
20)	Return on Capital Employed	$\dfrac{\text{Operating Profits}}{\text{Capital Employed}}$

21)	Return on Shareholders' Equity	$\dfrac{\text{Net Profit}}{\text{Shareholders' Fund}} \times 100$
22)	Stock Turnover Ratio	$\dfrac{\text{Cost of Goods Sold (or) Net Sales}}{\text{Average Inventory}}$
23)	Debtors Turnover Ratio	$\dfrac{\text{Credit Sales}}{\text{Average Debtors}}$ (or) $\dfrac{\text{Total Sales}}{\text{Closing Debtors}}$
24)	Debt Collection Period	$\dfrac{\text{Months (or) days in a year}}{\text{Debtors Turnover}}$
25)	Creditors Turnover Ratio	$\dfrac{\text{Net Credit Purchases}}{\text{Average Accounts Payable}}$
26)	Average Payment Period	$\dfrac{\text{Accounts Payable}}{\text{Net Credit Purchases}} \times 365$
27)	Working Capital Turnover Ratio	$\dfrac{\text{Cost of Sales}}{\text{Net Working Capital}}$
28)	Fixed Assets Turnover	$\dfrac{\text{Cost of Sales}}{\text{Net Fixed Assets}}$
29)	Total Capital Turnover	$\dfrac{\text{Cost of Sales}}{\text{Total Capital Employed}}$
30)	Capital Turnover	$\dfrac{\text{Cost of Sales}}{\text{Capital Employed}}$
31)	Interest Coverage	$\dfrac{\text{EBIT}}{\text{Fixed Interest Charges}}$
32)	Dividend Coverage	$\dfrac{\text{Net Profit after Tax and Interest}}{\text{Preference Dividend}}$
33)	Equity Shareholders' Coverage	$\dfrac{\text{Net Profit (after Interest, Tax and Pref. Dividend)}}{\text{Equity Dividend}}$
34)	Earning Per Equity Shares	$\dfrac{\text{Profits available for Equity Shares}}{\text{Number of Equity Shares}}$
35)	Dividend Yield	$\dfrac{\text{Dividend Per Share}}{\text{Market Price per Share}}$
36)	Price Earning Ratio	$\dfrac{\text{Market Price of a Share}}{\text{Earning per Share}}$
37)	Fixed Interest Coverage	$\dfrac{\text{Operating Income}}{\text{Annual Interest Expenses}}$
38)	Dividend Per Share	$\dfrac{\text{Dividend Paid to Equity Shareholders}}{\text{Number of Equity Shares}}$
39)	Dividend Payout Ratio	$\dfrac{\text{Dividend Per Share}}{\text{Earning Per Share}}$

5. MARGINAL COSTING

1) **Sales or Selling Price or Market Price or Value of Turnover or Invoice Price or Inflated Price or Loaded Price :**

    = Total Cost + Profit

    = Variable Cost + Fixed Cost + Profit

    = Contribution / P/V Ratio

    = Contribution + Variable Cost

    = Marginal Cost / Marginal Cost Ratio

2) **Profit or Net Margin or Net Income :**

    = Sales – Total Cost

    = Sales – (Variable Cost + Fixed Cost)

    = Contribution – Fixed Cost

    = Margin of Safety × P/V Ratio

3) **Loss :**   = Total Cost – Sales

    = Fixed Cost – Contribution

4) **Contribution or Gross Margin or Marginal Contribution :**

    = Sales – Variable Cost

    = Fixed Cost + Profit

    = Sales × P/V Ratio

    = Fixed Cost – Loss

    = Fixed Cost / Break-Even units

5) **Fixed Cost, Rigid Cost or Constant Cost :**

    = Total Cost – Variable Cost

    = Contribution – Profit

    = Contribution + Loss

    = Sales – (Variable Cost + Profit)

6) **Variable Cost or Marginal Cost or Differential Cost :**

    = Total Cost – Fixed Cost

    = Sales – Contribution

    = Sales – (Fixed Cost + Profit)

    = Direct Material + Direct Labour + Direct Expenses + Variable Overheads

Management Accounting   F.4   Formulae

7) **Break-Even Point i.e. BEP (in units) or (in output) :**

$$= \frac{\text{Total Fixed Cost}}{\text{Contribution per unit}}$$

$$= \frac{\text{Break-Even Sales in Rs.}}{\text{Selling Price per unit}}$$

8) **Break-Even Point i.e. BEP (Sales in Rupees) :**

$$= \frac{\text{Total Fixed Cost}}{\text{Contribution per unit}} \times \text{Selling Price per unit}$$

$$= \frac{\text{Total Fixed Cost}}{\text{Total Contribution}} \times \text{Total Sales}$$

$$= \frac{\text{Total Fixed Cost}}{\text{Profit/Volume Ratio}}$$

$$= \frac{\text{Total Fixed Cost}}{1 - \left(\frac{\text{Variable Cost}}{\text{Sales}}\right)}$$

$$= \text{Break-Even Point (Units)} \times \text{Selling Price per unit}$$

9) **Profit/Volume Ratio or Contribution to Sales Ratio or Contribution Ratio i.e. P/V Ratio :**

$$= \frac{\text{Contribution}}{\text{Sales}} \times 100$$

$$= \frac{\text{Change in Profits}}{\text{Change in Sales}} \times 100$$

$$= \frac{\text{Change in Contribution}}{\text{Change in Sales}} \times 100$$

10) **Margin of Safety :**

$$\text{MS} = \text{Actual Sales} - \text{Break-Even Sales}$$

$$\text{MS} = \frac{\text{Profit}}{\text{P/V Ratio}}$$

$$\text{MS Ratio} = \frac{\text{Profit}}{\text{P/V Ratio}} \times 100$$

$$\text{MS Ratio} = \frac{\text{Margin of Safety}}{\text{Actual Sales}} \times 100$$

11) **Sales volume to earn required profit (in units) or Sales for desired profit (in units) :**

$$= \frac{\text{Total Fixed Cost} + \text{Required Profit}}{\text{Contribution per unit}}$$

12) **Sales volume to earn required profit (in value) or Sales for desired profit (in ₹) :**

$$= \frac{(\text{Total Fixed Cost} + \text{Required Profit}) \times \text{Sales}}{\text{Total Contribution}}$$

$$= \frac{\text{Total Fixed Cost} + \text{Required Profit}}{\text{P/V Ratio}}$$

***

BIBLIOGRAPHY

1. R. N. Anthony, G. A. Walsh : Management Accounting.

2. M. Y. Khan, K. P. Jain : Management Accounting.

3. I. M. Pandey : Management Accounting.

4. J. Betty : Management Accounting.

5. Sr. K. Paul : Management Accounting.

6. Man Mohan Goyal : Management Accounting.

7. S. N. Maheshwari : Principles of Management Accounting.

8. R. K. Sharma and Shashi K. Gupta : Management Accounting.

9. Richard M. Lynch and Robert Williamson : Accounting for Management Planning and Control.

10. Horngren : Introduction to Management Accounting.

***

April 2015

MANAGEMENT ACCOUNTING

(2013 PATTERN)

Time: Three Hours   Maximum Marks: 80

N.B.:

(i) All questions are compulsory and carry equal marks.

(ii) Use of simple calculators is allowed.

1. Define the term "Management Accounting". Explain its need and importance.

   Or

   Distinguish between Financial Accounting and Management Accounting.

2. What do you understand by Financial Statement Analysis?

   Or

   The following is the Trading and Profit and Loss Account of Zodiac Ltd. as on 31st March, 2014

Trading and Profit & Loss A/c as on 31st March, 2014

Particulars	₹	Particulars		₹
To Opening Stock	5,00,000	By Sales	20,10,000	
To Purchase	11,00,000	- Returns	10,000	20,00,000
To Wages	3,00,000	By Closing Stock		6,00,000
To Factory Expenses	2,00,000			
To Gross Profit	5,00,000			
	26,00,000			26,00,000
To Administration Expenses	80,000	By Gross Profit		5,00,000
To Selling and Distribution Expenses	60,000	By Dividend		10,000
To Discount	5,000	By Profit on Sale of Furniture		20,000
To Depreciation	60,000			
To Loss on Sale of motor car	5,000			
To Provision for Taxation	1,76,000			
To Net Profit	1,44,000			
	5,30,000			5,30,000
To Interim Dividend	15,000	By Net Profit b/f		2,71,000
To Balance to Balance Sheet	4,00,000	By Net profit b/d		1,44,000
	4,15,000			4,15,000

You are required to redraft the above P&L A/c in a form suitable for analysis.

(P.1)

3. Define the term "Marginal Costing". State the advantages and limitations of Marginal Costing.

Or

'ABC' Ltd., a manufacturing company, furnishes the following information :

Year	Sales	Profit
2012-13	₹ 10,00,000	₹ 2,00,000
2013-14	₹ 12,00,000	₹ 2,50,000

Find out:

(a) Fixed Cost

(b) Break-even Point (BEP Sales)

(c) Sales required to earn a profit of ₹ 60,000

(d) Margin of safety for the year 2013-14.

4. Define the terms "Budgets" and "Budgetary Control". State the objectives and limitations of Budgetary Control.

Or

The following particulars are extracted from the books of Z Ltd. working at 50% capacity level producing 5000 units.

Particulars	₹
Direct Material per unit	100.00
Direct Labour per unit	150.00
Chargeable Expenses per unit	50.00
Factory Expenses (20% fixed)	1,00,000
Electricity (40% variable)	60,000
Administration expenses (fixed)	1,50,000
Selling Expenses (80% variable)	1,00,000

You are required to prepare a flexible budget for 60%, 70% and 80% capacity.

5. Write short notes on (any four) :
   (i) Funds Flow Statement
   (ii) Current Ratio
   (iii) Profit-Volume Ratio
   (iv) Balance Sheet Ratio
   (v) Steps in Budgetary Control
   (vi) Scope of Material Costing.

***

www.ingramcontent.com/pod-product-compliance
Lightning Source LLC
Chambersburg PA
CBHW080438230426
43662CB00015B/2317